ONE MAN'S WILDERNESS

If any of the company entertain a doubt of my veracity I shall only say I pity their want of faith. . . . I had the very sling in my pocket which assisted David in slaying Goliath.

Baron Munchausen

Do not believe what I tell you here any more than if it were some tale of a tub. . . .

François Rabelais

⚏⚏⚏⚏⚏ One Man's
WILDERNESS

Warren Page

Holt, Rinehart and Winston

NEW YORK   CHICAGO   SAN FRANCISCO

To all that vast body of wilderness lovers,
today maligned and sadly misunderstood,
who properly call themselves hunters, a breed of men who have
since the day of the cave lived more richly than most . . .

ISBN: 0-03-086009-1
Library of Congress Catalog Card Number: 72-91563
First Edition

Some of the stories in this volume first appeared in *Field &
Stream.*

Designer: RONALD FARBER

Printed in the United States of America

Contents

NORTH AMERICA

ANTIPODES

EUROPE

ASIA

AFRICA

Sixteen pages of photographs follow page 144.

Foreword

By John T. Amber
Editor, *Gun Digest*

I've been reading shooting columns and gun departments for a very long time—before the Hitler war those written by Ned Crossman, Townsend Whelen, Charles Askins the elder, Bob Nichols, and many others, all long gone to the Happy Hunting Grounds.

If you think that dates me, it does, but, because I'm going to tell you something about one of today's best-known—and best—writers on firearms and their manifold sporting uses, I want to establish the fact that I've been familiar with such writings for lo, these many years. Perhaps more to the point, my job being what it is, I've learned to cast a pretty critical eye over the wide range of stuff I read on my—and I imagine your—favorite subjects, guns and hunting.

In 1947, I think it was, a new writer appeared on the scene, a man who had already done a considerable amount of hunting and shooting before that time—and one who was to do much, much more of the same as the years went by.

That writer, to keep it a secret no longer, was Warren Kempton Page, if we set down his full handle, although in print he has dropped the middle section. He is also known as "Lefty" to a few intimates, among whom I'm proud to place myself. That nickname is an odd one, since he neither writes or shoots left handed, but certainly another individual oddity isn't strange among writers on hunting and firearms!

It wasn't until several years after Page's first stories and articles appeared in *Field & Stream* that I got to meet and know Warren, but I'd been reading his instructive and entertaining stuff in that magazine with increasing appreciation for the good job he was doing. Importantly, too, his material was even then consistently first class.

What he has had to say since has revealed an impressive knowledge of sporting arms, with a background obviously built on wide-ranging and constant experiences in the field, plus deep and objective delving into the lore of modern arms and ammunition. His cogent comments on their use and effectiveness have clearly helped his readers—or those who could be helped—to become better hunters, more knowledgeable and skilled gunners, and—best of all in my opinion—better sportsmen.

Now, after nearly twenty-five years of global experience, Warren Page has written this big and valuable book that brings together the top items from his tales of hunting 'round the world. It holds details of adventure on every continent plus a near-dozen freshly written chapters ranging from the nuts-and-bolts of game rifles and calibers to the strange psychology of the gun-haters, *New York Times* variety. It is second nature to Page to mix into his tales of derring-do sage and sound advice to the young Natty Bumppo making his first foray afield, as well as wryly amusing notes on the fads, foibles, and foolishments which are sometimes exhibited in our wonderful world of guns and shooting.

No writer in those purlieus today is better qualified than Warren Page either to excite the expert or to tell the aspiring and eager young hunter/ rifleman/shotgunner what he—or she—really needs to know. Page can draw on a uniquely well-rounded background, select from a tremendous fund of hard-won experiences around the globe. He is a top-ranking target rifleman who has collected no less than nine national championships in bench-rest competition.

Years ago, as early as 1958, Page won the famed Roy Weatherby Big Game Trophy, top accolade among serious hunters. A complete list of the record-book heads he has taken the world over is an impressive one indeed. He has been involved in the development of at least four of our best modern cartridges, is a deadly marksman on big game and an accomplished shotgunner.

Warren Page has been on thirteen African safaris, covering the Dark Continent from Abyssinia to Zambia, as well as on several shikars in India and other areas of Asia. He was pursuing Asiatic sheep types way back in the early 1950s, long before the present eastward rush. He has hunted quite literally all over the North American continent including sixteen trips in Alaska alone, and covering all the states and provinces from the Yukon Territory to British Honduras. The year 1970 was a slow one, he told me, since it involved hunts only in Spain, the Yakutat region of Alaska, British Columbia's Cassiar district, Scotland, Maryland, Texas, and New Mexico in that order. Looking for new worlds to conquer, Warren has lately turned to Europe. He has made highly successful hunts in Italy, Spain, Portugal, Austria, Norway, and Sweden—with ventures in the USSR and other Eastern countries on the agenda.

Probably more important to the future of the hunting and shooting world, in 1971 he took over leadership of the National Shooting Sports Foundation, and has made of it a major force in the development of sporting arms usage and ethical hunting. Not surprising, really, since he had been the essential founder of the organization a decade before and, unique among arms writers, had further pursued a conservation bent by being a founding trustee of such groups as the African Wildlife Leadership Foundation, the St. Hubert's Society, the International Professional Hunters Association, the African Safari Club of New York, and an officer of numerous others like the Campfire Club.

If this reads like an encomium, indeed it is one. Warren Page is a man unique in our society. In a word, he has been there and done it. Just about all of it.

Warren Page's writing is, I think you'll find, a delight to read. He is never stilted or pompous, never obscure. He writes clearly and objectively, invariably with humor and understanding—even when, now and again, he jets invective at certain eminently deserving targets.

I'm honored—and grateful—that I've had this opportunity to put down these few words about Warren Page's new book. I have enjoyed reading—and rereading—these tales and comments. I think you will, too.

Preface

The most expert travelers and hunters are always those who have been somewhere just once, or have done it just once. Perhaps a singular experience is so vivid that every element of its recollection becomes completely real, completely true. Whole books have been written about Africa after a single safari, for example, the author blithely sure that every word he has set down is gospel. The only way to beat that, I suspect, is to write a book about Africa without ever having been there, and believe it or not, this has also been done, the scrivener apparently feeling he approached truth by distilling everything everybody else had ever said on the subject.

Both such approaches, and certainly a third possible one, that of contriving outright fiction garnished with outrageous lies, do not seem to suit me very well. At least none has ever worked for me. After a baker's dozen of safaris in almost as many sections of Africa, fifteen or sixteen assorted hunts in Alaska, and similarly numerous investigations with a rifle into all manner of states and provinces, including those remote chunks of the globe where American is spoken only by the local rug dealers, I am thoroughly convinced that the more you travel, the more you hunt, the less you really and positively know.

That's one of the ironies of the opportunity to hunt worldwide today, made possible by the jet airplane. You can think you're pretty savvy about caribou hunting, for example, after you've racked up expeditions for Barren Ground types in upper Alaska, have sought long-racked mountain stags in the Cassiar, and walked up Christmas-tree woodland types in New-foundland, and perhaps even shot that new species created by Boone and Crockett Club fiat in Labrador. Then you try the European type, closest cousin to the reindeer, on the Norwegian uplands. At that point all your savvy goes out the window. Unlike our caribou, the super-racked Scandi-hoovian bull, master trophy beyond breeding age, cannot be stalked where he paws the tundra in frustrate solitude. On the Hardangervidda uplands he is still permitted to mingle in the herd, is part of a forest of antlers in the rear third of anywhere from five hundred to five thousand restlessly stir-ring, feeding bodies. Hunting caribou becomes a problem with several new twists. And by trying to solve it, if you are an individual with any degree of sensitivity, you become aware that we never know all. Usually we know less than we thought we did. The problem lies in recognizing that humbling fact.

We live in, there can be no doubt, the most intensive and extensive period of hunting for pure sport that the world has ever known. There may have been more lions or more oryx along Kenya's Uaso Nyiro fifty years ago, for example, but gun-and-camera safari tourism has recently come to mean a fifty-million-dollar addition to the Kenya economy, whereas it brought in a mere fifteen only a decade back. Early frontiersmen in this country undoubtedly had to hunt if they wanted to eat, but neither then nor later could their numbers have reached the twenty million or so Ameri-cans, with or without licenses, who now hunt in the fifty states.

This does not necessarily mean, alas, that the individual hunter is more highly skilled than was his counterpart of a half or whole century ago. He is vastly better equipped with rifles that shoot like laser beams, and clothes that are warm without weight, and machines that can take him into the game's very boudoir, but he isn't thereby automatically a better hunter. Probably the contrary is true. Hundreds go on safari or shikar as a social exercise. They first see their rifles when they are unpacked in a Nairobi outfitting office, are led around the bush by professionals who do all but aim their guns, and even that sometimes, alas. Hundreds more will climb dutifully up a sheep mountain behind a Yukon Territory Indian without having the slightest idea of why they are puffing up that particular ridge, or what they should do when they top it.

All this is too bad, since hunting is essentially an individual sport, some-thing a man does or can do by himself, and the deeper and more detailed any man's understanding of the sport, of the game, and the terrain, and his relation to them, the greater his pleasure. We who more or less hunt for a living and then write about it can only hope we've dropped a few bits of that understanding that others may pick up and gain thereby.

It is also quite possible, as will be developed later in this book, that we are living through the last great days of the hunting sport. I have for some years now thought myself most fortunate, for example, to have lived during this middle twentieth century, since in it we have seen incredible technological advances. Yet we are also seeing, or certainly may well be seeing, the end of the really wild places on our own planet. Not today, not tomorrow, but the fateful handwriting is on the wall. Unchecked population, the ravagement of resources for profit and "progress," the pointless consumption, the proliferation of gasoline-fueled machinery of many sorts that help man violate even the most secret places, the poisoning of earth, air, and water by human and industrial wastes—all these leave little hope for wild areas or the wild things, perhaps little for man himself.

The politicians have, of course, galloped to the rescue with strong statements praising motherhood and the flag while damning sin and pollution. And the people are perhaps aroused enough to take some of the steps necessary, though they'll probably not venture, alas, toward the fundamentally needed reduction of human population. There is a great new hue and cry for wilderness and green space and more and more parks.

All of this is fine, should indeed lighten the gloom. But in the cries for a green clean world, for areas of mountain and beach, lake and woods where the city-pent can come and somehow reestablish contact with a world not made of concrete, there seldom sounds the hunter's horn. The mountain-climber will, perhaps, be cared for; so indeed will the picnicker or the brave camper who carries his living room afield and sets it up in chummy elbow-knocking proximity to his fellows; but there seems little evidence that the planners plan a future for the hunters of this country. And herein lies an anomaly. Let's accept the usual estimates that some twenty million people do hunt in this land. If by some miracle that group of men and women, all of them by definition individualists, could be welded into an organized minority, it would be the greatest single political force this country has ever known.

They could, if that miracle were somehow achieved, themselves force the future conservation of our timber and our minerals and our wilderness glories even as they already have, without any real organization beyond a vague recognition of common interest, to date forced the conservation of the deer, the dove, the duck, and all those other game animals which can rationally exist in a world controlled by man. There has never been self-consciousness in the hunter's contribution of funds to conservation, be it in the excise tax on guns and ammunition, something over thirty-two million a year these days, or in license fees, funds today over a hundred million annually. He found out long ago that you couldn't really expect wilderness and wild things for free, and that a handful of dollars spent on buying marshlands or eradicating the srcewworm meant more ducks to watch—and shoot—or deer to hunt than do all the balloons of hot air sent up by the dickey-bird lovers and the professional hand-wringers. If our American ideas of hunting in a democratic way are to be maintained, the major task the hunting-minded face in the next decade or three will be that of winning acceptance by a preservation-oriented public of the idea that the sport hunter plays an important part in true conservation, and so must be admitted to all those newly established wild and green places. Otherwise the hunter could find himself on the outside looking in...

The urge to hunt, however, will never die. I firmly believe the Ardrey thesis that hunting has been part of the human heritage since that early day when an apelike creature konked his dinner with the thighbone of an antelope. It is an active part of the human culture today in those sections of earth like Central Europe which have often been thought more civilized than our American society. Hunting is there, oddly enough, accorded greater honor, and its practitioners are more highly regarded than they are in our own nation where wild meat was a necessary table staple only a few decades ago. No, I don't think men will ever quit wanting to hunt. It's just that today there are more people around who envy the hunter his individual freedom, wish he could be made to quit and join their dull gray mob.

I have been blessed indeed to have been able to dodge any such nondescript and maggoty existence and to have poked around as a man alone, if not completely free, in many of the strange and colorful corners of our globe. There have been times in the mountains when those hunting ventures were stark muscle-cracking work and times in the lowlands when they were mud-smeared, insect-bitten misery—but always the hunt has for me been a time of especially rich awareness, of being particularly alive. Perhaps this book will help you understand that, even share it.

To begin with, any man who hunts and then writes about it owes a vast debt to the outfitters and guides who have aided him in the search for trophies. They may have been paid in the coin of their respective realms, but it is my experience that the really top-notch guides and outfitters, whom the serious hunter must always seek out if he is to achieve much of a success rating, automatically and without being asked put forth that extra pinch of effort, use that extra bit of savvy of animal habits, that makes boom out of bust. Money cannot pay for that.

Nor, for that matter, can any outfitting fee pay for the associations with men who really know their country, their game, and their craft. The campfire hours spent together by a hunter and guide, be he an Indian who converses chiefly in pregnant grunts, or a British colonial who, on African beasts, knows natural history that has escaped the textbooks, are valuable beyond price.

So I am deeply grateful to the hundreds of outdoor-minded men who have flown me into camps, have loaded the packhorses toting my gear, have led me up mountains and through timber tangles, men who have enriched my understanding of the world and its big-game animals fully as much as their efforts have enlarged my trophy list. *Salud, amigos!*

In an immediate and practical sense I am, of course, indebted to *Field & Stream* for permitting the reuse of a large number of these chapters, which have appeared in the magazine in some form. In much the same way I am on the red-ink side to friends like John Amber whose criticism has been of very real help. I can even reckon a very different debt to surgeon Tod Craig for patching me up after I had variously overstressed one joint or another by chasing after game critters where even an angel would fear to tread! And in quite a different way I feel a great debt to my ever-loving spouse Martha, who has possessed patience and understanding enough to continue associating with a character who was either off in the boonies or at some shooting match half the year.

The list is too long. Any man, and any man's stories, can only be the final product of his friendships.

W.P.

New Canaan, Connecticut
January 1973

North America

1 : Ram with a Corset

It wouldn't have been a long fall. First a twenty-foot slide down a chute of polished rock sloping at seventy or eighty degrees, then a parabola out over the lip and a hundred feet of free drop onto jagged boulders. Of course, it's the sudden stop after the first hundred feet that kills. Another five hundred after the first bounce wouldn't matter much. As long as that one lump of hard rock midway of the chute held firm I'd be all right. But it was a mighty evil place for a man in a surgical corset.

The Mexicans watching me skitter across thought so too. Pancho and Daniel could toe-dance over rotten-rock cliffs and up the heart-pounding slopes of the Sierra de la Giganta, the prime desert-sheep range of Baja California, as if their feet wore wings instead of rubber-tire sandals. Yet they'd never hunted rams with a man whose back was ramrodded with a contraption of laced canvas and slim steel bars. Jorge Belloc, the stocky and purposeful chap who was outfitting the expedition, hadn't either. Seemed to them amazing, even a bit shocking.

But it wouldn't be to any serious sheep hunter. Such is the breed that the minor handicap of a sacroiliac shrieking with every jump would only slow him a bit, never stop him. Not if the back-stiffener could be hauled up tight.

"Doc Craig prescribed this contraption after I sprung a gasket hauling an elk over a log years ago," I had told Russ Cutter, my Colorado hunting buddy, at the base camp two days earlier. "It worked and I've lugged it in the duffel bag as insurance ever since. Excess baggage until this morning. But then, bending over my bedroll, I happened to sneeze. That slipped the frammister, I guess."

Russ didn't need to hand out sympathy. Fact was, we had both worked mighty hard for a chance at 100 percent legal desert rams. Annually he had put his money up for the Arizona drawings, never pulled a ticket. I'd done everything but create a bona fide natural-history museum trying to get a clean permit from Mexico City. Then word had leaked out that Dr. Corzo, whose job as Director General de Caza with the Mexican government approximates the position of Game Commissioner, was planning an experimental hunt for two optional ten-day periods in March of 1964.

The object of the hunt was only partly to provide more cash wherewithal to police an area and a species that has for years been poached left, right, and sideways. By putting enough experienced hunters and guides into the ranges south of the twenty-eighth parallel, Dr. Corzo hoped to get a mass of information on the distribution, numbers, and condition of the big-horned sheep type that battles for life in the toughest terrain this side of the moon. Richer by a six-inch pile of correspondence in both Spanish and English, and poorer by two C-notes apiece for the licenses, Russ and I had landed in Loreto ready for the first ten-day open period.

Almost ready. First we had to get into sheep country. South of Loreto the Range of the Giant spears upward out of the blue water of the Gulf of California, but there's no sense scaling those battlements from the front. Better to work back in, Belloc had explained, to jeep eighty road miles south, and then grind up a wash to a canyon goat ranch, where there'd be mules. Then three hours with mules and pack burros. Eventually we hit the main camp that Belloc had established, deep in a canyon where one of the rare water trickles, flavored with burro droppings, gave life to a monstrous fig tree.

Pancho and Daniel had earlier spotted two rams in that area, but they'd either spooked off or developed an uncanny knack for hiding in the gray-green fuzz of cactus, paloverde, and palo blanco that softened all but the most rugged cliffs. We could find only ewes and a few half-curl rams. But a ten-mile move to a spike camp several canyons north, from which we could reach a jumbled complex of ridges below the reserve area that has been established by Dr. Corzo's edict, produced more action.

Russ found gold in those mountains on the fourth day. With Belloc's friend Dr. Recio, a dentist with a passion for desert sheep who had been helpful in the prehunt assay of the Giganta range, he prospected a series of sawtooths inside the main range. Belloc and I were crawling precariously and fruitlessly around higher pinnacles that dropped straight into the gulf. It was Russ who hit the ram jackpot.

"I do now believe in Santa Claus," he said next morning, when we could see the massive head in daylight and run the tape over its battered curves. "I really do. If we hadn't stopped for lunch in just that spot and if the ram hadn't picked the precise moment to move off his bed, we'd never have seen him. And even after we sneaked around the back side of the next knob and I was all set to shoot, I still couldn't make him out in the tangle of organ cactus and monkey-tail except when the sun bounced off his horns."

Russ had been lucky. On the back, or westerly, side of the Giganta, the spiny mixture of brush and cactus was surprisingly dense. An army of sheep could hide in there.

"This ram was probably old enough and smart enough to know the odds ran his way if he stayed off the cleaner peaks. By the rings I make him thirteen or fourteen years anyway. And what a bruiser for horn weight!"

"Right now he scores around 171 on the Boone and Crockett scale," added George Parker, himself the owner of two grand slams on American sheep, one of them with every head beating forty inches, and likely the one man most experienced in Baja California hunting. As an old friend, George had come along to help with the Spanish and give his skilled advice. He wound up the steel tape and tossed it into my camera bag. "I get thirty-four inches on the longer horn. Both of them are broomed, but the bases go fifteen—betcha the final score is way over 165. Mighty fine *borrego*, Russ."

"*Macho borrrrrrrrrrego!*" rasped out Recio. "*Una cerveza, amigo?*"

Russ figured, and I agreed, that the occasion called for champagne rather than beer, but *cerveza* it was, for first blood.

Second blood, if you don't count skinned skins, blisters, and the cholla stickers that had to be tweezered out every evening, was slow in coming. It can be like that on desert sheep. There aren't many of them. Can't be, not in a country where water appears in dribbles fifteen or twenty miles apart, where the feed is sparse as hair on a Rolls-Royce fender, and the sun blasts like a blowtorch. Dr. Corzo's biologists estimate that the whole of Baja, all eight hundred miles of it, holds an estimated population of only fifteen hundred sheep, probably half of them concentrated between the Loreto reserve and La Paz.

We knew that for the 1964 spring hunt—the first such ever staged by the Subsecretaria de Recursos Forestales y de Caza of Mexico City, which is the department controlling forest and hunting resources—there had been issued a total of fifty-five permits, thirty to Mexican citizens, twenty to

U.S. hunters at two hundred dollars each, plus five special museum permits. The hunting pressure during the two ten-day periods in early and late March would not be great, not in that long wilderness of cactus and mountain.*

The Baja sheep have to be hunted. The white Dall rams of the far-north country may stand out like windmills in Texas, but the soft gray-blue-brown of the desert ram blends into the local rock coloring in perfect camouflage—all except for the cream-white fanny. That light-colored rear end is the giveaway. You spend hours laboriously examining a country everywhere gashed with concealing ravines and pockets of shadow, with caves and blowholes in the cliffs themselves, looking for sheep sterns. You sweat gallons climbing up to some point on the windy side—desert sheep seem to move more according to the wind than the sun, preferring to bed and feed in shelter—and then shiver while a half gale off the cool Pacific zips through your shirt. You sit there for longer hours, visually vacuum-cleaning the cactus-pocked slopes, trying to see the butt end of a ram sheltering under an ironwood a mile away.

We found sheep—Jorge and Pancho and Daniel and I. We saw a bunch or three of ewes every day, occasionally a half-curl ram. At rock-throwing range we blundered onto one ram that might—just might—have been shoot-able as a fully legal three-quarter curl, but he was clearly a young and un-broomed gentleman and, from the way he stared before whirling off the mountain, completely ignorant of man.

From every vantage point I was fascinated by the eastern end of the next range lying to the south. A smooth-topped five-thousand-foot ridge, it broke off toward the gulf in a pair of pointed towerlike peaks, each with a series of lesser castles, *morros*, marching up from the canyons on our side. In that country a ram could play hide-and-seek from two whole armies of hunters.

Belloc had the same idea. "Pancho says there is a way, though no trail in most parts. We must go back down to the ranch of the old man and the goats and then up the next canyon for two, maybe three hours and camp high in the *morros*. One pack burro only, so Señor Cutter and Señor Parker must stay here at the fig-tree camp. No water, unless we find some that Pancho does not know about, so we can stay only two days before we must get the mules back."

For only an evening and a morning hunt it was still worth the gamble. Those castellated peaks must hold sheep.

---

* Of the fifty-five permit-holders, only twenty-one bagged their rams on this first legal hunt. Several attained Boone and Crockett Club trophy listing. Later permit hunts have provided license income sufficient to assure protective control of the Baja sheep herd, so its future is reasonably well assured.

The dim trail up out of the canyon petered out at noon the next day, and we faced the problem of picking a way under beetling cliffs of rotten rock, across ledges so narrow that the overloaded burro was in constant danger of scraping himself off the face. Not even a goatherd had penetrated this country in years. And we found water. In the last basin before the mountain proper, a rain eight months before had left a jug-shaped pothole partly filled with algae-green fluid. It would keep men and beasts alive if we stayed an extra day, the last day my permit was good.

Sore from the long mule ride and stiffer yet, with the sacral pain only half allayed by the surgical belt, that afternoon I followed the Mexicans halfway around the first outlying peak, beyond the tricky chute crossing atop the last rim. The *morros* were rough, but they held sheep. We were positive of that from the dainty but blunt-toed tracks and moderately fresh droppings of at least two rams. The knowledge was worth all those dicey climbing situations where a man knows his cleated Vibram soles will hold, yet can't be sure of the rock underneath. The rams had to be somewhere in this tangle of pinnacles. But as we stumbled back down toward the tethered mules and the smatter of bedrolls we had seen only one. He, ironically enough, was feeding miles below us on a mountain we had already traversed coming up.

By midnight the wind raged across the flats so hard it rolled me off the air mattress. Jorge and the boys must be half frozen, I knew, but the violent blow carried a greater concern. Unless it dropped at dawn, the sheep would stay tucked into holes and be triply hard to locate.

But the air was still, or reasonably so, when we started the climb toward the second pinnacle, primed with jam-smeared tortillas and cups of the mud-thick jet brew the Mexicans call coffee. We had a chance. Two hours of puffing and still another crossing of that cursed chute and we topped the second peak. With heels jammed into rock that shattered off into amazingly regular one-inch cubes of shale, we could look over an entire world. But it was an empty world, peopled only by the occasional cruising buzzard that whipped past our silent, glassing figures. A half day down we could see a string of goats trailing out from the *cabrito* ranch. But nothing else. Certainly no sheep.

My heart was as heavy as my feet when the dropping sun said we must start down off the pinnacle. One day more, even if that pothole held water enough for our animals—and on the way back to our spike camp we'd be hunting terrain already twice covered. Perhaps I should have taken that first three-quarter curl and saved all this punishment. But it wouldn't have been a trophy. When you come right down to it, no trophy means much unless it is sauced by a fair mixture of blood, sweat, and tears. And we did have that one more day.

In the saddle between the inner peak and the outer tower, Jorge and Daniel paused in argument. My Spanish is largely profane, but their gestures made it clear that they were debating the best way to camp. Should we return by the known face or go around the back side of the pinnacle?

"Let's take the south side," was my vote. "We haven't touched that yet."

"Daniel says it will be rougher, and it's been in the sun all day. Not likely for sheep," Jorge said. "But there's always a chance. We bet our pesos on the south, no?"

"Fair enough, though we're betting this creaking frame rather than any pesos," I agreed, shouldering the 7 mm. magnum.

It began to look like a good bet, since even as we worked sidehill onto the canyon-slashed slope Pancho and Daniel carefully stepped around the tracks of a ram. With edges still sharp, unblurred by wind, they must have been made since sunup. Then Pancho, who had taken the lead when I passed my cameras over to Jorge to leave both hands free for the rifle, stopped on a teetering rock. He pointed out droppings in the shale, shiny and fresh. They weren't wet, since nothing can remain wet long under the Baja sun blaze, but they were clearly fresh. Then, for the first time in nine days of steady hunting, I fed a round into the rifle chamber and snicked on the safety.

The next canyon head was empty, and the next, and nothing moved either above or below us. But then the slope bulged out onto a rocky rib that would afford late-afternoon shade to any animal bedded in the far gully. The wind had died completely and we fairly tiptoed, stepping only on the heaviest rock outcrops lest a careless weight-shift set off a rattling downpour of shale. Like a bunch of Indians, I thought.

Finally Pancho could peer over the ridge to the opposite ledges. Slowly he lowered his head and beckoned, a white-toothed grin opening his craggy features. "*Un macho borrego*," he whispered needlessly.

Awkward with the rifle in one hand, and the steel-and-canvas belt around my middle hampering every movement, I wormed up the rocks until, plastered flat over the edge, I could see the ram, and could ease the rifle over into line. The sheep was dozing in the weakening sun, and the cross hairs had almost settled on the shoulder when he sprang into sudden alert. But it was too late. The 7 mm. T&R magnum barked and the ram staggered on his ledge, then pitched off in a rolling bone-shattering fall into the canyon.

When we'd made our way down for the picture taking and the cape skinning and the quartering of the carcass, Belloc suddenly banged me hard on the back and offered his hand for the second time. He knew, as I'd already discovered from a quick taping, that this ram could no more than barely score up to the 150 Boone and Crockett minimum; but his hunters had filled and his honor had been vindicated. Honor is important to the people of Mexico. And for the second time I accepted his hand gladly. Not because of any point of honor, but because the ram lying before us was a trophy in the best sense. It represented the triumph of mind over matter, the result of a lot of hard work, a little bit of luck, and two slim strips of canvas-covered steel.

---

2 : Glacier Bear

"See him? Just left of that patch of snow above the rockslide! That's our bear, all right—but I'll be darned if he doesn't look almost green!"

Neither guide Ralph Young nor I actually cared that a freak of lighting in Alaska's glacier country might make a blue bear glint green. We wouldn't have minded if the rare animal we were studying in our glasses had been as green as chlorophyll tooth paste or even striped like a barber pole! We'd finally spotted a glacier bear in an accessible position, feeding up where I might, if the red gods gave us one more smile, square my scope cross hairs on his shoulder.

I had come a long way for that bear, over thirty-six hundred miles. Most of the trip was a speedy ride in the comfort of Northwest Airlines. The last lap, into the very head of Disenchantment Bay, called for the slow sea-worthiness of a fifty-foot salmon boat, the *Alaska Maid*. For three years we had been contriving a meeting with a blue-pelted bruin. Back in 1949, while waiting for a brownie to come out onto a Baranof Island sedge flat, Young and I had first dreamed of hunting the blue bears. And if I could keep our date with the odd-colored gentleman up the rock slide, I'd be, as far as we knew, the first sportsman to take a glacier bear since 1906.

The glacier bear is a peculiar localized subspecies of black bear, found only in the glacier-gashed country behind Yakutat Bay, midway between Juneau and Anchorage. A few appear north of Glacier Bay, perhaps some on the Yagataga coast far beyond the fifty-mile radius of their central range. Their dense-furred hides vary in color from an off-white shaded with smoky gray-blue all the way to a grizzle-tipped blue-black almost like a silver fox. The typical specimen, if there be such, runs to the gray-blue of a roan horse, with darker muzzle and paws. Not grizzly bears nor yet polar bears despite their glacier-country habitat, but a peculiar form of *Euarctos* the black, they are extremely rare—a completely unique trophy.

For three years Young and I had quizzed scientists, Siwash Indians, and salmon fishermen for every crumb of information on these blue bears. Most printed material on the glacier bear—and there's very little—stems from a letter written by the naturalist Dall back in the 1890s. The original collection for museum use was made by a Lieutenant Emmons back in 1905. Our freshest material came from men like Frank Dufresne, twenty years in Alaska, and from Hardy Trefzger, almost fifty years in the Yakutat area. Since these blue bears do not summer on the coastal salmon streams with ordinary blacks and coastal grizzlies, but hang back closer to the towering St. Elias mountains, they are seldom seen, save by the local Indians who with Mongol patience take a hide or two each year. I was equipped, therefore, with an overlicense permit to collect for the Peabody Museum at Yale University a specimen of the strange blue bear, hide and every last bone.

And there he was, scratching out a spring breakfast from wild celery greens springing up under the snow line, far up a forty- to fifty-degree rockslide from where we drifted offshore in the *Alaska Maid*. The breeze was blowing down and across the mountain; we had several hours of daylight left for the stalk. Nothing to it but to struggle up there and bring down the blue bacon.

As we slipped the towline of one of the small power boats and sculled quietly ashore, I cleared my pockets of extra weight for the tough climb. Two rounds beyond the four in my 7 mm. Mashburn magnum would either be enough, or twenty wouldn't. A candid camera with one roll of fresh 35 mm. film. Binoculars around Ralph's neck. Rifle bore and scope clear.

The skiff's bow eased up onto shale at the foot of the treacherous slide and we stepped ashore, pausing only to shove it into deep water and fasten the mooring line. "Straight up the slide into that bunch of alders— then we'll check back with the boat," said Ralph, and dug his boot-sole edges into the loose gravel.

The rocks rolled and sweat started under our wool, but finally we heaved over the first hump, off the dangerously loose stuff to where we could catch a second wind and look for directions from Jack O'Donnell, the boat skipper. As we had arranged, he had the *Alaska Maid* hove to where his binoculars could pick out both us and the bear in the alder thickets above. He was waving a white dish towel up—and up some more.

We grunted our way up through tangles of alder and devil's club another quarter of a mile and checked back again. "What the . . . ? Now what does he mean?" Jack was perched up on the mast, his glasses apparently focused alongside us on a ledge that carried a few storm-dwarfed cottonwoods. At my whispered question, a pint-sized black bear burst out of the trees and crashed off down the slide. We found out afterwards that Jack was trying to tell us that the small black was perched up in a tree crotch looking at us, but at the time we were concerned only with the little devil's brush-busting racket. That had torn it, for sure—but the white cloth still waved up and left.

A few steps ahead, Ralph suddenly crouched and stared upwards. In the alder tangle I could make out a patch of light fur moving off. No shot. "Figure the wind shifted?" But it hadn't, and we began carefully to parallel the bear's apparent course, struggling toward a scour of snow a hundred yards long that had slid and ripped free the underbrush. Just as we reached its base, Young froze again, and my eye strained along his pointing finger.

There he was, only eighty yards or so above us, standing clear of dense brush that would have hidden him hopelessly five steps to either side. The blue bear!

I flopped onto the snow slant and willed the rifle muzzle steady. At the sharp whack of the 7 mm. magnum the glacier bear collapsed into a sliding, tumbling fall straight toward us. We scrambled aside just in time to dodge a cartwheeling blur of bear and flying snow that finally fetched up below us on a stout alder. Three years, thirty-six hundred miles, and eighty yards—and we'd done it!

I sat down with a cigarette, and when I could find the end with a match, shakily lighted it. Ralph scrambled down to inspect the bear and back up to bang me on the back and extend a hand in congratulation. "What's the matter with you? Stand up and yell! Realize you're the first dude that's killed one of these things in almost fifty years? Give out—or are you going to wait six months before you get excited?"

But the memory of three years of planning come to fruition in a few seconds of action left me without the capacity to dance and bellow, even if that tipped-up alder tangle had been any place for a jig.

This bear we estimated at roughly three hundred and fifty pounds, the size of a fine black bear, with a head seemingly heavier than normal, ears bigger, paws broader and somewhat more thickly furred under the toes. The pelt, luxuriant with soft, whitish underfur, carried long, blue-tipped guard hairs shading much darker on ears, paws, and muzzle. And sure enough, the greenish tinge we had observed through binoculars was still clear in close-up, no freak of lighting but of bear coloration.

So that the trophy hide would be unmarked save by the bullet entrance and exit holes in neck and back, where the one-hundred-and-sixty-grain

Barnes slug had driven through, the skinning job was done with surgery care and we started back down the slide. Ralph lugged the hide while I guided the carcass on its roll toward the beach. There we could bone it out in comfort next day.

But next day it wasn't where we'd left it, well above tide water, not by the time we got back from our overnight anchorage, took a few pictures, and inspected a very fine black bear which Jay Broome, the Texas representative in the party had taken with his trusty .300 H & H. A brownie had walked the beach during the night. As they will frequently do, he had carted off the blue-bear carcass for a light lunch.

"What about the museum people?" asked Ralph. "They need a skeleton, don't they?"

"Curator Ball insisted on hide, head and bones of the same glacier bear. Some scientific study of their anatomy in relation to other types of black. We'll just have to get another one for them and put this bear on my license." And nobody even laughed at me for being such a nincompoop as to think a man could get two glacier bears on one trip.

But this was no one-man blue-bear expedition anyway. The four-man party had both brownies and blacks to look over. In addition to his fine black, Jay had earlier dropped a creamy shouldered coastal grizzly with a neat sitting shot at one hundred and seventy-five yards. Remington gun-designer Mike Walker had picked up a slide-climbing black with some ultralong shooting, two lung hits at well over three hundred yards from his Model 721 in .300 H & H, and his friend George Hooker had salivated a brownie in a shooting affray below a glacial wash. In the Yakutat section, Alaska game laws as of 1953 permit the taking of two brownies or black bears on a nonresident license, and from the way blacks with unrubbed hides were showing we weren't going to have trouble filling out any rug requirements in the *Euarctos* division.

But the big brownies, the *Ursus* tribe, were coming hard. When our plane eased onto the Yakutat air strip on May seventh, we had found an extraordinarily late spring had left four feet of a twenty-two-foot snow-fall still piled beside the runways. Halfway to the bay head, in the Point La Touche section which Trefzger had tagged as the top brownie area, mountains and valleys alike were laden with snow over the ears of a tall Siwash Indian, too soft to support a man, slushy enough to make very heavy going on snowshoes.

We saw brownies in this wintry desolation, seventeen of them at various times, but could get into rifle shot of only a few, and not all of those proper trophies, who had crawled out of hibernation to scrounge a feed on willow buds. It was in this section, opposite where two huge glaciers dumped floes and bergs into the bay with constant thunder, that we encountered and failed to solve the mystery of a disappearing brown bear.

Picking a channel through the ice, with a fall of sticky snow cutting visibility on shore to a few hundred yards, we spotted a sizable brownie on a snowslide. He was working his way along under a sheer two-hundred-foot rock face, apparently insurmountable.

"Let's try for him," said Ralph. "Hooker, you come along but stay down on the beach by the skiff. Move fast—he's probably spotted us by now, but we may have him boxed under that cliff."

With two pairs of snowshoes in the skiff, we paddled ashore into a blinding flurry of stamp-sized snowflakes. For only a minute or two was that horse-bodied brown bear invisible, but when the snow curtain opened again, the slide was empty of movement. He couldn't have gone straight up; there wasn't time for him to get off to the higher end of the slide, nor could we see tracks leading over the snow shoulder that was his easiest route to safety; but the bear had plumb disappeared.

"He must be in next to the rock, Ralph. Maybe there's a shelf in behind the snow."

"Must be—I've seen bear do funny things, but sprouting wings isn't one of them. Want to take a look up there?"

My answer was to flounder up onto the snow and lash on a pair of webs, to start a zigzagging climb toward the shoulder where the brownie must have gone out, if he'd gone anywhere. Ralph slogged alongside, stumbling on the steeper spots.

Each of us tangled our webs and fell flat at least once but managed to reach the shoulder without jamming snow into our rifle muzzles.

Hooker's shout was faint but clear from his vantage point down on the beach. "Nothing moving so far! Any tracks where you are?"

But no bear had wallowed out over the shoulder. He must be under that cliff. Side by side, Young and I teetered out onto the snow slide, my .375 Weatherby at the ready. If the brownie boiled out from some cranny between rock and snow, either we'd stop him with a slug or somebody's widow would file a life-insurance claim. Stalking a bear on open ground is one thing; flopping around toward a boxed-in bear over ten feet of snow is another. A brownie can half swim through deep snow faster than a man can move on webs. The climb was not the only reason for the sweat trickling down my backbone.

But bruin was not at home. Either he had sprouted those wings or he had clawed straight up over an icy rock face that would have baffled a human fly. Common sense says he climbed but personally I prefer the other solution to the mystery—much more in keeping with that grim and barren point opposite Hubbard Glacier.

By May twentieth wind and tide had so jammed up the bergs in the narrows of Yakutat Bay that we couldn't make a second trip into the more open country at the very head, in the Russell Fiord area, without risking the *Alaska Maid* in an ice squeeze. Since by then the party was well filled up on blacks—and they're a story in themselves—the sensible thing was to keep watching those slides on the clear side of Point La Touche, and to hunt the beach and sloughs southwest from there. Best prospects were a grass-rich slough alongside the Roosevelt River, apparently named by an Indian who felt he'd been blessed by the New Deal, and a pair of slides, already green below the snow line, which rose behind Sitkagi Cove. Early in the hunt Young and I watched a very good sow bear prospecting a mussel bed along the beach with her yearling cubs, and we'd seen several sets of trophy-sized tracks above the surf. Since we were unable to land one of the fast outboards through the breakers pounding by the river, Ralph, Mike and I hiked the beach to the slough.

With Mike stationed on a point where he could glass the shoreline for two miles in either direction, Ralph and I found a soft stump near a brownie-tracked sedge patch in the meadow. Out of the wind, the rare sunshine was warm and we sleepily made plans for future assault on some virgin brown-bear country edging the biggest ice sheet on the North American continent proper, the Malespina Glacier, home of *Ursus dalli*.

"But there was half a mile of loose ice over on that shore the other day, when we got close enough for a look, and it was just as thick off to the west. How can that country be hunted, with no way to land a boat?" I asked.

"Maybe a helicopter, maybe you can land a skiff over there in the fall. I'll prospect the salmon creeks in that country one of these summers —mebbe so we can find a record bear over there . . ." dreamed Ralph.

Only a fat young black bear came out to disturb us. He meandered over the flat stuffing his belly full of spring greens, with not a care in the world. I watched him cropping sedge for half an hour, not because we wanted another black but in the hope that he might suddenly look over his shoulder and scram. Scram in fear of the boss brown bear who, by all the signs, held the lease on that grass patch. But he waddled off for a snooze and left the flat to us and a few early mosquitoes.

Out of a half-doze I spotted movement up where the creek came in. Like a sheep, was my sleepy thought. A blue sheep. Like a—"Hey—there's another glacier bear!"

Young took my glasses and quickly leveled them, but binoculars weren't needed on this fellow. Some four hundred yards upwind, too far for a dead-sure shot, a blue bear had nosed out into the open. This was a smaller animal than my first, but perfectly marked with dark head and legs, gray-blue body. The red gods were not only smiling on us—they were downright grinning. As the first killed by a sportsman in nearly fifty years, one glacier bear set some kind of record—two would be unheard of.

But by the time we could pussyfoot into shooting position, perhaps a hundred and fifty yards below the bear but as close as we could get without splashing through the hip-deep stream, that godly grin had turned into a leer. The bear had slouched back into the alders to dig out fresh skunk cabbage sprouts, and apparently there he was going to stay.

For half an hour I knelt in an icy mudhole behind a drift log, watching those light-colored blurs of movement in the brush. As they neared the edge of the thicket, up would come my rifle muzzle and tension would concentrate in sling and trigger finger. Then he'd turn back in and I could relax in the mud. This might go on forever.

"If he shows even halfway decently, Ralph, I'm going to take him. Another fifteen minutes of this and I won't be able to hit a barn," I whispered.

"Sure, go ahead. We can't get up further without crossing the creek. He's liable to duck into the timber permanently, so take whatever shot you can get," Ralph agreed. "A brownie might come out along here, too. Then whatcha going to do?"

That problem didn't need answering, fortunately, because just then the blue beast pushed his forequarters into the clear and my scope cross hairs swung onto them. Whomp! Not too sure of the placement of that first one-hundred-and-sixty-grain Barnes slug after a half hour of jittery waiting, I fed up a second round and slammed it into the blur of blue. That quieted matters at the edge of the alders.

"Brother," said Ralph, "you are a very lucky guy. We came up here figuring on a fifty-fifty chance of just *seeing* a blue bear, and now you've nailed two of 'em in less than three weeks!"

"But this one'll go to the Yale museum people," I replied. "I'm washed up for this trip, Ralph—if I push my luck any further it'll bust. Tomorrow you find a big old *Ursus* bear for one of the other guys. I'll hike back up here and bone out the carcass."

With the tide low, walking three miles back up the beach with only my lunch and a whetstone in the knapsack, the eight-pound Mashburn rifle over my shoulder, was easy next morning. But if anybody ever asks you to bone out the entire carcass of a bear, even if the skinning job is already done, you tell 'em you're going to a drapery salesmen's convention in Tucumcari. For six solid hours I pecked away at that corpse, first unjointing it to workable pieces, then whittling and carving to make smaller bony sculptures out of the chunks. Every ounce of flesh whittled off was one less ounce I'd have to pack three miles down the beach, stumbling over the rocks above the surf.

This meat probably smells pretty good to any wandering brown bear, too, I remember thinking as I heaved a hunk of flesh out into the alders. And if old long-claws walked in on me in this tangle, we'd have quite a go-around. It was quiet on the flat, not even a raven gloonking overhead —and a man's imagination gets pretty sharp under such circumstances.

Suddenly there was a horrendous scrabbling in the brush, right at the other end of the log I was using for a butcher's block. I dropped the knife and grabbed up my rifle, swinging its muzzle onto that meat-hungry brown bear.

Perched on the end of my log, much more surprised than I, sat a red squirrel, interrupted at his noisy business of scratching out a few comestibles among the dead leaves. Must have been a nervous little fellow, too, the way he was twitching his tail!

No brownie did come out. Perhaps one has since, because when I left that flat, with fifty or sixty pounds of bones—and the whetstone—sagging my packsack, the meat from that glacier bear was spread around for a hundred yards. Perhaps somebody from Young's next party of hunters met a brownie snuffling out that bait. I hope so—but with two blue-bear hides ready to salt down in their shipping kegs, I could let the brownies alone until some future trip up Yakutat way.

---

3 : King Caribou

"Look at him chasing that bull to the left!" Bob yelped, and squirmed around squarely behind the spotting scope. "Now he's shagging another one. That herd bull is going to be all pooped out before you can get down there to shoot him, Page. Take a look!"

There was no doubt about it. The king stag of that herd of caribou clustered in the bowl-shaped valley below us was wearing himself to a frazzle. By cracking down on all the other bulls in the country, bluffing or battering them into submission with a massive set of antlers pronged and palmated beyond any caribou head I'd ever before seen, he had amassed a harem of sixty cows. Yet six lesser stags still patrolled his herd, ambitious to cut out a few cows for themselves. The females, with complete disinterest, fed along quietly, hardly pausing even when the big bull jostled through them to chase off the hopefully loitering stags.

With that head, the king rated his superharem. His was just the rack I'd come five thousand miles to find. I'd traveled clear up into outfitter Bud Branham's Iliamna country, back of Kokhonak, with a rifle in one hand and the Boone and Crockett Club record listings in the other. We dropped into Round Lake in Branham's twin-engine Grumman and then slogged miles across frosted tundra to find the king caribou, but every mile and every step had been worth it, I decided as I watched him through the 20X glass.

"Brother! If you can only paint all this for Bob Kuhn. There he goes policing up the far side. See those two young bulls scram?"

Branham and I had already decided that this was the trophy bull—the best I or anyone else was likely to see during that season. Yet with our glasses focused on the herd a mile below us we almost dreaded the risky stalk that would begin once we edged over into the bowl.

"I can see six bull caribou hanging around that herd, Bud," I whispered, "and every one of them rates hanging on any man's wall. But he's the real boss, right enough. Wonder how come he doesn't chase that younger bull that's making time with some of the herd cows. What gives here, a partnership?"

In all my hunting experience I'd never seen the master male of any of the antlered animals, elk for example, let another buck or bull make passes at the females he'd collected—not without a drag-out battle. But it happens, Branham said. "Once in a while," he told me, "among the Barren Ground caribou. I've seen a setup where the king bull had collected so many cows that he gave a partner regal rights, made him sort of a crown prince."

"A share-the-wealth plan," cracked Kuhn as he set about loading his camera for the final stage of the hunt.

I tightened the caps on the spotting scope and handed the tripod to Branham. With my meat rifle, the 7 mm. Mashburn magnum, slung from the corner of my own packboard, I said, "Let's start after him." And we headed toward the line of alders that offered the only cover approaching the valley floor, toward the proud but harassed king bull.

Earlier on this same hunt both Bob and I had killed caribou. Bob's was a fine stag we'd spotted the day before a mile or two from Branham's tent camp by Round Lake. Mine had appeared three hundred miles north and a week earlier up in Rainy Pass, where Three Mile Creek cuts into Ptarmigan Valley. Both of these had been fair stags, but not real whoppers. Mine was a loner taken as he hounded his way down a mountain in search of amenable cows. But Bob's, already the boss of eight or ten females, had been impelled by curiosity or anxiety into leading his herd toward the crawling objects that were sneaking into shooting range.

In September we had seen lots of game; we even spotted half a dozen good moose on the flight into Rainy Pass, just hours after we'd stepped down onto Anchorage airport. Bob had made a try at a handsome blue-tipped Rainy Pass grizzly, only to lose him in a hundred-acre patch of alder. I had picked out a trophy moose from a score of great bulls that flashed their boards in the bush that edged Ptarmigan Valley. When you can see grizzly every day or two, and pass up sixty-five-inch moose, as I did several times, because they have a real or fancied imbalance in the antlers that might keep them from being Boone and Crockett winners, you're in real hunting country.

Despite all this, I had asked Branham to take us on the two-hour flight down to Kokhonak, because I was convinced that in the rolling tundra hills beyond Lake Iliamna, miles and miles of perfect caribou country, I'd find the really massive antlers I'd come to Alaska to get. And now we'd found them, proudly worn by the king bull below us.

From a high ridge we had first located his herd. It showed as a group of moving dots two hours from the ridge—hours, because movement across tundra country is better measured in time than in painfully counted steps or miles. There'd been another herd with at least one fair bull running it, but that bunch was even farther away and somehow we'd all felt that the larger bunch must have a real master stag bossing it.

The original landing on Round Lake to start the hunt had been tricky, calling for all the skill Branham had gained in seven thousand hours of piloting a Grumman. It was chancy because sharp frosts had rimmed the lake with ice, leaving only a dinky puddle in the center. But such concerns were now behind us; the camp was set, the game spotted, and we were ready for the final stalk.

Over the bulge and down through a patch of rich grass, where a sow brown bear and two cubs had bedded the night before, we made good time, knowing that the caribou would pay no attention to us nearly a mile away, openly visible as we were. The strip of alder-choked gully kept us in cover for a good distance down the slope, and Branham moved along fast, knowing that caribou are whimsical animals that often, for no reason, take off on sudden journeys at a high-kneed trot no man can pace. But while the herd kept on feeding, the cows with their heads down and the bulls absorbed in their rutting antics, we had a chance.

When the alders petered out, we were still seven or eight hundred yards from the bunch, and there was little cover between them and us.

Branham stopped, and again we brought the spotter and binoculars into play.

"If we can get to that cluster of moose willow over to their right, and then make like a walking blueberry bush from there to the next batch of willow, that should do it, don't you think?" I asked, puffing my wind back and easing my shoulders under the packboard drag. "Which way do you think they're feeding?"

Branham watched for a careful minute before answering. "The big bull is keeping his cows close-bunched and they seem to be working closer to those willows. We'll be moving crosswind, but that's all right if there's no freak shift. Might have to crawl some."

That didn't seem too rough, and I said so. Bob's response was something to the effect that most of us had started out in life crawling. Perhaps we had, but during the next twenty minutes I was to regret having abandoned crawling practice at the age of eighteen months or thereabouts. A grown man forgets to exercise those hands-and-knees muscles.

We made the first clump of willows in fine shape, simply by walking in a fast lockstep in full view of the herd. We looked like either a bear—of which the caribou have little fear—or three men imitating marching convicts, and that they'd probably never seen before. At any rate, we reached the dense willow brush and rested for a short blow.

Branham led the way out for the next lap, ambling on hands and knees low behind a sheltering swell of tundra. My turn came next to crawl. The first ten yards were easy, but then the packboard started to work up, first onto my shoulders, then so high as to edge my cap off into the muskeg. My rifle flopped forward and tangled an elbow, the sling strap and a blueberry bush in neat confusion. Every placement of my knees was either on a crosshatch of edged twigs or onto a blob of frost-juicy berries that blued trousers and longjohns clear to the skin.

At the fifty-yard mark I could see Branham ahead in the sheltering willows, doubled in a frenzy of silent laughter. Behind me, Bob lumbered along with troubles identical to mine, save that he fought cameras instead of pack and rifle.

By snaking through the screen of tangled willows we had earned ringside seats for a domestic comedy, caribou style. The stage was still almost four hundred yards away, and we couldn't hear any dialogue, but the king bull was busily chasing one ambitious stag, then another, trying to keep his harem clustered. Yet he paid no attention to the "crown prince" bull, which was actively favoring the cows that pleased him. The wind held steady crosswise as we watched, and the caribou seemed to be shifting slightly toward the hump of tundra, perhaps fifty yards ahead of our hideout in the willows, from which I planned to shoot. Time for another check on the stag.

Bob was monkeying with the telephoto on his single-lens reflex, and Branham had the spotter lined up. "I can see only one brow palm," the outfitter muttered to me, "but it's a good foot wide and I'd guess seven or eight points. Now, if he'll stand for a moment. . . . The beams aren't the longest I've ever seen, but the spread will be terrific, close to fifty—and those tops are the heaviest I ever saw. Palmated like a moose. He'll tally well over four hundred points. Might be a record——"

By now my eye was behind the rifle-scope eyepiece. It's tough evaluating a caribou trophy, what with all the odd sprockets and difficult measurements, even when the bull is dead and will hold still for a steel tape. I certainly couldn't judge this great stag by eighths of an inch while he was busy bluffing off the bulls that threatened his throne. But he was all I wanted in a caribou. "Let's go," I said. "I'll never be any readier."

We bellied out to the next hump and I got the rifle steady, my left hand solid in the moss for the three-hundred-and-fifty-yard shot. But the bull wouldn't stand still. The white of his cape kept disappearing behind a screen of feeding cows as he edged the pretenders away from his boundaries. Whenever he stopped, with his head low, rack back and mouth open, in the manner of all rutting caribou, a cow or a yearling would move to a new moss patch and blank him from the lens of my 4X. Branham lay beside me, glasses on the herd, calling the plays like a sportscaster. This first shot had to be right, had to stop the stag cold, because if he ran with the herd I could never pick him out of the clutter.

"Calf in front of him now," shouted Branham. "He's starting to come out through the little bunch in the center of the herd and I think he'll stand. Sure ought to!"

Seemed so to me, too, after all the exercise that bull had had, and ten minutes more of suspenseful watching, even on the soft tundra, would have exhausted a stone man. My forefinger had taken up all but the last few ounces of trigger pull, and the cross hairs were following the gray-white cape as the bull worked our way. He was clear, almost broadside—and he stood.

The whang of the rifle sent the whole herd off fifty yards. Then they turned in confusion and stood watching the master bull as he staggered in circles. The 7 mm. magnum jarred again and he crumpled to the moss. The king was dead.

But long live the king! Even as the second shot stirred the caribou herd into confused flight the crown prince, the partner stag, took control. He herded up the stragglers, pushed the cows up over the tundra roll and out of sight, and even as he turned for the last look of caribou curiosity he dropped his muzzle and rushed at one of the hanger-on stags. The king might be dead, but his throne was filled again, the kingdom secure.

All else was anticlimactic—the dazed inspection of the boss bull, the discovery that my rifle fitted inside his basket with half a foot to spare, the job of caping him out and packing trophy and meat over five miles of hilly, mushy tundra to Round Lake. Then we got out the tape, the Boone and Crockett blanks, and a pencil. The big bull was a hard one to measure, with the wide palmation in his tops, but as the figures were added the tension began to mount again to a new climax. He might conceivably go into the No. 2 spot in the printed records. Or then he might not, depending on how the difficult measurement rules were interpreted.* But there couldn't be too much anticlimax there, no matter what official figures eventually come from the judges, because this is a fine trophy caribou, king size.

"Did you see the way that other bull took over instantly?" murmured Bob as we sank back to rest that night. "Just like humans these caribou, no?" On that the artist and the hunter could find no argument.

4 : On Your Feet

Since childhood days, when real basketball sneakers were the *sine qua non,* I have always been strenuously interested in footgear, some say abnormally so. But a concern with boots and shoes is proper to the man who hunts seriously and wants to do it in comfort.

Most of our nimrods have the idea that a pair of moccasin-toed boots eight or ten inches high, with more-or-less hubbly soles, or a pair of rubber-bottomed, leather-topped boots, such as were two generations back developed by the original L. L. Bean, answer all our hunting needs and most of those overseas. Would this were true, since life would then be simple. But the first type, comfortable enough though they be, like the rubber jobs give your feet little protection or support. They are essentially correct footgear only for the mild usages of bird shooting, and largely dry-ground bird shooting at that. The second, originally conceived for the wet-or-snowy-underfoot situations of Maine deer hunting, are excellent

---

* The official score tallied 419⅝".

for just that, north-country deer hunting in early or midseason before the thermometer really drops to the iron-cold or toe-freezing level. For wet-ground bird shooting, spring turkey hunting and such, they're fine too.

But they have no place on the mountain. The soft-bottomed boot in high country can bruise your feet, means needless sprains and sorenesses from uneven ground. In sections where you climb hard, use your feet hard, the rubber-bottom shoe merely adds the problem of perspiration-soaked socks. And finally, equipping such rubber-bottoms with Vibram-style cleated soles, so they'll stick on the mountains, is a snare and a delusion. They stick, yes, but then the soft top of the boot slides around so your cleated sole is flat on the slope and you're walking the sidehill not on the hooflike edge of a properly stiff boot, but on the side of your foot. And will probably fall on your butt, too.

The best boot for the goat hunter and the sheep hunter who is going to work steep territory, with all the mountain attributes of shale slides, slopes so steep they'll hold only grass, rock ledges, and such is the mountain boot. That is the boot developed for maneuvering around in mountains by the people who do it, originally by the Swiss, Italians, Austrians, the alpine types. Hunting sheep is perhaps not quite the same thing as making an ascent of the Grand Tetons, to be sure, but essentially the same shoes work just dandy.

These are normally six to eight inches high, which is plenty, unless you're wading around in snow, and for that the combination of scree-tight tops and thick wool socks works out about as dry as ten-inch boots anyway. They are stiff-soled, with cleated Vibram. They are stiff-toed, against rock bruises. They are stiff-countered, so your ankles will stay upright on a hillside, the cleated edge of the boot dig in. Ever notice how a horse can walk calmly across an incredibly steep hillside?

Mountain boots are internally padded for comfort and support, and often the laces are covered against wet by a protective flap. Such boots need a lot of breaking in, should be used over two pairs of socks, are as waterproof when correctly treated as any other waterproof boot. All but one of the types made in these United States are needlessly heavy; rough-side-out types are reasonably light and fine in dry weather but will soak up water like a blotter. If you can latch onto European-made climbing boots you'll be better satisfied.

In the fall of 1969 I was lucky enough to be in Vienna for a few days. The time netted me two pairs of boots which will assuredly last out my hunting life. One pair was handmade by expedition-supplier Mortz, cost only twenty-four dollars, which would likely be three times that over here. I wore them chamois hunting for three days with no break-in but without blisters or any significant foot soreness, and enjoyed sure stability in a section of the Austrian Alps which is hardly a staircase. They've since been to the Corzala ranges of Spain for ibex and to the Cassiars of British Columbia for stone sheep.

The one major drawback of any Vibram-soled boot—which remember should be of a stiffly supportive design—is evident in riding. Those sharp cleat corners do not slip readily out of a stirrup, so that a horse that falls on a bad place or suddenly goes into a rodeo frenzy can give you a really bad time. I compromise. That is, I usually tote along smooth-soled boots, even riding boots, for pack trips in and out, use the cleated jobs only on the shorter hunting rides.

Years back there was considerable noise made in print about logger boots, with or without hobs. These are fine for the man who has all his life worn a high-heeled boot. For the city-dweller used to flat heels and flat pavements they are unmitigated disaster, and hobs—either soft iron hobs or the sharp steel spikes used by timber-workers—should never be used by the average Joe Hunter. He'll make a lot of noise on the rocks, and more after he lands on his ear a few times.

Don't expect too much by way of waterproofing, either. Several brands of leather boot today make flat guarantees about being waterproof. Could be they are, if the boot is left standing in a bucket. They may stay nicely dry during casual wading in and out of the creek. But I have never yet, in a lifetime of hunting, found *any* leather boot or any compound to treat leather boots that would stand more than two days of steady hiking through slushy snow, or through soaked forest moss. The combination of steady rubbing and soaking will leak right through the guarantee!

A year or two back I was in Montana during the elk-bugling season, hunting a section of the Bob Marshall Wilderness which gets abnormally heavy rainfall, is brushy, and in many areas is floored in moss. It rained on us for eight straight days. I was wearing a new pair of boots 100 per-cent waterproof, so the ads said. At midday of the third day they gave up entirely, became as waterproof as a lace curtain, and thereafter my feet were wet, save when I was in the sleeping bag. Those boots were still wet inside when they returned to the maker's plant.

Of course the only decent thing to do is to help the guarantor along, keep your boots treated daily. Silicone sprays or swab-on fluids work best on siliconized and welded boots like those from Browning or Dunham. On other leathers, a greasy dubbin like the Arctic Dubbing obtainable in Canada, or any other boot grease, will work after a fashion, the method of application being as important as the formula. Put it on and rub it in only when the boots are warm and dry. Repeat treatments, and repeat again before you leave on a trip.

The general-purpose U.S. hunting boot is becoming this "waterproof" leather type, with a medium-soft, mildly cleated sole, lined, insulated or not as the climate indicates, between eight and ten inches high. Daniel Boone would've given up all his raccoon tails for a pair of these, believe me. They work fine, so long as you don't expect them to do specialized jobs or believe the bunkum about their being waterproof.

Siliconized or even oil-tanned leathers are an abomination in Africa, of course. If your safari is headed for stony country like the NFD a pair of World War II GI shoes, rough side out, is just dandy. The blucher-style moccasin, about five or six inches high, such as those made by Bean and other mail-order outfits, works fine once the oil is out of the leather. Typical bird-shooter boots are needlessly high, and, since their hides are oily, will make your feet sweat unpleasantly. I once experimented with Corfam boots on a Uganda safari in a semidesert area and nearly ruined my feet in the Corfam. Waterproofing limits breathing—precisely opposite to what you need under hot and dry circumstances.

One of the handiest of shoes for mild-country Africa is the desert sandal, the crepe-soled, chukka-height shoe made with sueded leather. As turned out by Clark's of England in the original model these go for about fifteen dollars the pair, by Bata of Czechoslovakia for half that in a cheap but practical imitation available in most African towns, and in skived elephant hide, handmade by assorted Hindu gentlemen in Nairobi, for about twenty-five dollars. These are all moderately cool, sloppy enough to be comfortable, but should you chase an elephant for fifteen or twenty miles in them you'll create new blisters on the old ones.

For really wet country, bongo hunting, swampy jungle, the best footgear is a six- or seven-inch shoe of canvas and cleated soft rubber made in France and sold by Abercrombie and Fitch in the States. The hemp insoles are removable to speed the drying-out process. I suspect our military Viet Nam boots are a derivative.

None of the literature ever mentions what to me is one of the most important forms of footgear, the aprés-hunt shoe, if we may swipe a phrase from the skiing fraternity. Guides and outfitters—and also horses—seem to be happy to spend the evening wearing the same clodhoppers they've hunted in all day; but most ordinary citizens enjoy a switch to dry socks and restfully light slip-ons. These must have enough top and enough sole to be reasonably wetproof since campgrounds are forever damp.

Heavy socks, worn inside the low topless rubbers, such as appear in Bean and Bauer catalogs, aren't bad; the fleece-lined soled slippers with zipper fronts, as made to wear inside duck boots, are fine, especially if you have the local cobbler add thin rubber soles. So are cheap stadium boots. Or moccasins with socks. Ordinary house slippers are not worth duffel-bag room, since a gentle dew will soak their soles through during your first jaunt to enjoy the 3 A.M. scenery.

All rubber or rubber-bottomed hunting footgear should be equipped with insoles, their function being partly to reinforce the sole, add some protection against stone bruises, partly to serve to soak up the dampness inevitable inside rubber. About 1960 I turned up in Norway, a country where 99 44/100 percent of the hunting is necessarily done in knee-length rubbers, a type of plastic insole called Skankes, and I have been using these ever since. About three-sixteenths of an inch thick, these are slashed in a herringbone pattern with slots which are broad on the side toward the boot sole, narrow toward the foot. They create an air space between foot and boot, and hiking produces a pumping action which means your socks end up dry and the boot sole wet, so your feet stay warm. Bob Hinman of Peoria, Illinois, sells these but makes little money out of them because one pair lasts a hunting lifetime.

Insulated rubbers ten to twelve inches long have their place in goose pits, some duck blinds, in stump-sitting for whitetail deer, in late-season horseback hunting in the western states when it is really cold. Nothing is better for these. But they are not worth a damn if you must walk more than a mile. They're heavy and awkward, and if you move hard enough to work up a sweat, the insides become so clammy there's question as to which you'd rather be, cold or wet. In recent years, incidentally, the U.S. market has seen a flood of cold-weather boots made in Japan, fancily molded and lined with phony fleece. Unless you have short feet like a Japanese, forget 'em. And remember that once that fleecy lining is wet with sweat, it's damp forevermore.

Items like mukluks for the Arctic ice, wirelined leggings or loose-legged, Gokey-type leather boots for quail operations in rattlesnake country, the tight-ankled hip boots (today made only by Red Ball) so suitable for most Alaskan hunting, are all highly specialized, and ordinarily the outfitter will specify to his customers any such type of footgear needed to be comfortable in.

But the general subject certainly merits hard thought during packing for a trip. You can get along with the wrong pants, and the wrong shirts, or the wrong jacket, but your sleeping bag or bed accommodations must be up to snuff and suit the climate or you'll run out of poop in short order; your underwear must be right or you'll be highly uncomfortable from heat or cold; and if your footgear isn't correct, you'll fall on your face or at best hunt at far below peak efficiency. Don't be a boob about boots.

5 : The Lazarus Bull

The dead elk wasn't there. When Roy and I finally worked our way down the sixty-degree hogback to the snow-filled chute bottom, the dead bull had vanished. But the six-pointer had neither evaporated nor ascended into elk heaven. He had walked off, the tracks said, first staggering for a few yards, then moving out strongly, leaving behind a few spots of blood at the top end of a melted-in and flattened body shape in the snow.

"I saw him go down flat. He didn't move for five minutes. Dead as a doornail," muttered Roy Feutz, my Lander-based guide on a 1968 hunt in the Gros Ventre Range. Then, his voice rising, "Why that colorful language offspring of a colorful language canine was DEAD!"

"And like Lazarus he rose," I agreed solemnly. But it wasn't funny at all.

Two hours and about two miles of black timber blowdowns later we were licked. The "dead" bull had traveled steadily. He had left no further blood, had neither slipped nor stumbled in the hard places, and the spike we had earlier seen with this six-pointer had rejoined him. The bull, however defunct he had been for five minutes, was healthier and traveling faster than we were. Total frustration.

In what is now a full generation of what some think of as professional hunting, this misery has happened to me twice before, and I have witnessed it one other time. The trouble is not the fault of the bullet or the caliber or the rifle but solely of the hunter. He has shot a mite high.

Next time you quarter an elk—or trot down to the nearest wholesale beef distributor if elk aren't handy—note that between the forequarters that hump we call the withers is created by a series of fingerlike bony processes, or vertebrae extensions, which stick straight up from the spine. They project upwards at that point, more or less between the shoulder blades, where the spine crooks down decidedly between neck and back line. Shoot too high, bang a bullet in where it will jar those bony fingers yet will not actually break up the spine proper, and you do the beast no really permanent damage. But you will very probably stun him into immobility, create the effect of a Dempsey-like punch on a Milquetoast jaw.

Years ago in Quebec it took only a matter of seconds for the moose I'd hit too high to fall flat and wave his feet in the air before coming to, perhaps fifteen seconds; and the zebra in Zambia had managed to recover from spine shock collapse in moments, to sprint off while I was rounding a litter of mopane brush. The Lazarus elk just broke all the records by being down and presumably dead for at least three minutes, indeed more like five. And he was long gone.

Getting even that one chance had come hard. The year before, during the 1967 season, late October had seen Wyoming's upper Gros Ventre trails choked with snow belly-deep on a horse. The elk were out of the timber, congregating in bunches of a hundred or more, pawing out feed on the high alpine meadows where wind had blown the snow thin. Cold, and tough going—but pick your bull. In 1968, at October's end, however, there could be no selection, just a sweaty scramble to find any elk. Warm weather, actually hot at midday, had the herds scattered over north-slope bedding grounds, steep as a barn roof and everywhere tangled with blow-downs impassable to horses and at nine thousand feet nearly impossible for men. Prying elk out of the cool darkness of those spruce fastnesses takes either dynamite or a heavy, cold snow, and we hadn't much luck in finding the fuse for either.

The high Gros Ventre where the river flows southeast from its source before whiplashing around the foot of Sportsman's Ridge northwest toward the Snake and the valley before the Tetons, is superb elk country. It holds the classic mixture of high meadows, forested slopes dotted with little parks where the grass grows fat, peaks high enough to keep the bulls fly-free in summer. The elk have a fine route out to Jackson Hole wintering grounds, and a good way in over spring calving areas. And most important, four-wheel-drive vehicles are out. They can make it only to a point some eight miles downstream of the hook-shaped bend, or onto Bacon Ridge lying east. All the other country northwesterly up beyond the ultimate Gros Ventre spring, onto Darwin Peak toward Pyramid and the rest, is horse country.

"And it will stay that way, too," said Loring Woodman, the young man who operates the Darwin Ranch for a few dudes and fishermen in summer, and a half dozen hunters at a time in the fall. "This quarter section is totally surrounded by national forest land untouched for generations. Unless Union Plywood, which has already logged off the Union Pass country to the east, manages to bamboozle the Forest Service into letting them cut up the Gros Ventre, just to keep their Dubois mill operating, it may stay that way. The game commission people seem to think chopping up this area with roads and lumbered-over areas would be the end of the Gros Ventre elk herd. From what I hear, there's some small chance that the elk and deer range between here and Jackson may end up as primitive or wilderness area."

"That would get my vote," I agreed. "Mighty little country left without the stench of gasoline. And lumbering this range would be a vile sin."

The Lazarus bull who grew up in it had been a dandy. Actually he was a raunchy, rangy old bull, probably totally bereft of fat after a season of running a harem of a dozen or so cows, but his head sprouted widespread antlers with six long points on a side, a proper trophy. Theoretically, of course, I hadn't come out to Wyoming to bust any monstrous old bull whose gravy would bend a fork, but to bag a first-rate chunk of meat. At least, the heap-big chief of the local gun club back home had so requested.

"You get a fat young bull down as far as the freezer in Pinedale," he instructed, "and we'll pay for the packaging and shipping of all the elk steaks you can't use at home. Our February stag party will be big enough this year to eat a whole elk."

Of course he didn't understand the trophy hunter's natural instincts. Faced with a quick choice between a fat spike and that stringy old hat-rack, I had automatically chosen the trophy-horned bull—and then flubbed even that. From here on out I'd better be looking for a tender one.

Even that was tantalizing. We kept seeing elk. One midmorning from one glassing spot we picked up two cows and a spike, then a dozen cows, then a bunch over two dozen, all heading off the open park country down into spruce thickets on the north slopes. We rode within knife-throwing range of seven cows so suddenly they stood in bug-eyed horror almost long enough for me to get the camera working. But only the moose common to the Gros Ventre region, at this season up into the mountains for the rut, would stand to have their pictures taken. One dawn we rode up the steep section of Sportsman's Ridge. No one could account for that corn-ball name, but I have a sneaking suspicion it dates back to the days shortly after the century's turn, when on behalf of one of his Rough Rider buddies, Fred Darwin, Teddy Roosevelt used a spot of influence to carve out of national forest for him the unique quarter section on which Woodman's ranch house now stands. During the climb Roy Feutz saw a bull with real hip-scratching horns melt down into the forest. I didn't see it. My noble steed, a lazy female correctly named Nasty Biter, wouldn't get up within thirty yards of Roy's gelding. Perhaps they'd feuded previously.

We were certain that victory was ours when the glasses picked up the creamy body of a bull deep in timber across a steep-sided gully. But he wouldn't stay put while we tiptoed into range. Since tiptoeing on a forty-five-degree slope heavy with crusted snow and blowdowns is noisier than falling off a tin roof, that wasn't surprising.

Roy was getting discouraged. So was I. We spotted three cows one late afternoon, bedded or lazily feeding on a grassy bench a full mile across a timber-filled basin from us. There had to be more elk in that bunch, hidden in the shadows. If we could work our way across and up to that higher level where a shadow rimrock slanted uphill, we would strike a fringe of timber right above 'em. It took over an hour, since the basin had a canyon down its middle that human flies could negotiate better than horses. The stalk was perfect. We sneaked into within forty feet. But there were still only those three cows. Not even a spike, and my license called for an antlered critter.

"We've tried Grizzly Basin and Alpine Meadows and Pine Meadows and those parks down the Hollow Log Trail and Bugle Basin and Hungry Meadows and a dozen other good spots," Roy summarized after dinner one evening, a ranch meal rendered no less palatable by the fact that Woodman's idea of a proper cook is a sharp-looking ski instructress waiting for snow. "I am stuck."

"How about Sleepy Hollow?" asked Woodman, who had somehow managed to get a piano into his remote ranch, and had been exercising it with the works of Johann Sebastian Bach, no connection with the Beatles. "Have you tried up there?"

After the first day or so that hadn't occurred to us. The high hollow was the largest grass and sagebrush park really near the ranch, only a half hour up the ridge, and while we had on occasion seen night-before elk sign as we passed through it, certainly no area tagged Sleepy Hollow could hold elk. That name belonged to a place on the Hudson River, two thousand five hundred miles to the east, where a skinny character named Ichabod Crane met up with the Headless Horseman. I didn't dare ask Woodman why the name. I had asked why one horse was named Public Enemy No. 1, and his answer to that one showed why foolish questions get foolish answers.

"Earlier this season elk fed in there every morning," Woodman continued. "Why not ride up in the dark and watch it at dawn?"

We'd tried all the hard places, made all the ten- and twelve-hour rides. Maybe an easy one would produce.

It was less than full dark when we eased into the lower edge of the park, having left our horses tied well back. Scattered patches of old snow crunched under our boots. The sun had already broken the eastern horizon, threw flatly horizontal rays of gold across the up-sloping park. The place was empty. No. Not empty. My glasses showed elk hazy in the cold shadows halfway up the park. Cows. Five cows. But one was light-colored. The sun had lifted by inches and a beam cut sharply through the timber to cross that animal. It was a bull! Not a big one, a five-pointer, but seemingly fat. Probably he had been no Casanova during the earlier month.

There can be something of anticlimax, I discover as I get older in hunting years, in the actual dropping of a game animal once the search and the stalk are done. There was a snag a few feet from where we lurked in the concealing timber. I crawled over to it, still in the shade, and slipped a round into the chamber of the 7 mm. Taylor and Robbins wild-cat. Roy was whispering that his idea of the range was two hundred and fifty yards. I didn't agree. It was well over three hundred, unless the early light was fooling both of us. But with the help of the snag the cross hairs steadied and the rifle bucked. Should be good, I thought, as we heard the zop of the bullet striking home. The cows ran but the bull stayed right there, staggering. None of that guessing he's dead, I muttered. This must be sure, and the rifle zipped another one-hundred-and-sixty-grain Nosler across the sage. The bull went down.

And then the work began. A trip down for pack horses, a trip back up and then down again with the meat. I just hope those gun-club guys enjoy their elk steaks next February. I may be chewing along with the rest, but I'll be thinking of the Lazarus bull, the long-horned one that died and then ran away. Like to meet him again next year.

---

6 : Snowshoe Grizzly

By the time Bob Kuhn, Bud Branham, and I had zipped up our sleeping bags we'd made a fair start on the subject of bears. We'd covered bloody-fanged charges real and imaginary, agreed that no North American animal stirs a hunter's adrenalin like a husky grizzly, and that bears are more fun than people.

But we still weren't much closer to a record-quality spring grizzly than when we first stepped off a plane at Anchorage on April ninth—into a foot of new snow. That had meant three to ten feet in the mountains. During the ski-plane flights in to Branham's Rainy Pass Lodge and then to one of Bud's trapping cabins, we'd seen little sign of bear. Sheep on the peaks, moose and caribou tracking up the valleys, but only at one spot the wallowing "road" a big bruin makes through the spring thaw. Binocular prospecting had located one bear trail across Portage Creek. We'd try him in the morning.

Before the bacon sizzled we were back in the ursine debate of the evening before. This time on the differences, if any, between brownies and grizzlies.

"Back at Rainy Pass," Bob said, "Ray Harris told me coastal bears chase salmon three hundred miles up the Kuskokwim. They brownies or grizzlies?"

"All the straight-snouted, big-headed, hump-shouldered bears along the Rockies and along into Siberia are of the grizzly family, Bob," I replied. "Thirty-odd types according to one naturalist, fortunately now discredited. A Cold Bay bear fat on salmon naturally grows a bigger skull than a timberline grizzly living on berries. The Boone and Crockett Club people had to draw a line somewhere."

"Well," put in Bud, "I've seen saltwater bears back pretty high, but it's reasonable to classify as brownies all the grizzly types within seventy-five miles of tidewater and those further back as grizzlies. These critters come in half the colors in your paintbox, Bob, but any grizzly you find up here, a hundred and fifty miles in, will be a mountain bear." *

And so we snowshoed around the mountain toward the old tracks. They crossed Portage Creek above where it flows into the upper Skwentna. Downstream five moose humped black against the snow. Moose were old stuff. But then my 7 X 35's picked out a new trail wallowing upcreek. The bear had started across the frozen stream, but the drag of wet-thawed snow or the icy bluff of the south bank had turned him back to our side. Where?

"I don't think he went over the range," said Bud. "Fresh out of hibernation, his pads will be tender. Let's go."

Noon sun had us shedding jackets before we reached the new tracks. They were fresh. No crusting around the edges, great dishpan-sized wallows. In deep snow a thousand-pound bear—and the paw marks bottoming each hole showed this one was a buster—can't walk on top. He swims along, bulldozing his way with brute strength.

Nothing to it but point our snowshoes along the trail up a scramble-and-grab gully into the timber. The bear's broad-beamed road wound aimlessly to a low-branched spruce where he'd dug out a snoozing place. He'd left there only minutes before. Silver-tipped chocolate hairs were still unfrozen where body heat had thawed the snow. But he'd torn out at a swimming gallop, ramming his way straight up the steep mountainside.

A half hour of trailing through frost-squeaky snow only proved what we already knew. "He's taken out," decided Bud. "Bedded close to the

* Since the writing of this story, and since the occurrences therein, Boone and Crockett has twice altered the brownie-grizzly line. The present line of distinction is generally the crest of the Alaska and Chugach ranges, little more realistic than the original seventy-five-mile line.

creek, he scented us when we battled up that gully. No sense in a marathon."

Fagged out, we stopped on a bald ridge for another look over the country, but every sagging muscle snapped alive when Bob muttered under his binoculars, "What's that on the edge of the timber, in that fringe of alders?"

Bud and I followed his direction to a sentinel spruce just below the bare snow-sweep of the peak. We could pick out a dark blob.

"Winter-killed moose, Bud?" I queried. "Live one wouldn't feed that high in April."

"Nope, that's your bear—see how light he shows? He's going to lie down. Think you can make it?"

No need to answer—we'd come too far to let aching ankles keep my scope cross hairs off that bear.

Stripped of all surplus gear, we followed the ridge toward that marker spruce. Wind in our faces was a help when the fast pace meant opened shirts.

The timber thinned, and we shuffled up through patches of cottonwoods and alder tangles. Fifteen minutes' climb and then a puff. Repeat, endlessly. No admiring the scenery, though we were not far west of Mount McKinley. Just snowshoe up.

Closer now and I was easing each web into Bud's tracks to make the least possible snow-squeak. A mess of alders and the single spruce. In this tangle, if I flubbed the shot, we'd be under an avalanche of mad grizzly.

Bud stopped. There was a lump in the brush snarl ahead a hundred yards. A brownish lump, silvery.

No time for binoculars—up with the .35 magnum and look through the scope. Thank heaven for 4X at such times. We were on the grizzly. But no killing shot from there. Through calf-thick alder stems only his head showed clear. I couldn't smash a bullet into that skull, not when I knew he was a record-sized bear.

Up the slope to get a clear angle. Now turn slow. And my left snowshoe trembled down across the right just as the bear came up! Broadside, clear. Tanglefoot or not, my two-hundred-and-seventy-five-grain slug cannoned into his shoulder.

With a bawling roar the grizzly flinched, sagged, struggled into the finisher. A last kick sent snow flying. We had a bear, half a ton of square-headed grizzly.

The fading afternoon left time for Bob to sketch only a few pictures if we were to make the cabin before black dark. Next day it was a long haul to skin out the perfect hide and an anxious wait until we could boil the skull and measure it on the square. 15⅛ x 10 meant 25⅛ points raw.

'Way up on the list. It could shrink only a hair before the official measurement, I knew.

So there was nothing shrinking about the chap who later boarded the Anchorage-Seattle flight and tenderly stowed a carton under his seat. With that bear-smelling package, he was no violet either. But he was happy.

---

7 : Moving over Snow

For my money there's a world of difference between snowmobiles and snowshoes, and in this day and age the gasoline-powered beltmobile is the popular choice. This is too bad. A man doesn't know wilderness until he has ghosted through it on slats or webs, the only sound the faint powdery crunch of his footgear. Certainly such personal contact with the snowy world is totally lost if you whiz through it with a smelly buzz-saw roar.

The two-cycle engine has a unique ability to make nasty noises, which is bad enough in itself, as the ultimate invasion of privacy, but even worse is the list of uses to which the snowbuggies are put by those who have no sense of responsibility, or even in some cases by those who do. State troopers have a new problem, with camps and summer homes stripped in January by snowmobilers. Passing laws about running down snowbound deer or elk with vehicles, with which the ability to outlast the game is limited only by the fuel supply, is a waste of time. No game commission or conservation department has the manpower to enforce such regulations, even if income from the gas buggies came into such departments, as ordinarily it does not. Nor is there much point in establishing rules about what roads or trails can and cannot be used by the rackety belt-drives, for the same reason. If people are going to cheat on snowmobiles, if they are going to use them in hunting during the legal season or even afterwards, they're going to cheat.

A simpler way as far as the National Forest and BLM areas of the West are concerned—and there the negative effects of the vehicles are greater than in most sections of the eastern states—would be to keep the devices completely out of said areas, save perhaps for official vehicles. It's all very fine to have Glacier Park operating in midwinter for the snowmobile enthusiasts, if there can be—and there can't—absolute guarantees they won't violate decency by bothering game beasts that are only just about cutting it in deep snow anyway. A hateful attitude, mine, say the manufacturers—but they certainly rate no kudoes for what might laughingly be called the educational campaigns they have mounted, or failed to mount, to indicate fitting use of their equipment.

8 : Big Red's Jaguar

Curtis Prock looked worried when I first saw him across the customs barrier at Belize. Glad to see me, but deeply worried. I had finished clearing my cameras and the .44 Ruger carbine before I found out why.

"Gotta get right back to camp," the hound man explained hurriedly. "Three dogs down from a big cat. I don't think we can save Joe and Big Red. Both badly cut up and in shock."

As we rattled for miles across the Honduran flatlands behind the hurricane-wracked town of Belize I got the whole story, in bits and pieces. "We'd run this *tigre* three or four times in the past two seasons. A big one, biggest track I ever saw. But he got smart. Won't tree. Won't even bay up. Runs about so far, then turns back into the dogs and just cuts 'em to pieces. I sewed up a slash in Big Red's neck you could put your fist in." He cursed as the Land Rover jounced through a pothole, but he was damning the dog-killing jaguar, not the local road mender.

Prock's feelings were reasonable enough. He had started the season—November through May in British Honduras—with forty-four dogs, and saw them reduced to twenty-six by disease and the lightning claws of jaguars. The bloody damage inflicted by the cat he had come to call Bigfoot was the crowning blow, because two of the dogs cut up were prized animals, long with him on mountain lions and *tigre* from the southwestern states on down into Central America. And top jaguar dogs do not come cheap.

I knew that the going price for completely trained, trail-reliable hounds with just the right amount of fear of the big spotted cats mixed with their bawling bravery, was from three hundred to eight hundred dollars. Hardly mutts! Poor hounds won't push a jaguar .hard enough to force him to tree; good dogs that are too brave will live through only one short bout with the leopard of the Americas. It takes just the right mixture of scent-ing ability, deep-lunged drive, and sense to make the perfect jaguar dog.

That evening we took a gasoline lantern into the shack where the wounded hounds lay. Queenie, a bluetick bitch, had already recovered from her few scratches and came to greet us. But Joe, the huge black-and-tan, and Red, the stout-legged redbone, only lethargically thumped their tails in the dirt as the lantern gleam hit their eyes. They were sick dogs. But both had come out of shock, guide Dave Shaw told us. Joe, he re-ported, had not only taken water but had eaten, despite the great vertical gouge sewn up across the shoulder muscles. And Red finally raised his head to meet Prock's caressing hand. Barring infection, they'd both make it. The relief was clear in Prock's weatherbeaten face.

"But I doubt they'll be able to run while you're here," he gloomed as we sat over coffee in the dining tent of his safari-style camp layout. Then he brightened. "Plenty of dogs left, though, and tomorrow morning I'll send out Charro with one pack and Dave Shaw with another while you go quail shooting. This late in the season we've pretty well worked over the area between here and Orange Walk, but there have been two *tigre* periodically moving around not far from camp. They might make con-tact."

The jaguar shares one trait with the tiger of India. He tends to hunt his own area, moving in an irregular circuit; his prints may appear on a mahogany-cutting trail or on the edges of an orange plantation at eight- or ten-day intervals. Hence the jaguar hunter needs, other than good hounds, a kind of intuitive sense of the big cat's habits.

He must also make it his business to be friendly with the local people over a wide region, to establish a network of reliable jungle-wise natives and gum-collecting *chicleros* who will pass on reports of fresh tracks seen. And he must know the terrain, every last swampy pond and every one of the grown-over trails made by the mahogany cutters and occasionally used by rosetted cats. Prock had all these elements under control. His clients had scored 100 percent the first season in Honduras and more than 80 per-cent the second—incredibly high performance on jaguars.

"Not that we can't strike out," I assured him after three days of hunt-ing over road and drawing a blank on cat tracks. We'd had a good time in the afternoons with the Central American quail, like our bobwhite but an ounce or two smaller. They coveyed up everywhere on the grassy pine ridges. "Last jaguar hunt I was on, down in Bolivia, we worked two weeks and Dale Lee wore out two mules without finding a track made since the Gran Chaco war."

"Then let's change our luck," smiled Curtis. "Lots of this country you haven't seen yet."

I suspect there's a certain amount of British Honduras that nobody has seen, save for the wandering *chicleros* who tap the chewing gum trees scattered through the country. But we were to see considerable of it in the next five days.

To the first stop was six hours at truck speed, back toward Belize, then south through billowing dust on the Humming Bird Highway, which was named by some gent with more imagination than sense, and then west again to a river. There a hand-powered ferry crossed us to Banana Walk Plantation. No bananas, but many bulls and more cows, Banana Walk being a cattle ranch hacked out of the bush by Dave Shaw's family. This should be sure pop. Everybody knows jaguars like stray calves. But apparently Dave's sister, who could run cattle through the tick dip better than the *vaqueros*, had all the loose calves protectively penned. Or perhaps the local jaguars had switched to a diet of brocket deer, peccary, or the tasty *gibnat* or *paca*, which looks like a cross between a spotted young pig and a hamster, and makes better fried chicken than either. The big cats certainly weren't around the cattle-growing area.

We even prospected the steep-banked river, sliding a dugout canoe onto the bars and cuts where a jaguar might drop down from the jungle to drink. No tracks fresher than three or four days. Plenty of iguanas, though.

"Like iguana?" asked Prock. "Bust that one on the log for supper."

I gulped, recalling all too vividly the taste of the roast alligator tail we'd tried in Bolivia when supplies ran low. That was protein and edible, even if it did taste like a codfish reared in a henyard. But Curtis and Dave and the boys could have the iguana. The steel-jacketed Norma softnose from the .44 magnum carbine might be considered proper lizard medicine for iguana, however, because when the slug went in one end and out the other, it left nothing but skin and about four feet of whiplike tail. Precleaned iguana. Personally, I still prefer a good bait of rattlesnake meat.

There had been late rains, so there was no reason why either the jaguar's natural game or the cats themselves should stay near the river. Perhaps we'd better move farther back in toward the hills we could see rising blue in the west, out among the mahogany cutters. The soft-spoken Honduran who drove their supply tractor had reported jaguar prints along the main track.

What he neglected to tell us was that said main track had become gluey mud, impassable for either the Land Rover or our truck of camp gear, several miles short of the clear jungle stream that bordered the country we wanted to hunt. So we made a dry camp, and had the choice of either extra foot mileage every day or the borrowing of a ranch tractor as basic transport. Our vote on that was unanimous.

On the hill trails that are slashed through the jungle to get out the four-foot logs of mahogany, we found the smaller pad marks of mountain lion, reasonably fresh, and both older tracks and scratchings of *Felis onca*, the jaguar. But the jinx persisted. Jaguars were ranging somewhere else.

"I stink," I announced to Curtis one evening as we arranged the mosquito netting around our cots.

"So do I," he agreed.

"Then let's travel back to the main camp tomorrow," I suggested. "We can wash off the jungle with three consecutive hot showers, get fresh dogs and grub, start all over again. I'll even buy you a beer in Belize on the way."

"Can't change your luck on beer, even in Belize," Curtis muttered. "But we'd have to move anyway in another day or so. Tomorrow it is."

There is something about a refit that changes a hunter's outlook on life. It's like baseball, which becomes a brand new game once the score is tied. Trouble was, our score was still 0–0. But the attitude turned fresh and willing.

And more to the point, when we rolled into the main camp Joe and Red had come out to bay deep greetings. The bigger black dog wasn't going to help us, because he had gnawed out his stitches and the handlers had rigged a collar like a picket fence to keep his teeth and tongue away from the shoulder wound. But Red was as frisky as a puppy. His cuts were all healed and his general condition was good. He could hunt. In Prock's mind that changed the whole picture. Somehow I shared his hunch.

The tenth day dawned for me at 1:30 A.M. Curtis had already been stirring around for an hour getting things organized so we could leave camp by 2:30 A.M. This was to be the big push, he announced.

"We'll take two Rovers and three packs of dogs, and really work the ridges beyond Rock Stone Pond. Eat your breakfast."

In three hours of travel through black dark, the last hour of it in a low-low-gear battle along an overgrown track that wrenched through near-bottomless mudholes and over rutted ridges, I never did see Rock Stone Pond. Didn't make much difference, because the track broke out into a half mile of clear savanna ridge just as the sun cracked the eastern horizon. It was a fresh day, and a fresh start.

One of the three packs struck a trace within minutes of leaving the vehicles. Eureka! But the older dogs quickly lost interest, and tiny cat prints in the mud showed it was a margay, an inveterate tree climber, handsomely spotted, but only the size of an ordinary house cat. A waste of time.

With three groups of men and dogs circling the area there was no point in our trying to stay up with any one. Better to wait and listen near the Rovers, see what happened. Besides, it was cool in the quiet shade.

At eleven the northernmost pack struck again, their baying whisper-faint in the distance. I got up, ready to go.

"Hold your horses," advised Prock. "They're only cold-trailing, from the sound. Might lose it, or sniff around for hours without starting the *tigre*. Wait."

When the hound note passed from earshot I wasn't sure Prock was right, but when at noon Charro brought his five dogs, headed by the fully recovered Red, in from a fruitless swing to the south I came to realize that Prock knew exactly what he was doing.

"Dave's bunch are cold-trailing," he told the Honduran. "I reckon they're in the area of those two big ponds beyond the *chiclero* camp we found two years ago. Take your bunch over there and find 'em," he ordered. "Maybe with fresh dogs you'll catch the *tigre*."

It was 2 o'clock, really too late in the day to expect to run a jaguar, when one of the boys came trotting in from the north. "Treed," he announced. "Big *tigre*, but very far."

Honduran speech has a faintly British flavor, a leftover from colonial days, like that of the Jamaicans, and apparently Hondurans are also given to British understatement. Very far to him was a helluva way to me.

We walked fast, pantingly fast, across the easy going of the savanna and then plunged into dark jungle where progress could be measured only in machete swings. The dog handlers seemed able to slip through the tangle like smoky ghosts, but I could only crash through it, tangled in lianas, forever tripped by roots that looped above the ground like croquet wickets. We slobbered through a swamp—six inches of water over two feet of soft mud—where trying to leap from one dry bush clump to the next meant an inevitable sprawl in the muck. It was a relief to break out into the first of the two ponds. Wading was slow, with the soft bottom and foot-clogging reeds, and the water came up to my shirt pockets. But it was cool, blissfully cool.

"Tell that guy to keep the camera pack above water," I implored Curtis. "Biggest reason I'm down here is to get a picture of a jaguar in a tree —hardly ever been done. And we'd better start praying we get to him before the light fails."

But there was more deep cob-webbed jungle and more swamp and still another pond before we could hear the dogs ahead of us. They were mouthing dire threats at a huge spotted cat in a tree. It was his fourth tree, Charro told us as we panted onto the scene. The redbone hound had never let the *tigre* settle into a longer run.

It was 5 o'clock. We'd been going three hours. And under the leafy canopy the light was lousy. The needle of my light meter barely jiggled.

But the jaguar was there, about thirty feet up. I tossed the .44 carbine to Prock, took out the camera with the long lens. But even as I raised it to focus I realized that the cat was moving restlessly, ready to jump down out of the tree. Worse, he'd shifted so that the lens showed only his stern end and handsomely marked tail. Male, all right, I noted. Time for only one or two exposures, and no chance to try moving around the tree for a clearer view. If the cat jumped while I was armed only with a camera, there'd be *tigre* and dogs and people all in a slashing tangle. Somebody'd get hurt.

Prock was frantically waving the carbine at me. "Drop that damned camera and shoot!"

His urging was wasted. I'd already realized that the cat had shifted around in the tree, was bunching his feet and leg muscles for a leap. The handy carbine came up and the sights settled on his neck. Mustn't smash the skull—this one surely rated measuring for Boone and Crockett.

I'll never know whether I fired first or the cat jumped first. I know I got off another shot at him in midair and still another as he hit the ground, but which bullet hit his forepaw and which slammed through his chest will forever remain a mystery. The neck shot would have been enough, anyway.

The raving dogs were given their privilege of wooling the *tigre* a bit before we stretched him out. A big male. Well over seven feet and stocky, certainly heavier than any African or Indian leopard I'd ever seen. Maybe two hundred pounds, at a guess. And a beautiful hide. Golden with black rosettes, differing from leopard markings in that the major rosettes along the back had central spots.

Even with the underbrush slashed away, it was too dark for good trophy pictures. Doubling the speed rating of my film gave a meter reading of only f3.5 at a quarter of a second. Flashgun? That was useless, full of water from that last pond we'd waded.

"We'll take some anyway," I told Curtis. "But there's no way in the world to be sure we're getting anything in this light."

Curtis had another solution. "Then we'll tote him out of here," he announced as the dog handlers groaned. "Get more pictures in camp tomorrow."

We came out of the jungle in the dark, slowly, with two tiring flashlights and occasional torches of bunched grass to light the way. We slipped and scrambled and waded and finally made it back to the Land Rovers an hour short of midnight. Tough going. Big Red trotted along with me most of the way. Seemed we shared a feeling of accomplishment, of which that big spotted cat, swaying on the pole ahead, was the symbol. But Red rated the larger share.

---

9 : When Is a Jaguar Something Else?

Ever since the Boone and Crockett Club started its biennial contest for trophies to go into its official North American record list, this world-famous club has faced the problems of all contest sponsors. Chief among these is enforcement, since humans are of such a nature that you cannot have a ball game without an umpire, a fight even under the Marquis of Queensbury rules without a referee.

Policing contests can become a major bugaboo, one certainly familiar enough to *Field & Stream* personnel, since our fishing contest, in action for two generations, on occasion requires policework worthy of the FBI. The gentlemen of the Boone and Crockett Club, essentially a conservation-oriented organization, wanted no part of such rather unpleasant activity. Hence their constant policy has been to set up rules and trophy species definitions, handy, if at times artificial, to eliminate the dirty business.

The British Columbia–Yukon line was made the demarcation line to differentiate between mountain and Barren Ground caribou, for example, which the white-necked stags certainly did not know. The brownie-grizzly distinction, tough enough at best in Alaska, went from a limit of seventy-five miles from tidewater, to a situation under which grizzlies were not found in Alaska with the result that such bears got tossed into limbo, to its present range-crest limitation. This has a level of accuracy at least equal to the other two, but puts the coastal bears of British Columbia where they don't belong. Since float-plane hunts into the Ungava shield began producing caribou too big to compete against the woodland race to which they were for a time thought to belong, a new brand of caribou was established. This left only Newfoundland as the place to look for a fine woodland head.

Then quite recently the jaguar was defined as a North American animal only if he lived north of the bottom edge of Mexico. That, someone had suddenly apparently decided, was the dividing line between North and South America, though most of the rest of the world puts that line at the Panama Canal or thereabouts.

Obviously the larger jaguar of Brazil's Matto Grosso should not compete with more northerly types. The effect of the new look at geography was, of course, to throw out of the contest and the records jaguar that had come or might later come in from British Honduras. That area, which is largely north of the southern panhandle of Mexico, has been most productive of big cats in recent years. The real background reasons have, alas, been left a mite obscure, though there are some unkind souls who whisper that the geographical distinction saved the possibility of having to investigate the legitimacy of one outfitter's cats.

This is too bad. There are cheats in every business, every walk of life, but that is no reason to penalize the legitimate sportsman or to duck the demands of running a contest of great influence. The Boone and Crockett Club doctrines of fair chase and of selective hunting are above reproach; the organization is vastly respected by all hunters and sportsmen. Yet oddly enough with that respect comes, it must be realized, a responsibility to the sportsmen themselves. It's rather like the story about saving the life of a Chinaman—if you haul him back from death's door you're responsible for him thereafter.

---

10 : Two for the Book

Little Joe was a very confused grizzly. He had been snuffling along a British Columbia hogback, moving with that cocker-spaniel scurry so typical of young bears, when two hunters and a guide popped up on the ridge and began snapping pictures of him. The three human figures, Russ Cutter and I and one of the Indian guides, had shown him no harmful intent even though we moved constantly closer upwind, and the other two-legged figure standing back with the horses was too far away to menace even a two-year-old grizzly. So Little Joe had peeked and sniffed and scuttled and stared while we used up Ektachrome. He never did make up his mind to lollop off down the rockslide until John the Indian heedlessly bounced a fist-size rock off his ribs. Then he looked back with a hurt expression. Things had certainly changed since his mother had met that big boar bear and bounced Joe out to meet the world.

I guess we all have to be disillusioned sometime. But I for one will never forget Little Joe's disillusionment, not because I think all grizzlies are Bambi-type bears, since they aren't, but because it started a streak of luck for the disillusioners. Five minutes after leaving the gold-caped young bear we were looking at a record-quality Stone ram. And chasing Little Joe had brought us straight to that particular basin in the Cassiar.

The rams—there were four—must already have seen the horses, since we were skylined as well as they, though on the opposite shoulder of a broad cup in the mountain. They may also have watched while we set up the spotting scope and argued the quality of their horns. But the sheep seemed unconcerned while Cutter took the time to decide that the lead ram, surely over forty inches, was for him, even though this was the first day of hunting. The rams paid no attention when he and John eased over the lip and onto tumbled rocks, gave no heed when the hunters disappeared from their sight down into the bowl of the basin, and continued to rest in easy disdain on their grassy shelf as my own Indian, Perry, and I settled back to watch the stalk.

"That pile of boulders like a castle just below them," Russ and I had agreed, "that's the spot. If a man could crawl up the gully into that without their spotting him he'd have the shot made. About two hundred and fifty yards, what?"

The stalk into range wasn't quite that simple. For Russ and John to climb down, cross the moraine a long-dead glacier had left in the basin, and start up again took nearly an hour. Then their chosen gully turned out to be full of loose and noisy shale. Part way up they discovered that all the rams except one were obscured by their own ledge, and that one, the trophy, was lying in a position from which one jump would take him behind solid rock. And before the hunters could belly into hiding behind the castlelike promontory, the wind began whisking over them straight toward the dozing sheep. The ram got up, nervous.

But with his 6.5 wildcat slung tight over a handy boulder Russ made the shot. He had only the one chance, but as Perry and I held our glasses on the ram it was clear that the sheep had fallen, not jumped, behind the arresting ledge. For his photograph, Little Joe had paid us with good fortune, plus interest.

And that was only the first day of hunting from Frank Cooke's base camp. We were half done already. When Russ and John, laden with hindquarters, ribs, and the cape and head of the ram, staggered down off the mountain to meet us and the horses, it was evident that the spotting scope hadn't fibbed a bit. Our field measurements gave the splendidly wide ram a score of more than 173, easily into the Boone and Crockett record list, beyond forty-two inches around the curl and a trophy for anybody's wall.

"So now you've got to complete that trophy-room addition," I chaffed the Coloradan.

"Nope, not unless I find a mountain caribou. That's postponed until tomorrow," he smiled.

He might do it at that, I thought, the way things were going. We certainly had all the advantages.

Outfitter Frank Cooke's upper British Columbia hunting territory, lying west of the Kechika and south of the Turnagain, almost had to be prime Stone sheep country. A whole series of ranges on the sunset side of the Rocky Mountain Trench, it had been the western half of the famous Skook Davidson's hunting grounds, which have in recent years produced so many of the record Stone rams, four or five out of the top twenty.

Skook had raised Frank much as a son, Cooke having run away from home at fifteen to see the north country, eventually to become Davidson's chief packer and general right-hand man. As Skook tired in his middle seventies he had turned the western half of his hunting domain over to Frank. With Hal Komish's B.C.–Y.T. Flying Service in Watson Lake to charter-fly hunters in and out and regular radio contact to advise them what groceries to load into the Beaver float plane, Frank was set up in a hunting paradise, quite probably the best Stone sheep area on the continent. And he had firmly in mind the idea of keeping it as prime country.

"Be pretty easy for a fly-by-night operator to clean out terrain like this," he told me one morning as we lay flat on a rockslide. We'd been caught in the open by one of the three goats we were stalking, a billy that fed out from under a ledge when it should have been sleeping through noonday. "Much of this area can be ridden clear to the mountaintops, and some outfitters would run people through here in mobs on short-term hunts. The sheep would be cut back in a few years. I'd rather have fewer customers on longer hunts, and everybody with a forty-inch ram or better. What do you think?"

"Wiser words were never spoken, Frank," I agreed. "Let the young rams add on years until they're ten or twelve years old and up in the trophy class. Real clients are willing to pay big dough for big rams—you'd go broke offering them trash," I added. "Our goats have moved out of sight again."

Bent over both for concealment and for balance, we teetered another two hundred yards across the shifting slab, edging closer to the three goats we had spotted from the lower basin. A few more such careful moves and I'd be in sure shooting range. Then we saw a movement of white down below the ledge, and froze into immobility again.

"Not much good country left for Stone sheep," I offered during that pause. "Still good rams down in the Stikine and Klappan areas, and some big ones in the Prophet and Muskwa country if a man has the time to pack back that far, but I'd say yours is prime territory. It will produce record rams as long as you can take care of it. Now, if we can see the best goat from that next ridge, I'll be ready to shoot."

The goats were ready before I was. We had just started the final sneak across sharp rocks when they fed out from below the overhang, their heads fortunately down. I dropped into a sitting position; Frank lined up his binoculars. For once, picking out the best goat would be no problem, since the two larger ones were at least two inches different in horn length.

"Take the one on the right," he whispered.

The cross hairs had already steadied, and at the shot the goat dropped over the ledge. We sprinted downhill as fast as one can on a rockslide, thinking to cut off any flight around the basin edge, but there was no need to risk breaking a leg. The goat was right there. The tape said ten and a half inches, but the black horns were a shade too slim to make the record book. A nice goat, and the hide would make a warm bedside tootsie rug for wintry mornings, but in truth, this was just a goat. It had cost us a five-hour climb and stalk, however, and that makes any goat a trophy.

That same day Russ had picked up his first mountain caribou, a fine stag still wearing old velvet, but with multipointed horns clean and hard after they'd been stripped and soaked a day or so in the lake. He himself was looking over goats as I turned back to serious sheep hunting. There were lots of rams to examine, nineteen or twenty a day sometimes, but I wasn't going to settle for anything less than Russ's forty-two-incher. Full-curl rams we studied carefully, but though there were several that looked like forty inches we had not, from the base camp, seen another with the flaring tips that should markedly hoist that measurement, making a shot worthwhile.

So we moved westerly some six hours' ride and set up a spike camp, where from one valley we could easily hunt three ridges all hooked into the divide behind us. The area looked like excellent sheep country.

Indian John and I glassed eighteen rams the first try from that camp, but the sun was burning down so fiercely, the mirage so bad, that anything beyond a half mile was a dancing blur, identifiable as a Stone ram only because it had horns on one end and a light-colored rump on the other. We had been on the wrong side of the wind to try closer stalks—

better to leave those bunches for a day when the odds ran our way. Russ and Frank had ridden up out of the valley into another range to glass some goat cliffs. Near sunset (which is midevening in those latitudes in August) they jogged back into camp. Russ was excited; Frank just looked smugly happy.

Before he had stripped his saddle horse, Cutter hauled me off into the backbrush. Judging from his manner this was strictly a CIA item, most secret, the real hot poop.

"Remember Frank said he'd seen sixteen rams last fall over by those goat bluffs beyond the divide, with one that looked like the Chadwick sheep?" he whispered hoarsely. "Well, we didn't find the sixteen, but we found five whoppers, every one of 'em over forty inches and I think the pappy ram will make forty-eight!"

"Doubt that," smiled Cooke as he joined the planning session. "Might go for forty-five, though. We watched 'em almost all day."

"Yeah, and there's a bloody big billy goat for me bedding not a quarter mile away. Mebbe we can get 'em both. But you take first cracks for the ram," Russ finished more seriously.

We both understood. Even if the sheep and the billy goat were in similar positions when we found them next day, a simultaneous try on both by two hunters was almost surely doomed to failure, would probably ruin the chances for either. And as a longtime friend Russ knew that a possible record ram for me, another one for the book, was more important than any goat, thick-horned billy or not. Friends think that way.

We had ridden out of our valley, through another drainage, and into a third, then switched back up a mountain, clearly marked by sheep trails, into a pocket under the cliffs where the horses would stay hidden. Russ volunteered to watch the saddle stock while we crawled around the mountain bulge on all fours to look down into a long valley with a lake at its far end. Its westerly slopes dropped in a series of steep slides, with knobs of harder rock bulging up to make little grassy points. The willowbrush of a tiny creek bed meandered down the middle. A beautiful hidden basin.

"And there are the rams," whispered Frank, as we crawled up behind the last protecting boulder. "Within a hundred yards of where we first spotted them yesterday."

My heart pounded a bit as my binoculars centered on the little group of dark-bodied sheep. Three were lying motionless; two picked about restlessly. They were down almost to the floor of the valley, perhaps five hundred feet below our level and a half mile away. Even with only 7X, the glasses showed their horns, all of them, to be majestic in weight and sweep. And when Frank got the Bushnell spotter screwed onto its tripod and motioned me over for a look, the view through 20X spurted another shot of adrenalin through my veins. Every one of those rams was a full curl; every one was in or above the forty-inch class.

One rather light-bodied oldster showed some brooming on the left side. We must avoid him. But there was another with the light coloring occasional this far north, where the all-white Dall sheep and its cousin the blue-gray *stonei* begin to intergrade, and he was almost as long in the horn as the master ram. The best of the bunch, darker and seemingly a trifle heavier than the others, surely over two hundred pounds, had bedded slightly apart. As I watched he slowly turned his head so that I could see the distinct outward flare of the horn tips.

Feeling the wind in my face I shakily lighted a cigarette. "I see why you watched 'em all day, Frank. That bunch would keep any sheep hunter staring. The best one may not be the fifty-inch Chadwick ram of thirty years ago but he's terrific, might go forty-five, will surely beat forty-three. Hard to guess even with the others for comparison. But on this wide-open slope we can't get within five hundred yards."

Frank considered. "We'll wait. Before noon they'll move again to a midday bedding area. If they come up this side, we'll go back around the peak and climb down behind that far ridge. If they cross, bed where they did yesterday, and if the wind doesn't shift, perhaps we can get around behind the valley head and traverse those slides above them."

"And if they bed in a bad spot, we'll pass them up until tomorrow, right? Unspooked, they won't leave this pocket. So we wait," I agreed.

But the waiting was interminable. The rams shifted around, alternately fed and rested, occasionally stretching their heads along the ground, as if to ease the horn weight. A small band of ewes—probably old dry ewes long past bearing, since seldom do the sexes mix this early in the season—wandered down to join the party. They could be a complicating factor. Then the whole bunch moved down into the scrubby growth in the dry creek bottom to fiddle around there for an endless half hour.

"Ah, now they're moving. The big ram just crossed the creek but the ewes are staying on this side," grunted Frank from behind the spotter.

The next fifteen minutes would tell the story. There were four likely bedding areas on the steep slope opposite us, little grassy flats in the shale. Two would be impossible to stalk, atop hard-rock promontories that broke the slides, but two other lying-up spots showed under those bluffs. These lower ones would be in shade the rest of the day, and we could work in over them without being seen. At least, I was keeping my fingers crossed.

"Okay," Frank said finally. "They're not going to climb high. Let's back out of here while we can."

Carefully low, we scurried back toward the horses. We hadn't spotted

Russ's goat, we told him, but the billy might be farther down the valley, toward the lake, and hidden in a cave or behind some rock edge. "Forget the goat," he said. "Go get the ram."

On the way across the valley head, a wolverine humped along within fifty yards ahead of us. I had long wanted one of the rare big weasels, but not today, not with that big ram a possibility. Best Stone ram I had ever seen, for sure. That realization kept me light-footed as we finger-and-toed around a dangerous cornice, scrambled down a noisy slide of small rock and sweated a quarter mile up the other side. Slowly we traversed the first grassy bluff. The rams hadn't bedded under that one. Must be under the next. Had to be quiet.

The steep slope between was nasty. A different sort of claylike rock, it was sun-hardened to the consistency of concrete, with a top layer of scattered pebbles that rolled underfoot like marbles. A fall would be easy, and disastrously noisy, but the edges of my Vibram-soled climbing boots bit and held, and finally we were peering over the edge of the bluff.

Too much overhang. If the rams were below, they were in out of sight. Carefully, we edged down a series of grassy steps to a second level. There they were.

Four of the five rams dozed in clear sight almost directly below, placidly ignorant that we were looking nearly straight down on them from perhaps two hundred and twenty-five yards. Which was which?

With the rifle still unloaded, I edged my binoculars over the bluff. The three closest all looked good. One was light-bodied, therefore the other light ram, apparently the broomed one, was in out of sight. One of the three dark rams must be our quarry. Not enough flare on that left-hand one, so the choice lay between two. One gray ram had picked the prime resting spot, farthest from the cliff on a flat shelf. Surely he must be the boss ram. If they'd only shift a bit, give us a view other than straight down.

I was considering rolling a pebble or making some natural nonhuman noise when the problem was solved for us. The outside ram stood up, turned around. Then he looked straight up at us. No doubt about that flare. That one. The rifle was already loaded and lined on him when I realized the problems in the shot. At some two hundred yards of range on the flat my bullet path should still be about three inches above point of aim. But shooting downhill at easily sixty degrees it would hit even higher. How much higher? If I held too low, any slight miscalculation could mean hitting, perhaps smashing, one of those magnificent horns. Better figure six inches, at a guess. A backbone hit would be fine anyway.

With the blast of the 7 mm. Remington magnum the big ram dropped. The others started to their feet in confusion and the other light-bodied ram appeared from under the cliff. Good. But then my ram started to his feet, moving in toward the overhang. I had missed the backbone and had to fire again.

After we had worked our way circuitously down, the tape showed forty-three and a half inches around the longer curl, with fourteen-and-three-quarter-inch bases, and the symmetry was close enough so that when we had completed the field scoring it tallied over 175 Boone and Crockett points, up in the top quarter. I knew it might lose some in drying, but that in no sense lessened the wave of satisfaction that swept over me. Frank was pleased, too. He'd done his job, and done it properly. We had the best ram, but there were four more moving off across the valley, every one of which will be as good or better with another year's growth, come the fall of 1966.

11 : Thoughts on Technique

Hunters are by their very nature those who must see the other side of the mountain; yet when they discover that new country, be it a remote slope in Asia or a fresh acreage of Maine timber, the observant ones will also discover that the methods of hunting the animals in it have certain basic similarities to those of more familiar hunting grounds. Glassing and stalking a bearded urial ram in the spurs of the Elburz is essentially the same as hunting Stone sheep above the Kechika. That in the one case you are crouching alongside a reformed Persian poacher, and in the other by an Indian named George, doesn't much alter matters. Likewise, the essential difference between a tiger beat in the Madhya Pradesh and a deer drive on the New Jersey pine barrens is that, whereas tigers have been known to chew on beaters or even shikarists, nobody ever heard of a deer eating anybody, even from New Jersey!

As I look at matters after a lifetime of hunting, there are a half dozen basic systems, each with local variants according to topography and game type. First there's spying and stalking, the approach of the mountain-country hunter, who must spend hours looking for his trophy before even deciding to try moving into possible range. Then there's spooring up, the technique of the African safarist—or the Adirondack deer hunter after an inch of fresh snow—who follows alongside a track of promising size until, hopefully, he comes up with his quarry. Doesn't always work. An elephant may just keep on dawdling along at a five-mile-an-hour amble, stopping neither to drink nor feed, while you fall farther and farther behind with mouth full of cotton and feet puffed with blisters. Or the smart buck deer may swing a downwind circle just to see and smell who is rude enough to tail him. Third, there's beating and driving, the only resort for country too dense for men to move in quietly yet restricted enough by roads or local topography so that a smart tactician can reasonably guess where game will move under pressure. This is a sociable scheme but doesn't rate really high on the hunting scale, since almost any idiot in new Abercrombie and Fitch clothes can be persuaded to stand by an indicated tree until he's picked up. Calling, a method almost viciously effective with varmints, is on the rise for coyotes and bobcats but falling into relative disuse for bigger game, partly because the presence in the field of too many elk hunters with plastic bugles nullifies the calling skill of the rare real expert. Sitka deer in southeastern Alaska respond to a blatting fawn call with motherly anxiety, but a whitetail deer coming to the same call in Pennsylvania would have to fight its way through half a dozen hunters. And finally there's waiting 'em out, the patient sitting by trail or known hangout until the game wanders into view. The Texan perched on a ladder stand in the mesquite or the Walengula crouched by a northern frontier water hole are working the same method.

Hunting with dogs, whether rabbits with beagles or jaguar with Plott hounds, is, I think, a system in some ways marginally beyond the province of this book. As a sport it belongs primarily to the men who love the dogs, who revel in their music and so would almost rather let the fox go to earth to run another night. Hence this method is less the property of those whose interest lies in the trophy itself.

One of the major challenges and charms of hunting on a world scale has been to note how all hunting everywhere relies on these basic schemes, used alone or in combination but always adapted to the local terrain.

In the course of the average Wyoming elk hunt, for example, it is almost certain that you'll glass parks and slides for bulls, will locate elk at least in areas by noticing tracks. In the early season you may bugle up a bull or may wait by a grassy park for dawn light to reveal a late-feeding six-pointer with his harem. You will probably try a spot of elk-pushing if you think you have a bunch located where they must flee across an opening.

Yet it's interesting to note that in working on the *hirsch*, our wapiti's close European cousin, alpine jaegers, or guides, stick chiefly to the waiting-out system in the dawn and dark with an occasional spot of spying and stalking. Seldom do they either refer to tracks or attempt even casual driving. In Spain and in some sections of Eastern Europe, of course, the superdrive or *monteria* involving up to fifty riflemen is still in use, but, as a general thing, Central Europe demands more selective techniques. The jaeger and his hunter, for example, must see and positively identify the stag as the correct stag for the license or for the health of the herd before a shot is fired. How many U.S. elk hunters would be successful if they were working under such requirements? I have often wondered.

It has always struck me as a sad commentary, incidentally, that in gatherings of superhunters, at affairs like the dinners staged for the Weatherby Trophy presentation or the Boone and Crockett awards, for example, this whole area of hunting techniques rates too little attention. At these affairs mutual brags and effusive congratulations are exchanged about remarkable trophies taken or expeditions made, but seldom do we hear any nitty-gritty analysis of approach procedures or the locating methods used in taking those trophies. It is perfectly possible, of course, for a hunter to have been conducted into sure range of a record head by a competent guide, and to dispatch that record, without possessing the remotest idea of how the whole thing was done or why he could walk upright at four hundred yards but must crawl like a snake at forty, why it was necessary to go half a mile back down the mountain before cutting up toward the herd. Yet the hunter who understands not those how's and why's experiences little of his hunt. It is therefore almost a duty of those who have indeed tramped the world to emphasize less the magnitude of their deeds than the way of doing them. The waste of sheer hunting savvy at these splendid gatherings is nothing short of sinful.

Written exchange of technical hunting matter, however, belongs in the last century. We don't have time for it today, so you should not expect it, save very indirectly, in this book. The embryonic hunter is, to be sure, loaded with wise counsel in his earlier years. His father or his Uncle Samuel, or, as in my own case, the fathers of my two grade-school chums, will instruct him up to a point in the ways of game and of the men who hunt game. But the grown-up hunter, or the guy who has been at it for only part of his lifetime, must expect to be on his own, to gain wisdom not by advice from others but from observation by himself.

And for my money, that is what distinguishes the successful hunter: ability at observation, muscle to climb mountains, money to travel the remote outback, skill to shoot straight. These are all hardy attributes but are of themselves no guarantees of success or satisfaction. Being able to note animal traits and proceed accordingly, to spot and to read minute signs that betray the whereabouts of game, to note automatically details of terrain so that game movements whether spooked or peaceful can be predicted, such Natty Bumppo abilities are in the long run the earmark of the skilled and successful hunter. The sheep hunter can be as strong of foot as Sir Edmund Hillary, but if he has not observed the morning and afternoon wind switches normal to a mountain slope, he'll find it hard to crawl into range of a ram. The safarist who hasn't observed how far a rhino can and cannot see or who hasn't come to realize that the movements of a pride of lions may be traced by the reactions of lesser game, even when cat prints are invisible, is not a hunter but a dude relying totally on some professional's services.

To observe sharply, a man must be alive, all his senses working at high pitch. And very possibly that is why so many of us so deeply enjoy the oldest of all sports. When hunting we live, we live totally, and only then.

12 : Guessing the Giants

Like the pay-phone user who never gets his dime back, each of us has his pet frustrations. One of mine, which is rapidly becoming an obsession, stems from a yen to nail a true Boone and Crockett mule deer. There have been big bucks to gladden any hunter's eye, to be sure. In the past couple of decades I've glassed hundreds, probably well over a thousand, and have shot my share of the hatrack kind so wide as to jam in the average door. But never has appeared that perfectly proportioned monster, not only wide but also heavy in the beam and neatly balanced in the prongs, the type that will beat the minimum in the Boone and Crockett Club's listing of record mule deer.

Whenever I shot a good deer against a 175 minimum, that was the year in which Boone and Crockett raised the ante to 180, or to 185, which was the minimum in the year we're concerned with in this story. It has now been hoisted to the absurd figure of 195, at which level you don't hunt for record-list deer. You just read crystal balls, collect four leaf clovers, and pray a lot. Fate certainly conspired against me in such matters.

"Or you just don't live right," said Russ Cutter, with whom much of this trophy-deer search has been shared. We were buying my nonresident tickets in a gunshop on the main street of Craig, up in Colorado's deer corner. On the counter lay the rack of a buster buck brought in earlier in the season. It would obviously score well over 190. "Some ranch kid shot this one ten miles out of town—caught it mooching around a haystack and busted it for freezer meat."

"With my luck I could park on that haystack for the next twenty years and never see one like it," I muttered angrily.

"Maybe you should take up Yoga," helpfully offered the shopowner, as he rang up my deer-license money.

That wasn't so funny. I hadn't tried either Yoga or a touch of Buddhism, to be sure, figuring that Asia and its deities couldn't know much about Rocky Mountain deer, but I'd long since gone through wishing on the evening star, dodging black cats, throwing salt over the left shoulder— and I can't remember breaking a mirror for well beyond the mystic seven years. But maybe a touch of Yoga or a Tibetan prayer wheel would turn the trick. Bagging a mule deer over the 185 score at the time called for a special kind of luck.

"And that we haven't had much of," agreed Russ several mornings later, as we drove out of Craig toward deer country.

The thermometer outside Jim Monger's Crosgriff Motel had read sixteen below when the starter of Cutter's beefed-up International growled the motor into reluctant life. More snow was falling, as it had off and on for days, to fill up old ruts. On the high benches it would be making white mounds over the sagebrush, soft-looking lumps that often hid boulders. We'd have to chain up when we left the highway, possibly chain all four wheels and certainly the front pair for the morning climb.

"I dunno—we were pretty lucky yesterday to get out, what with the forward-drive line smashed over that rock. Even with the big jack and the winch I didn't think we'd squeeze out of that one, not with the front end hanging half over that coulee edge."

"Wasn't even thinking of that," said Russ. "I had in mind various unlucky goings-on in the years past."

I knew what he referred to. One season we had made the long haul up into the Dinosaur National Monument country, to get into a little-hunted strip of Colorado between the closed monument, with its mile-deep Green River Canyon, and the Utah line. Scenery? Terrific. Deer? By the hundreds, and plenty of good bucks. The superbuck? Twice seen. Each time he stood a hundred yards inside a shiny new Park Service fence. If bucks wore fingers he'd have thumbed his Roman nose!

There'd been a hunt in the Southern Ute Indian Reservation, high in the longleaf pine and mountain mahogany, with deer everywhere and three on a license, even a special dance put on for us by the Utes themselves— but nary a rack of Boone and Crockett stature could we spot.

And the quick swing just south of Russ's home town of Grand Junction, into Area 62 on the Uncompahgre, where he was pretty darn sure of the hangouts of four first-quality bucks. But my two hunting buddies had found and busted two, wounded and lost the third, and we never could locate the fourth, though we looked over dozens that to most people would have been worth taxidermy charges.

And on a half dozen other tries in five mule-deer states the hunter's gods had not seen fit to give me the nod. Plenty of fine deer but always some bad break on the whopper.

The odds should run my way on this operation, however. Conditions were really right. During the regular season the Colorado country around Craig and Meeker, from Piceance Creek to Black Mountain and Greystone, is overrun by an army of hunters, most of 'em from sunny California. In mild October they swarm up into and beyond the aspens, see deer in quantity, shoot deer in quantity. But when it turns iron cold and the snow starts piling, they pull out their pickups and trailers and campers. Theirs is the regular season, and for my money it is all theirs.

We were operating during one of the postseasons of very late November and early December. Then extreme temperatures and snow to wading depth will push off the foothills all but the most rugged vehicles and savviest hunters, just as the cold and drifts will force off the high country the final migration of deer, bring down the last old timberline bucks. Tough going but lots of muleys.

"How many'd we see yesterday?" I wondered idly as we climbed back into the *jaegerwagen* after clamping on the chains to start up a drifted track.

Russ looked down at the counting device hanging under the choke knob. "I punched 114," he said, "but that doesn't include the mob we saw along the Willow Creek bottoms. Gave up on them."

"I'd say conservatively that two hundred walked by that fence-corner marker," I added. "And there must have been twice that many higher up the creek where that other guy got himself stuck."

We settled for an average of two hundred and fifty head a day, mixed bunches of bucks, does, and youngsters, with the bucks showing in good numbers even in the low sagebrush country. And in the past two days, with the snow already so heavy that any vehicle lighter than the big International would slide up onto it, lose traction, we'd spotted only three sets of hunters. We'd heard a few distant shots, but only once in the glass had observed hunters in action, a three-man cannonade that chased a good buck and his does into a remote patch of oak brush.

There was no point in battering our way up to aspen level. We'd seen elk that high, but not even old mule-deer bucks will stay long in thirty inches of snow unless they are hard pushed. With light hunting pressure the major herds were down closer to sagebrush level looking for feed and easier going.

Russ had already taken his trophy, and he made a very fancy shot doing it. The rancher who let us through his corral gates to reach the Willow Creek bottoms had mentioned two heavy bucks sheltering there. We had eased carefully over that last rise, but even so flushed out of the frozen creek a whole procession of deer. The two good ones came out last; for some reason they did not catch the fever of fright that kept the rest of the herd filtering off up the opposite cedar slope. On the lowest bench they stood staring back at us from fully four hundred and fifty yards.

"Which is the better?" asked Cutter from where he had bellied into the snow in order to use the lowest fence strand as a rifle rest.

For once I had found myself wishing for a binocular of higher power than 7X or 8X. They were both trophy-size deer, the rangily built animals that often carry a lot of antler bone. The right-hand buck showed taller and wider antlers, no doubt about that, but was he too slender? The left-hand buck seemed shorter in the points but was clearly heavier, and his top points appeared bladed a bit.

"Damfiknow," I grunted. "Think I'd take the taller one, on the right."

Russ had apparently decided the same way, or perhaps the long-pronged buck looked restless, about to run. Cutter had certainly done some quick and accurate range and holding calculations, because my words were scarcely out before the frosty air was blasted by his 6.5 Stegall wildcat. Moments later, after we'd already seen the buck sag and pitch into a sliding fall, the plop of the one-hundred-and-forty-grain Nosler bullet came back.

We finally worked the International over to load him, but before I fished out the steel tape it was obvious we'd made a bad guess. Regardless of how good or bad the heavy-antlered buck had been, and regardless of how tall and wide this one was, it couldn't cut 185 Boone and Crockett points. Reason? One supplementary prong, seven or eight inches long, sprang from the left antler. Neither one of us had spotted that even with the glasses.

"Not your fault," said Russ when we'd eaten a disconsolate lunch and started to clean the fine buck. "From what I could see I'd have shot anyway. To judge these boys right you've either got to be lucky or have a half hour of careful scope work."

"Strikes me they have to be laid down on the ground first," I commented ruefully.

"Something in that," Russ agreed, as indeed there is.

It's no great stunt to select a *good* mule-deer rack, one worth hanging on the wall. One that to most hunters merely looks terrific will qualify on that score. Let's put aside for the moment those multipronged heads, glandular freaks, that belong in what Boone and Crockett rules set apart as the nontypical class, which can be gauged on the hoof only by a crystal-ball gazer. The good typical mule-deer head will carry four or perhaps at most five prongs plus the brow points on each side; it will stand high; it will spread beyond the belly bulge when the buck is facing away, and will seem wider than the buck's ears when he's staring at you. A good honest muley, guessed this way, will score somewhere between 140 and 170. It's when you're looking for *better* than just a good head, are seeking one of true record quality, that the estimation turns really tough.

First off, it is not outside spread that cuts the mustard. The handsomely proportioned world-record muley, now in the museum at Jackson Hole, is only 30¾ inches on the outside. Overall spread may be a fancy figure just because extra points—which are probably debits on your score—stick out in some bizarre fashion.

It's the *inside* spread that has meaning—and believe you me, the buck with adequate air space inside the main beams of his rack will from the rear view still look like an off-breed of the Texas longhorn.

How to judge it? Friends, I wish I knew a method as quick and simple as making instant coffee! By the ears, probably. The mature mule-deer buck may tape anywhere from twenty-one to twenty-three inches across his ear tips, unless he's a stunted or small-bodied type as sometimes found in desert areas. The mounted world-record buck, however, is only 20½ inches from ear tip to ear tip. There are trophy deer registered in the most recent Boone and Crockett book, *Records of North American Big Game,* published in 1964 by Holt, Rinehart and Winston, Inc., that show inner spreads as small as nineteen inches or as large as thirty-plus; but those narrow ones must be a yard tall and the superwide ones probably score up in spite of rather than because of their wide-open baskets.

Where the ordinarily good deer gives the impression that his floppy ears—and a buck carries his listening apparatus at a flatter angle than does the antlerless doe—are inside his general rack, then a superdeer will look in your glasses or spotting scope as if the ear tips are actually narrower than the main stem of his up-projecting rear or topmost point. Mighty few look like that! What the record-list hunter searches for is a buck showing an honest two feet of spread *between* the two main beams, since the odds are that this will hit the superdeer category.

Beam length? You'll need the crystal ball again, because antler beams swing in a curve, so appear foreshortened from most angles. The best answer I know is to try for a side view, so that you can judge the forward swing of the beam in relation to the buck's Roman nose.

If the prong count is uneven, with more sprockets on one side than the other, of course the odds are against his qualifying. The unbalanced head must be remarkable in other measurements, since those extra spikes count against, not for.

And the prongs must be long, high. The higher the better. The back point, the one the Boone and Crockett record blank refers to as G-2 or the second point, must rise from sixteen to twenty inches off the main beam, and the point forking off it should seem to rise eighteen to twenty inches or a shade more off the buck's head, and remember that a husky buck goes nearly a foot from his shiny black schnozzola back to where the antlers sprout.

Since three circumference measurements are to be taken on each main beam, antler weight is vital.

"Think in terms of your rifle stock," was my suggestion when Russ and I were discussing beam circumference. "Around the pistol grip the stock measures somewhere between 4¾ and 5⅛ inches. The beam of a record buck will tape at least that for circumference between his hair and the brow prong."

"Could be," he agreed. "But who can see fractions of an inch at five hundred yards?"

As a matter of fact, even with a good binocular nobody can. You can't be positive with a rock-steady 20X spotter. Neither can we be dead certain of the other dimensions, since the difference between good, excellent, and superbuck is a matter of inches here and there.

"But the really fine ones all look unbelievable at any range," we both agreed.

The proof of the pudding came two days later. We had worn the coating off our binocular lenses looking over deer, had frazzled the ends off our tongues debating their point counts. We'd long since learned not to mention the sighting of ordinary bucks and to disregard does entirely, by keeping our eyes attuned only to the extra size, the blocky body and heavy, low-carried neck that spells a big deer. Even the best ones didn't seem quite good enough.

With all four wheels spinning snowballs we had battled our way over trails untouched since the snows began, fought into basins that hadn't been glassed by man for weeks. But finally, trying to break through a side-hill tangle of cedars to a point overlooking the head of Willow Creek, we reached the end of navigation; we could go no farther on wheels.

I clambered down out of the International, somehow instinctively shouldering my rifle, to check on the turn-around possibilities behind us. I had waded back along the tracks perhaps fifty yards when I heard Russ blip the horn. This was no accident of his elbow. Russ was leaning halfway out of the window, pointing frantically up the cedar-choked ridge. I heard four words.

"Big one! Shoot him!"

When men have hunted together often they operate on trust. I caught a fleeting movement two hundred yards above us and realized that Russ could have had no chance really to study any buck that was sneaking off. But he'd gambled on my word, and we'd examined so many deer that I was certainly prepared to gamble on his. Holding the rifle muzzle high to keep it free of snow, I dropped into a sitting position. It was awkward on an uphill try but still steadier than offhand.

Flicks of gray and white moved toward an opening. I lined on that clear spot. Two does came through first, plunging in deep snow. Then the buck, and the 7 mm. Remington magnum kicked back just as the cross hairs swung in front of him.

We pulled the heavy animal back downhill to smoother ground before reading his story off the tape. Weight? Enough to make the list. Inside spread? Adequate, a bit wider than the 22½ inches across the ear tips. Height? More than enough, with a back prong reaching up 20½ inches, longer than the world record. Beam length? Ah, there it was. The left beam read twenty-five inches. Not bad. But the right? It was short, the tip almost deformed. Damnation. The field score of over 185 would in drying out shrink a couple of inches or so. The buck wouldn't quite make it—all because of some minor accident way back in the growth history of his 1964 antlers, a fluke that had cut back that right beam's normal development. And how could any ordinarily luckless guy see such a fault in the rack of a buck flitting off through cedars?

No doubt about it, guessing the superbucks is a real job, with or without luck. But there's one nice thing about hunting hatrack deer. There's always another chance next year. I've already placed my orders for a Tibetan prayer wheel and a new rabbit's foot.

13 : Reunion with Lumpjaw

The droop-snooted, lop-eared, stilt-legged old cow moose was in a frightful tizzy. She had backed her mismatched frame out to the very tip of a peninsula stretching halfway across a shallow tundra lake. With the hair along her neck and withers bristling, she was making angry dashes, first back toward the brush and then out into the pond. Bud Branham and I watched her in puzzlement. I figured that the hot, bright May weather, unusual for the Alaska Peninsula, must be giving the Aniakchak Bay moose spring fever. Then we saw the reason for her frenzy. Two slick-haired calf moose, so wobbly legged they could be only hours old, stumbled up from their grassy bed and made an awkward effort to follow the cow.

"Darned if I know why she's in such a swivet even with the calves," Bud puzzled.

"Could be our bear went through here," I whispered.

But the bear hadn't gone through. He had been lurking there in the brush all the time. We didn't know it, however, until we had topped out onto a little knoll above the lake and the tableau of the moose. Then we saw the bear, a brown streak humping himself into deeper brush away from the human scent. My rifle came up automatically.

"No—he's not good enough," said Bud, and I could see that the Alaska brownie was not in any real sense a trophy.

"The son of a gun is a meat eater, though," I said. "He was figuring to pick off those calves for lunch."

"Peninsula bears aren't normally meat eaters, certainly nothing like mountain grizzlies," answered the outfitter, a veteran of long years in Alaska. "But as you've already discovered, things aren't normal out here this spring. And with so many moose moving in, the bears are changing their habits."

To begin with, the 1959 spring was late in Alaska. When we began our hunt, heavy snows were still hanging on at the hibernation level, which ranges from fifteen hundred to two thousand feet on the peninsula home of the big coastal brownies. During the first two weeks of May few bears had crawled out of their dens. Then when the weather did change, it turned spring with a vengeance, day after day of brilliant sunshine. It was hot—sixty degrees in the shade of the plane wing, half again hotter after we'd slogged up a couple of miles of mountain to investigate tracks shadowing across the snow. Fresh from hibernation, the heavy-coated brownies spent the warm days snoozing under alder clumps, where the sharpest binoculars or the best spotting scope couldn't find them.

The hunt, my sixth in Alaska, had started with plenty of fast action. Late on May fourteenth, I boarded a Northwest Airlines plane in New York, stopped to swap hunting lies in Seattle that evening with Bill Niemi, the maker of Eddie Bauer down jackets, stepped down in Anchorage on the fifteenth at 5 A.M., local time. A commercial flight to Naknek and a charter hop brought me to Branham's base camp on Chiginagak Bay, roughly five hundred miles west of Anchorage. There an Alaskan surgeon, Dr. Hale, and another medico, Dr. Sparks of Ohio, would hunt their brownies. Bud and I loaded up his Super Cub and flew to our own camp on Nakalilok Bay. At 6 o'clock on the evening of May sixteenth we were glassing a handsomely furred brownie. By 8, Bud was skinning the hide he wanted to lay before his Rainy Pass Lodge fireplace.

Thereafter matters slowed to an amble—which is about all the pace I figured to maintain for the first couple of days of Alaskan climbing with hip boots and a packboard sagging with camera gear. To begin, we hooked half a barrel of five-pound Dolly Varden trout, tossing back all but the two we'd use for supper and breakfast. Then we made a three- or four-mile jaunt across Nakalilok Bay to a butte of volcanic rock to watch the high snow slopes until sundown, which comes late up there in May, around 10 P.M., with sunrise around 2:30 A.M., and no real darkness between. We saw tracks traversing the glittering white slides but no bears.

Most of the tracks were old. One set, however, stayed strong and clear under the bright sun of the next two days. "A big bear made that trail," mused Bud as we focused a 60 mm. spotter on the high country one morning. "His tread is as wide as a Sherman tank's!"

"Then he's the guy we're looking for," I answered. "Old Lumpjaw himself."

"Who's Old Lumpjaw?"

"Remember the big bad bear in the Disney film?"

Branham remembered, all right, and the name "Old Lumpjaw" stuck. He was our meat—maybe.

We almost found him, too. A real Alaskan williwaw cut loose somewhere west of us, and next day we were stormbound. As the storm slacked during the brief Arctic night Old Lumpjaw must have moved through our country, for when we made a fifteen-mile circuit of the hills lying west of camp we found his clean-edged tracks up near the snow line. The fore pads printed a full nine inches across and his hind paws dented hard gravel in a deep fifteen-inch print. He was on the move, stopping nowhere to chop off mouthfuls of early grass or wild celery tops, or to nip the willow buds that fattened faster every day.

In the unseasonably hot weather, the brownies were moving only during the brief night. They were bedding in rock crannies or in alder clumps throughout the day, we concluded after a ten-hour stretch of eyestrain from a butte we called Eagle Rock because we'd never seen an eagle within miles of it.

The tide was nearly full down by then in the bay, and it seemed sensible to cross the Nakalilok flats back to camp for some hot grub and a few more battles with sea-run trout.

Bud suddenly punched me out of a half doze. "See him?"

I couldn't see anything but that same wall of slides and gullies and snow-filled basins we'd been watching fruitlessly all day. "Where?"

On the line of Bud's finger I picked up a spot of brown as it showed briefly on a slope far up the valley, perhaps two miles away. Too far to tell whether he was good, bad, or indifferent—Lumpjaw or his kid brother. We'd have to climb up there.

Hot and winded from fast travel, we finally made it to a knoll some three hundred yards below an alder strip into which, from the halfway point, we'd seen the bear go. Shrugging off packboards and rifles, we went to work with the glasses. No bear, not even a suspicious spot of brown.

"He must've moved while we were wading the river, Bud."

"Doubt it. He's asleep in there somewhere."

Believe me, we'd never have seen that bear if he'd stayed asleep. Only when he rolled flat onto his back, then calmly reached up and pulled down an alder branch to scratch his belly, did we catch the movement. He had scraped out a cool hole in the brush roots, for all the world like a dog under a hydrangea bush, and sprawled to blend into the slope.

"Too small," said Bud. I had to agree; perhaps an eight-footer but no Lumpjaw by a long mile. "Good chance for pictures if we can get him down this way, though," Bud concluded.

Knowing he always carried a long-lensed movie camera, I suggested, "What if I slam a bullet into that rock right over him? He'll move downhill."

"Do that," said Bud, and he worked his way over to the left nearer the line the bear would probably take.

The clap of the two-hundred-and-seventy-five-grain slug from the .35 Mashburn magnum, powdering rock a foot or two over the bear's head, brought him out of there faster than any fireman ever slid down the brass pole. He burst across the slope for fifty yards in one rolling rush, whirled, and looked back toward his bed in angry inquiry, hackles high over his hump and lips pouting in a bear's piggy snarl. Then he turned again into downhill flight another hundred yards or so onto a half-acre patch of snow directly ahead of Bud, pausing there to growl and cuss at the loud noise that had disturbed his siesta, displaying himself nicely for the camera before dropping over the edge of a concealing gully and out of our sight.

So Bud got his movies and we started down the mountain. Then one of those ever-loving alders reached out and grabbed my left boot. I flipped and landed hard on a right foot that gave way with a ripping ankle tear all too easily remembered from school football days. A sprain, and a bad one, I could tell with the first few limping steps. Nothing to do about it but keep going, however. It might work itself out. But after we'd hiked the four or five miles back off the range and across the tide flats to camp, hurrying a bit to catch the 8 o'clock radio schedule maintained each night among all parts of the Rainy Pass operation, I knew it wouldn't. The swelling was coming up too fast.

I was sitting outside our camp the next morning, soaking the ankle in thirty-five-degree seawater, when another brownie paraded out across the bay. Just over the flats he was, ambling along in broad daylight. We had the spotter aligned on him in minutes. "Pretty bear," said Bud. "Looks like a rangy young boar, but he'll square only nine feet at best."

Foot and ankle half numb from the cold water, I hobbled over to the scope. He was a handsome bear, all right, in good coat. But even without any nearby object with which to compare him for size it was obvious that he wasn't even close to the record class—he hadn't the ponderous dignity, the belly sag, and the massive rear-end waddle of a really big old boar. I couldn't have made it over there anyway.

That evening the Chiginagak Bay transmitter told us that the two doctors, their brownie hunt over, would be flown over to Bud's lodge at Kakhonak to smash up some fishing tackle on the leg-long rainbow trout of the Iliamna area. So Bud suggested that we shift our base to the larger bay. Since the move would mean another day of rest for my gimpy ankle, that made good sense. Off we went in the morning, arriving in time to help load the flat-equipped Taylorcraft that Dennis Branham, Bud's brother, was flying to ferry the doctors and their guides to Kakhonak.

"Fresh tracks showing on the snow slopes up here every day now," reported nephew Dean Branham as we waited between flights. "You fellows will find a bear, all right."

Bud and I weren't worried. We'd been yakking about finding Old Lumpjaw, but we really didn't have to find the biggest bear on the peninsula. This hunt was a sort of reunion between a couple of characters who liked to be with each other in the wild country, to drop a quiet rock in the other guy's packsack when he wasn't looking, and to experiment with new ways of making bannock biscuits. We were in no sweat.

Wind and tide stayed right only a couple of days. One day produced the encounter with the cow moose and the calf-hunting bear, another developed into a mad footrace across the beach of Yentarny. Bruin won the race without even knowing he was in it, nonchalantly swimming the river five hundred yards ahead of us—a river too deep to wade and too cold for ordinary mortals to swim. Then the wind switched around to come from the west, straight out of the mountains, in a near gale, to end hunting for the day.

So next morning we left the Piper, our transportation back to civilization, safely lashed to waterlogged timbers, under the bluff that protected our camp, and started up the mountain on shanks' mare. The wind hadn't changed except to ease, nor the weather. It was still incredibly bright and sunny. The sky carried only puffy flecks of those gray masses of cloud that usually squat on the peninsula range, when warm air from the Japan current to the south runs into the colder flow from the Bering Sea. By the time we had reached a protected spot just under the peak, we were both soaked with sweat. Heavily taped, my ankle had stood up well.

We could see part way into a big valley. Enough snow was melting off its upper basins to raise its river to flood level. No bears moved there, though, and we could see no fresh traces across the high snow sweeps, save for one lightly dotted line that ended in a caribou which was grazing a mossy outcrop five hundred or a thousand feet higher than a caribou should be at this season.

It was warm there in the sun, sleepy-warm after a couple of sandwiches.

Alternately glassing the area and dozing, we spent hours in the drowsy heat, overlooking a stretch of bear country seemingly half the size of Rhode Island. No soap. I was dozing off again when Bud grunted in excitement. "A bear!" he said. "A big one. Take a line down off the right corner of that second peak. Under the snow there's a steep rockslide— gray rock. Got it?"

I had my binoculars on that slide.

"Now, down and right of it there's a long escarpment, about a third of the way up from the river, with a waterfall in the middle of it, right? Just below the left edge of the rocks—"

"I've got him—feeding in that green patch. He must have parachuted in."

"More likely came up out of a gully."

It was too far to judge the bear's size with any but a wild guess, but he had the ponderous and deliberate air about him that characterizes a big boar. Chances were he'd clean out that little patch of green and then move slowly around the slope under the steep escarpment. Or he might just take it into his head to walk straight out of the country.

We had something like three miles to go. Down off our mountain, which would be easy, then down into the canyon of the river, which might or might not be wadable at this point. Finally, part way up the opposite mountain to the top fringe of alders. And for half the trip the bear would almost surely be out of our sight. In thirty minutes he could vanish. Both of us knew the dire risk of letting a stalked animal out of sight for long, but we had to take that chance.

We waded the boiling river at a point above a rapid, and were winded and slowing down, my ankle screaming protests, when we crawled up toward the green patch. There had been no sight of the bear for nearly half an hour, and on his side of the river the breeze was switching around, one moment cooling our brows, the next pushing gently on our pack-boards. Be a miracle if the bear was still out on the little flat.

He wasn't. Not there or behind any of the minor humps and gullies that chopped up the area. We could see where he had been feeding, and the softer spots showed tears in the moss and the flat-crushed traces left by a heavy brownie. Heading off below the escarpment and then down-slope toward the bay flats ran a regular bear road, the broad-beamed trail the big coastal grizzlies make as they travel the country, each bear step-ping more or less in the tracks of those who came before, so that the road is a double dotted line of worn spots each the size of a washbasin. He should logically have followed the road.

But he hadn't. There were no fresh tracks on it.

"Think he dropped down toward the flat?" I queried Bud.

"More likely moved left of the track and around under the escarp-ment, either toward the fall, in which case we may spot him, or up and completely out of this round basin."

To get a better view of the alder-grown slopes under the frowning rock cliffs, we climbed a bare knoll at the edge of the bowl. If the bear hadn't topped out or wasn't lying down up there, we should spot him. And we did, briefly—caught just a glimpse of chocolate brown moving slowly through alders a thousand yards ahead of our elevation. Again no chance to estimate size and hide condition accurately. And the bear's direction could, if he continued moving at the feeding amble, which is fully as fast as a man can scramble through alders, carry him out of the far side of the basin.

"If I can see him from that next hump, it won't be too long a shot, Bud," I proposed.

To drop off one hill and race up the other would mean arriving too winded to shoot at any range, especially at a target that would appear only through openings. So we cut around the steep sidehill, fighting cling-ing alder branches every step of the way for twenty minutes. No use. When we finally staggered out into the hill clearing, the bear was not in sight. He could have dropped behind a rise of ground or into one of the gullies that ran down toward the small creek at our right. He might have topped out of the basin completely if the wind had fluked our scent in his direction, or he might still be there in the brush, sleeping or feeding.

"To climb around on top of the escarpment would take almost an hour," mused Bud, "and in that time the bear could leave the country. Probably wouldn't be able to see him from there anyway. Let's try drop-ping down to where we can see the whole slope, locate him properly, and see if a stalk makes sense."

We had dropped off the hill and crossed the small creek, at every step watching the left-hand face of the basin as it opened up, when the bear made his move.

Bud's shout came as I was fighting free of brush edging the creek. "There he goes!"

The brownie had fed until his belly was full, then settled down below a standing rock for a nap. He had been lying hidden only a matter of yards from our colloquy on the second hill, hadn't heard our whispers there, but had caught the human taint as sun-warmed air carried it up the side of the bowl. The bear was off and running.

My first slug from the hard-hitting .35 Mashburn magnum caught him solidly as he showed in a room-size clear spot. Down he went, rolling twice on the steep slope. Then he was up again in dense alders and making good time slanting down across the sidehill. I caught him with a second bullet but didn't slow him much. A third turned him, though, and at sixty or seventy yards the big brownie swung downslope directly toward us, bellowing in pain and anger with every jump.

Not a charge, though it looked like one. He was hurt too badly to climb, and had to go downhill. It just happened that the easy path was straight down toward where Bud and I stood in a little spot of clear tundra. The bear's broad head and driving shoulders looked huge in the 4X scope as he lunged off the hill and showed clear for an instant as he broke out of a brush patch. I cut loose the fourth and last round in the rifle. It hit, but we were so close that any bullet smack was lost in the muzzle blast. The bear rolled again, recovered, finally stopped about fifteen yards away, out of sight on the other side of a clump of scrubby willows by the creek. All went oddly quiet.

Dead? Or still alive and full of steam and waiting for us to come get him? No way of telling; there was not even a patch of chocolate hair to be seen. No sound save the clicks as I slipped a couple of fresh cartridges into the Mashburn and rammed the bolt shut. Two would be either plenty or by no means enough. If he came, there'd be time for only one shot at best.

But two were more than enough. The brownie, finally running out of steam, had piled up by the creek edge. Just the faintest twitch of life remained, the last vestige of the tremendous stamina that had carried the bear fully two hundred yards on his arcing course while his forebody was absorbing three solid hits, over ten thousand pounds of tearing bullet energy. Tough bear.

A good bear, too, with the spread of hide that can square out at half an acre if soaked rubbery overnight in saltwater and then stretched on an A-frame, as some do it. It figured a strong 9½ feet as hides should be measured, laid hair side down on the grass and not hauled out of shape.

Not a record skull, alas; so Bert Klineburger of Jonas Brothers wouldn't be calling the Seattle papers about this one. No deformation of the jaw or dental equipment; so it certainly wasn't Old Lumpjaw. But one odd thing: two toes had long been missing from the left front foot. It could just have been Old Lumpjaw's first cousin, Old Threetoes, slightly wounded in some battle between the sexes. A fine ending for a reunion of good friends and hunting companions, however—that's for sure.

---

14 : Much Ado About Bears

A minor crusade for the *New York Times* and all its "sistern and brethren" has been the parlous state of the polar bear, usually described by that paper as destined for extinction within the week, because vile hunters shoot bears from airplanes. This is, of course, nonsense. Bang a bear from an open plane door over Arctic ice and then what? Do you fly away and leave the hide you spent several thousand dollars to hunt?

In point of truth, the polar bear—about which mighty little was known until recent hunter-financed studies, by Lentfer of the Alaska Game Commission for example—is menaced primarily by Norwegian sealers. Understandably, since the white bears eat seals, Scandinavians regard them as a commercial menace. To the sealers they likewise look like a commercial bonus, since the world hide market is supplied from the Spitzbergen region. No solid evidence exists that the white bears of the Alaska-Russian section, the Chignik Sea, which from the Alaskan side is indeed hunted by paired small aircraft that locate bears and land hunters near them, face any problem of numbers. Men like Bob Curtis, who have thus hunted Nanook for over fifteen years, see no slackening in population, and that feeling is borne out so far by the more academic studies being conducted with radio tracings, paint markings, and such. Alaska's own earlier regulation that limited the number of Arctic-licensed guides kept the kill well within bounds and worked as intended far better than has the permit system evolved in response to preservationist uproar.

The only real menace to the white bears of our side of the pole—and there has been developed no evidence that these bears live on a circumpolar merry-go-round as once thought—is the snowmobile. Some year the good seal and bear ice will be on the Alaska side. Then our native population, operating under virtually no restriction, will create a profitable slaughter on bears for once within range of their gas-powered vehicles.

The status of the brown bear, however, seems somewhat different to me. As one who can clearly remember hunting them at a time when the license was good for two, when the salmon industry was demanding brown bears be considered vermin, when to suit the embryonic cattle industry bears were being officially shot off islands like Afogniak, I've been watching them for some time. Perhaps I have slain more than some would consider my share. But the brownie's troubles today stem from more than mere hunting pressure.

In southeastern Alaska, the Forest Service is merrily selling off stumpage rights for pulp and saw logs, some say to Japanese interests and certainly for Japanese use, as in the Tongass National Forest. Cutting will injure the salmon runs and hence eventually the big coastal bears. Kodiak is becoming "civilized," with cattle ranches. The peninsula is close enough to Anchorage and its air-minded gentry to permit casual weekend hunting by the area's growing population.

Evidence of damage to the brownies is clear enough. The Alaska Game and Fish Commission has been requiring the "sealing" or reporting of all such hides, and recently skulls, for some ten years. Over that period the average length-plus-width measurement of peninsula hides has shrunk from 16.4 to 15.8 feet. The measurements of hides from Kodiak Island have shrunk from 16.9 to 15.9, a whole foot. Obviously, and taxidermists have been reporting this all along, the bears taken today are steadily younger, smaller. Since there is no vast dietary change, the difference must be that the bears don't get to live long enough to grow to trophy size. And a trophy brownie is no spring chicken. He may have twenty or more candles on his cake.

Steady shortening of the season, reduction of open areas, and all the obvious medicines have been and are being tried. But these do not strike at the real menace to the big brown coastal grizzlies. This is the "vacuum-cleaner" outfitter who guarantees a bear, flies his customer out to find one, lands, and illegally shoots the first available, be it big, small, or medium, so that he can return his client to Anchorage and jump off with another customer. This breed of men have no investment in the country and its game, no conception of ethics. The understaffed game department, no matter what devices of airplane law are contrived, is nearly helpless in enforcement. I cannot remember a single successful prosecution for hunting from an airplane, though there must somehow have been at least one. The present law, which essentially prohibits hunting on the same day you fly, makes sense. If only there were some way of making it work!

This same breed of unethical professional, or reformed bartender as many of them seem to be, was found under the rocks turned over by the Game Commission when it was discovered that upwards of 25 percent of the brownie and grizzly hides shot in Alaska had been bootlegged down to "lower 48" taxidermists without the required sealing, so that, to say the very least, their studies of the area kills were out of kilter.

It goes without saying that violation of the law on such a scale cannot exist without demands by hunting clients equally lacking in ethics, it being axiomatic that a parlor house must go bankrupt without free-spending customers, so that problem is not easy. Essentially the guiding/outfitting profession in Alaska must sweep its own Augean stables. There is some hope that through the recent affiliation with the International Professional Hunters Association one local group may do just that. But reformation of the character who flies into Anchorage, buys a guaranteed if illegal "trophy," and then scoots home again is a problem of vastly greater complexity. Apples so rarely toss their own rotten brethren out of the barrel.

Once in a blue moon even today bears squaring an honest ten feet (nose to tail plus fore claw to claw divided by two) are taken, but there never were too many, and today they are rare as teeth in peacocks, despite what some guides would have their clients believe. The brown-bear hunter of the 1970s can hope for nine feet but if he flatly refuses to shoot at anything around eight he may go home empty-handed. Even so, that is probably better than sending to a taxidermist the six- or seven-foot hide of a sow or a two-year-old, and obviously vastly better for the future of our most imposing North American beast.

---

15 : Whitetails Along the Border

Loud the songs and long the stories about the cunning of the buck whitetail in his native habitat, the North and East. I should know. Over the years I've sung plenty of those paeans of praise. But I just quit. Heresy it may be for a Yankee raised on hunting beech-ridge whitetail, but I hereby hand the laurels for smartness and general hunter-challenge to the Coues deer, that pint-sized spook buck of the South and West.

"At least that's the way it looks right now," I said to George Parker, the Arizonan whose ranch is not named Hacienda del Cazador by accident, since George has in his time "cazadored" about every animal worth hunting. "That buck today made monkeys out of both of us."

He had, at that. We had been hunting alone, Doc Rusten of the Boone and Crockett Club Records Committee and Parker's ranching friend, Pollard, having left camp for areas more civilized than this quarter of the Santa Ritas. The terrain was typical of Arizona mountains. From the spiny point where I perched on a sharp rock, I could see both sides of the little draw George was poking out, could cover the canyon in front of me with its few cottonwoods shading the dry creek bed, and could watch the draw opposite making up into the far hills. It all looked to be wide open. Yet somehow that buck had stayed concealed from the time he first bounded out in front of George until I had finally spotted him halfway up the far draw, way out of range. Neither of us had seen him come down the draw, cross the canyon, and begin the far-side climb.

"The little sonsaguns sneak like ghosts. I'll bet that a full-sized Coues buck, big as they go at a hundred and twenty-five or so, can hide behind one pad of a prickly pear!"

"Behind one mighty small clump of grass, that's for sure," agreed Parker.

And he should know. I doubt that any living man has spent more time pursuing the Coues deer on both sides of the border than has George. Not always to hunt for himself, usually to help other people hunt. That takes even better knowledge of animal habits. George agrees with me that the Coues deer is a tough nut to crack. A buck that has fooled men for years, long enough to grow eight points and have the Boone and Crockett record-book enthusiast fumbling for his tape, the points all warty and gnarled so that the deer rates the "cactus buck" sobriquet often given him, is a worthwhile antagonist, believe you me.

Arizona's desert mountains, typical Coues country, from far away may look utterly barren, utterly empty. Closer, it becomes evident that what looked like smooth slopes are actually ravine-gashed jumbles of wind-worn rock, and what looked from afar like the faint green of dusty grass is actually the fuzz of palo verde, ironwood, cactus, occasional mesquite. Closer yet, actually back into the mountains, grass does grow rank enough to hide animals far larger than deer, grass not green but sun-blasted into a bone tan. The crevices between the boulders become full-sized alleys; the brush in some sections actually tangles; gladed pockets, flower-grown at certain seasons of the year, open in the canyons. When you are deepest into the jumbled mountains there is water, year-round water. It disappears now and again into the canyon sand, only to ooze up again several hundred yards below. But there's always water somewhere. Like the Apaches, the deer know where it is. What was utter emptiness from far away becomes, close up, full of surprising life. These mountains are the hideout of the Coues deer. And he *hides* in them.

"Remember those two I watched yesterday, the young buck and the doe? You screeled and squawled on that bobcat call, which you say sometimes will start deer out of a brushy pocket, but they never moved an ear no matter what horrible racket you made. Probably wouldn't have shifted until you walked right onto 'em."

"Don't your eastern whitetail do the same way?" asked George.

"Never tried scaring 'em to death with a racket like the rape and murder of two dozen rabbits—but the difference is that the whitetail back home have something to hide in, a spruce thicket or laurel clump, or a swamp—these little gents hide out where there seems to be nothing to hide behind!"

These deer, as I came to realize, use their eyes to a far greater degree than do the timber-loving Virginia deer. They often move out so far ahead of hunters that very evidently sight, not scent or sound, alerts them.

That reliance on sight in a way handed me my first chance of the year on a Coues buck. George and I had nooned up on the peak, snoozing an hour or two out of the wind, and had actually blown the game, or so we thought, when we came over the crest and were momentarily skylined. A band of several deer had already moved out from under the rimrock, a favorite lying-up spot, for a midafternoon snack. Seeing us they had spilled off down the slope and disappeared beyond two gullies. It appeared they were going to run off the entire range.

On the way across the jagged sidehill, however, we hastened not, nor did we forget to move as quietly as Vibram-soled boots and sun-rotted granite would permit. There was no reason why an intervening Coues or two might either be staying hidden behind some eroded boulder or be lying like gray camouflage cloth in the sparse shade of an ocotillo clump. There weren't, but in Coues deer country, even when a chunk of mountain acreage seems as bare as Jimmy Durante's skull, you must continue to expect to see deer. Because you often will. Not this time, however.

We finally made out the little band of departing deer. They'd run farther than usual; had actually slipped down off the mountain into a tangle of juniper-clad sidehills, mule-deer country. But busily engaged in watching them was a fair buck, the best we'd seen in rifle range. He was so engrossed in using his eyes on the movement below that he momentarily forgot to look high and behind. This was his fatal error.

I almost missed him at that, guessing the range at three hundred when it was less than two hundred and fifty, simply because I found it hard to believe that a perfectly formed buck could be so small. The first shot went over his back, the next two were misses as he skedaddled toward better cover, but the fourth put a one-hundred-grain Nosler bullet through his chest. He still made another fifty yards, finally pitched into a sheer-sided gully where without the telltale blood I'd never have found him. A representative eight-point only, he had knocked off several sprockets in the tumble.

"And given us a merry chase, too," I said to Parker. "Let's see, now. We've been on this range for seven days of hunting, five with Doc Rusten, two more ending tonight. By my reckoning I've seen perhaps a dozen bucks, two the first evening that were in easy range, this one, and eight or ten more either on the next mountain and running or slipping out around a corner so quick as to give no shot. Yet you say this is the best Coues deer area in the state."

"Close to it," answered George. "Years back I often spotted that many in a day. Of course the thing on Coues is not what you see but the deer you don't see!

"Come back in January, you and Russ Cutter," said George, "and we'll go down into the Sierra Madre, look up another brand of Coues deer. They run pretty far down into Mexico, you know."

I couldn't fail to agree with an excuse for another hunt as valid as that one. We'd take in the goose shooting at Babicora on the way. Meanwhile we had the job of toting out the buck. A carcass hefting only a hundred with the innards dropped and the legs off at the hock gets heavy within a quarter mile, even downhill.

When later George went to find the jeep and drive it up the wash, there was time to think a little bit about Coues deer. Several oddities about them appeared. Their ears, for example, seemed to stick out far more than do those of the woods-loving whitetail breeds, almost as if mule-deer bucks had made a sashay or two up into Coues country. They were grayer than any northern whitetail, even the whitetail of Texas, and a mite more smooth-coated. They were obviously able to get along with little or no water, but gained needed moisture from the pulpy insides of pawed-apart barrel cactus. All the hide-and-sneak stunts of the regular whitetail were theirs, but refined and adapted to the arid Arizona terrain.

Staying put seemed to me more a trait of the Coues deer, though their cold-country cousins will often lay doggo if they think a hunter may walk on past. Parker and I had rolled tons of boulders over rimrock edges to go slamming on down slopes, blasting into noisy dust. But only once so far had this bombardment, usually so efficacious on high-country mule-deer bucks, pushed out deer lying in under us. Then a doe had moved off casually, as if rolling rocks were normal to the desert sidehills.

It struck me also that the Coues deer are more sensitive to human noise, even conversation, than are their eastern cousins, I suspect primarily because they hear less of it in the sunlit ranges. I couldn't agree with George that his beloved varmint call would surely move them out of thickets and canyon pockets because we tried that dozens of times. More often than not it produced not deer but a boar javelina or two, trotting in to see what noisy critter was upsetting his harem of sows and piglets. But metallic clicks, or any of those noises associated with humans rather than with nature, would rouse instant reaction from the delicately attuned Coues deer.

When in January we rode Cutter's Cessna down into Mexico to find the ranch far back into the Sierras where Parker's *amigos* had promised to show us zillions of Coues deer, it looked as if hunting them would also be tough on airplanes. The strip below us looked impossible. It was short, though Russ and I had come in smoothly on landings as short before. It was high, too, at seven thousand or better, up where the air is thin and a plane's performance falls off. But worse, a hot afternoon breeze was blowing crosswise to the ridge of which the strip, hacked out with shovel and wheelbarrow, scarred the side as it ran down to the edge of a two-thousand-foot dropoff. That would create a strong down draft. We made one pass. That was enough to see the men and mules awaiting us, but also enough to feel the plane mushing away under us, sensitive to the hot air and cross-wind. Only an angel could land on that strip under those conditions. If we tried it, we'd become angels.

"Not today, boys," said Cutter. "Tomorrow at dawn, mebbe. Better we spend the night at Madera, eighty miles east."

The next morning was anticlimactic. In the heavy, cool air, with no upsetting side wind, we put ourselves and our gear onto the strip handily, and loaded up mules for an hour of travel to the ranch. It, with a worked-out silver mine down near river level, was the reason for the strip.

There was an abandoned building on the mountain *estancia* where we could live, said the *vaqueros*, and there were many deer in the hills surrounding it, *mucho venado*. But in two days of hard hunting it became evident to us that though the Coues may earlier have been dwelling in the foothills, they had moved somewhere else, very likely straight up. We could see tall long-needled pines darkening the topmost ridges.

"Maybe they just got sick of cactus and sun-blasted rocks," I suggested, "and went home, went back to cool timber, where whitetail ought to be anyway."

Could be, George and Russ agreed, but we'd have to change our method of operation to hunt that country. Too far from the *rancho*. Why not base on the airstrip, which was halfway up the mountain?

But even with our bedrolls laid out in an abandoned corral near the strip, it was still a long way to the crest of the sierra, four hours on bony saddle animals whose decrepit appearance belied the stamina that kept them shuffling upward. The country changed as we climbed, the brush beginning to show leaves as well as thorns. Where the trail wound back into the head of a canyon, sizable oaks proved that there was ample water underground, and in the dry stream bed a succession of low stone dams showed where some prehistoric Indian race had tried to hold back floodwaters for the drier seasons.

It was noon when we heard the faint echoes of two shots coming from the ridge series that Russ and one of the *vaqueros* had elected to climb. Two shots is usually bad news, but from the spacing the second was probably a finisher and he had his buck.

The trail we were using had been cut in centuries long past by mule trains carrying high-grade silver ore out over the mountains. It was clean but had washed away to one-hoof width in the steeper spots. There were few places to stop and glass the country.

But we didn't need glasses to see a bunch of deer moving up through the timber to the right. They had obviously been watching us, finally decided that we were coming too close even at six hundred or seven hundred yards.

"Might stop on the far side of the hogback," said George, swinging down alongside me. "If they do, they can't move left, and if we work along to the right, we might stop 'em again. One pretty good buck. He'll be staying close to his does at this season."

It seemed worth the climb. A great fault in the mountain shoulder impassably isolated that ridge from the main peak, eliminating one path of escape. We'd try it.

Beyond the knife-edge of the ridge, when we puffed up onto it, was nothing but blue mountain air. A near-cliff off a hundred yards under our feet to a narrow bench. Below that was emptiness for a thousand feet or more, the cliffs forming the rim of a vast valley accessible only if we dropped back almost off the range. The deer had disappeared completely.

Or had they? Suddenly from directly under us a doe stepped daintily away from the rock wall. Then she broke into a playful run, heading to the left, around that corner which we knew ended in a cliff impassable even by goats. Then a buck trotted purposefully after her, head low in the attitude typical of the rutting chase. That doe wanted to be caught!

But I was not interested in love among the *venados*. If the buck wanted to chase the doe into a cul-de-sac, that was his private business. I'd merely get set and wait for them to come back onto the bench. But both deer heard gravel slide under my boots before they had turned the rock corner, stopped and looked back. Maybe there was some way for deer to get off that last cliff. Better shoot.

The 6 mm. bullet sliced neatly through the little buck's neck and he dropped, kicking, each kick carrying him nearer the cliff edge. He hung up only on the final clump of prickly pear.

"Lucky you," said George. "One wiggle more and he'd have dropped into that chasm. We never could have found him. Worst place I ever saw a critter shot in. Worse'n goat cliffs."

Maybe there is a bit of goat blood mixed into the Coues deer. The rutting buck smelled goaty and certainly the rockpile he lived on was billy heaven. But goats are a mite dumb, or at least nonsmart. And the Coues deer is smart. That is, he's smarter than a human unless there's a pretty doe to run after. Then he can be almost as dumb as a man.

---

16 : A Muzzle of Meese

Bud stood the Cessna up on one wing, and at just above stalling speed we circled across the flats to where the floor of Moose Creek Valley pitched upward into the Alaska Range. "Never saw anything like it," he marveled. "I'll come around the other way so they show on your side."

I'd never seen so many in one mob either. There were at least forty bunched into a half mile of willows and stunted spruces. An amazing crowd—bull moose, cow moose, and last spring's calves, all mixed up in one great conglomeration, standing up, lying down, feeding. Here and there odd pairs of bulls battered at each other in the shoving matches of the early rut.

"Incredible," was all I could say until we had straightened up on course to the cabin by Moose Creek Lake. "I've seen gaggles of geese and sounders of pigs and nyes of pheasants and coveys of quail—reckon that herd must be a muzzle of meese?"

"Certainly a tremendous batch of bulls," agreed Bud over the roar of the plane motor. "Two or three of those in the center were whoppers, up around the seventy-inch mark and heavy in the boards. No use bothering them now, though. We'd never pick a way through that mob without spooking the whole—what'd you call it?—muzzle of meese. Let's go on and drop the supplies at the cabin. Then in three or four days, when the herd is scattered into individual harems, we can come back, move into the cabin, and hunt down Moose Creek on foot, what?"

That would have to be the scheme. It made sense because when the bulls spread around, each with his own hard-won group of cows, we could set up the spotting scope and perhaps pick a monster for the record book.

Old friends after half a dozen hunts together, Bud and I had already looked over hundreds of moose scattered through the maze of valleys that lead up toward Rainy Pass. We had watched through binoculars as the bulls began their search for interested cows, had counted points and estimated spreads. We'd even had grunting matches with rutting bulls that pushed without fear to within thirty or forty yards. One young stud, with the longest bell I'd ever seen hanging below a moose throat, had snorted clear around me in a seventy-five-foot circle before he finally decided I neither looked nor smelled like a maiden moose dreaming of love.

The country was full of moose. We had checked out at least two dozen that would beat sixty-five inches. Ed Luckenbach, who had left his steamship lines long enough to try hunting the Rainy Pass section of Alaska with me, had one evening trudged back to the lodge on Puntilla Lake wearing a broad grin. On his off shoulder he toted Vern Ross's glasses and rifle, while the guide plodded along behind. Vern's packboard strained beneath the cape and antlers of a very handsome old moose, a rack broad and heavy enough to score above the pre-1963 Boone and Crockett Club minimum of two hundred points. But it wouldn't tape the seventy inches or more that Bud and I sought.

From a camp on Styx Lake, so high in the main valley that its waters flow not south into Cook Inlet but northerly into the Kuskokwim, Ed had also picked out and dropped with his '06 a pair of trophy-quality stag caribou. Since Alaska law properly requires that all possible meat from antlered and horned game be backpacked, flown, or somehow lugged to camp, Ed had already finished the hard-work section of his hunt. He had only the more pleasant—but usually more difficult—job of locating a proper grizzly.

"And as far as I'm concerned," he maintained one evening, "any big old bear I find this far back into the Alaska Range is a grizzly, not a brown bear, no matter what the Boone and Crockett Club says."

That remark brought a chorus of agreement. In minutes we had spread out detailed topographical maps of the area, to check the ruling, under which both the Boone and Crockett Club and the Alaska Big Game Trophy Club have of late operated, that draws an arbitrary distinction between brown bear and grizzly.

"They say the difference follows the crest of the Alaska Range," explained Bud. "Any bear shot on a slope finally draining into Cook Inlet is a brown bear; one killed in the northerly drainage going into the Kusko-kwim, for example, suddenly becomes a grizzly. That's the rule until you get as far west as Houston Pass, to the sixty-second parallel, south of which all hump-shouldered bears are classed as brown bear."

"From which we must assume that any bear who goes up the mountain never goes over, always comes back on the same side," I put in facetiously. "What about a bear shot by Marsh Lake? That one drains both ways, doesn't it? And the bears up there don't see salmon one year to the next."

"I'd call him a brizzly or a grownie," put in Bud's brother Dennis. "Or mebbe we should stick up a lot of flags as markers along the range."

"Well, it's my personal opinion that the big difference lies in whether or not a bear can load up on salmon," I submitted more seriously. "High-country bears that never see a salmon all summer and have to rustle berries and rock rabbits for a living, aren't about to grow up to brown-bear size, not in forty generations. But the bears that hang near enough the coast to beef up on a four- or five-month salmon run are brownies and should be called such clear down into British Columbia. Most of these mountain locals up here get no fish at all. You shoot your bear first, Ed, and worry about what category he falls into later."

"What about you?" asked Dennis.

"Why don't you and Dennis move into that camp up on Jimmy Lake?" suggested Bud. "I've got to spend a day or so in Anchorage, and Ed and Vern really should check on what little is left of the old moose carcasses within striking distance of the lodge. We know there's one bear over by Three-Mile because we know he chased off a sow and a cub. As long as they hang around hopefully he's still parked by the remains."

On the way up to Jimmy Lake, Dennis and I proved once again the reasoning behind the plane-usage rulings of both the Boone and Crockett Club and the Alaska Big Game Trophy group. From the air we could hardly miss spotting any number of caribou. It would have been a lead-pipe cinch to drop down onto one of the lakes with the Helio-Courier, which can land in a good-sized bathtub, and to pot a caribou within a quarter mile. But as we climbed higher onto the Kuskokwim drainage and the willows and alders gave way to stunted mountain buckbrush the game grew sparser. Near the alpine lake nothing moved at all.

Not so next morning, however. A casual glassing from our campsite brought a bear into focus. He was higher yet, in a berry patch, but if we climbed his mountain by staying in a gully it would be an easy stalk.

Perhaps it was too easy, or perhaps he was too interestingly close to that imaginary grizzly-brownie dividing line. Perhaps from that first look I was so confident he was a whopper that we didn't check again from closer in; or maybe it was the richly heavy coat, inordinately long for a September bear, that fooled both Dennis and me. Whatever the reason, when we popped over the last ridge and a one-hundred-and-seventy-five-grain Nosler from my 7 mm. Remington magnum had rolled the bear off his berrying ground, we knew this bruin would never establish any fine point of law in the grizzly-brownie hassle. He was a good boar in superb coat, but as Dennis put it when he finished the skinning, "If a hide won't square better than eight or eight and a half feet, and this one won't, there's mighty small chance that the skull will make either minimum." And Dennis was, alas, all too right.

"Doesn't bother me, though," I told Bud Branham when we met back at Rainy Pass Lodge a day later. "A good excuse to come up again for a superbear right on the boundary line. Now what about our muzzle of meese? Time to look into them?"

"Since tomorrow is the next-to-last day of the moose season in this area, I'd say you and young Mike and I should move into the Moose Creek cabin this afternoon. For all we know, that whole mob has left the valley," said Bud. "Get your warbag rolled and let's go moose hunting."

The moose hadn't left, but they had done precisely what we had hoped. The mob had split into small groups, harems of three to six cows, each with one prime bull as master and one or two younger bulls prying around the edges. That much we could see flying in, and we needed no more evidence to convince us that conditions were right.

But there's many a slip. Next morning dawned cloudy, and as the three of us left the cabin a solid breeze blew from the lake straight down the valley. Alaskan bull moose in the rut are very *macho*, as the Spanish say—too busy being great lovers to fear much of anything. But if the cows and young bulls got a snootful of man-stink they would sound the sirens and our hunt would be a bust.

There were two young bulls feeding in the lake, and we blundered onto a small bunch in the creekside willows before we had moved down creek a half mile, but evidently our scheme of wading much of the time was working in that both wind and human scent stayed within the windings of the creek itself. The bulls seemed to have driven their cows up off the valley floor into brush pockets along the foothills above the wind drift. Within a mile or so we had checked over several with the glasses and left them undisturbed.

"Mike," I said to the young husky from Utah who had come along with us two old-timers to help with the packing, "today you'll get some exercise."

"In fact," added Bud as he stopped and put his binoculars on a small batch of moose that showed across the creek, "you may get it lugging just that set of antlers there."

The lad and I lifted our own glasses. I crowed but young Mike groaned.

On the rise beyond yellow-leaved alders paced a splendid bull. The light glinting off his boards showed them both long and broad, heavy. They'd weigh over a hundred pounds just with the cape and antlers. And that would be only the first load, we all realized.

With the spotter set up next to an antler-rubbed spruce, we counted points carefully, watched to guess the width as the bull moved around his cows, and tried to answer the difficult but critical question of whether or not the palms continued down into the brow points in unbroken sweep. At half a mile and with brush intervening it wasn't easy. Bud and I were engrossed.

"How about this other bull?" asked Mike quietly. "This one right here?"

Standing two hundred yards off to our right, watching us over the clubbed willow tips, stood a really tremendous bull. Since both he and his cows had been lying down on the brushy flat, we might well have walked straight past without ever seeing them.

Bud hesitated not at all. "That's him. He'll break seventy inches for sure."

I was busy slipping off scope caps and feeding a round up from the magazine. "Points good? Palms go all the way down?" I whispered.

"He'll score well up. Take him," urged Bud.

As I swung the rifle up and looked through the 4X, I could see the reason for his urgency. This head was obviously better than anything we had seen. But the scope also showed that between the muzzle of the 7 mm. and the moose grew a haze of willow tips that might well deflect the bullet. One hole did open clear to the bulge of shoulder, but at that range the opening was too small for an offhand hold. I stepped back to the little spruce and leaned against it. Better.

At the shot the bull staggered and lunged forward, then dropped as a second one-hundred-and-seventy-five-grain Nosler slammed in alongside the first. When we trotted in through the willows, four cows and a mulligan bull stood there, moving off only as we came alongside the great bull.

Bud was as exultant as I. "A good six feet across!" he crowed. "Probably the best bull in the whole valley." As we roughed out measurements with the tape, he added, "Seventy-two inches—he'll make the new Boone and Crockett book for sure."

But young Mike looked at the downed moose more practically. "And it'll take me two days to pack him out piecemeal," he muttered.

It did, at that. But you could hardly expect the boss bull of a whole muzzle of meese to cut up into less than a meat market full of steaks and mooseburger, could you?

17 : Reservation Hunting

The business of hunting on hitherto closed reservations has become Indian business in a big way, especially among those tribal groups who didn't happen to be shoved onto "worthless" land that turned out to be rich in oil and uranium, but who happened to end up where the deer and the antelope play. At least one group, the Mescalero Apaches, own, and essentially operate, a first-rate ski resort, complete with all needed tows, motels, and Purple Dog gin mills. On the northern edge of their reservation their "worthless" mountain happened to rear up twelve thousand feet, and that means snow even in southeastern New Mexico.

Reservation hunting has become standard operational procedure where the game supply will bear it, and sometimes when it won't. The Northern Utes, up near Vernal in Utah, had hatrack mule deer by dozens when they first began to sell permits and to guide hunts. Last word was they'd oversold the idea a bit, yet control should be easy. The Southern Utes, in a strip along the bottom edge of Colorado below Durango, have for years been running a highly productive mule-deer hunt on their acreage. Perhaps the area that has been the most famous for the longest time, the Jicarilla Apache country of northwestern New Mexico, is perennially being "discovered" by ambitious young outdoor writers as a "new" area for whopper muleys, primarily because its broken country and rich feed continue to produce big deer no matter what. The ski-oriented Mescaleros have both mule deer and a smattering of whitetail on their land, with both permits and guide services available.

Our red brethren do not give their game away, permit fees running on the high side, up to two hundred dollars per deer in one instance. Nor should they. And they charge for guiding. And why not. But, especially in the earlier years, the hunting in areas that are not pounded by mobs of deer-minded nimrods is good, worth every nickle of your outlay. Today—check with somebody who has been there during the past couple of seasons. It may be excellent, or only fair.

18 : Pappy Checks the Bet

My father, may he rest in peace, long ago advised me to check the bet to the poker player who draws one or two cards. The odds are, he said, that your opponent is trying to fill a straight or flush, or turn three of a kind into a full house. Let him show his strength first, so that you can either retire gracefully or display your own muscle. If you're a father out with your son on a big-game hunt, always check the bet to him.

This bit of practical wisdom occurred to me when four of us lay sprawled over a basin edge in Yukon Territory's Arkell Range in August of 1961. Seven Dall rams fed quietly in the bowl of the basin under us. My guide, George Sydney, and I had carefully glassed them and confirmed what the spotting scope had told us before we started the two-hour climb from Meat Creek. The sharp-eyed Indian agreed that the second from the left was a corker—forty-two, perhaps forty-three, inches on the curl, and heavy-based—a cinch for Boone and Crockett listing.

"I'll check the bet to you, Kem," I whispered to my son, lying over beside his young guide, John Bob. "He's your ram. The range is about two hundred and fifty. Your .280 is dead on at three hundred, and you're shooting downhill, so hold on the bottom edge of his body, just behind the shoulder. Crawl up and get a good rest over the rocks."

I wanted that ram so bad I could taste it. His head would make the middle of the record list for sure, and my last Yukon sheep had missed its bottom end. I was cocksure I could drop this one in his tracks. But you don't bring your eighteen-year-old on his first major hunt and then shoot the good ones out from under him, do you?

No matter he'd banged pheasants and ducks and hunted deer and potted home-territory woodchucks since he was old enough to pull a trigger. No matter that he could shoot hundred-yard possibles one after the other with a rimfire target rifle, with half a dozen X's in each string. This was different. This was the Yukon. That animal looking so small in the scope was his first sheep. So he got jittery.

His first one-hundred-and-fifty-grain pill splashed inches over the sheep's withers. But the second—after the ram had trotted a few steps, then stood bewildered—missed by five or six yards. That was it. In seconds

the ram and his pals were around a bulge and out of sight. After the first
great pang of disappointment, a light dawned on me. Why shouldn't the
boy have been jittery? It was tough enough to be on his first big hunt, to
be lining up on his first sheep, and that obviously a first-class trophy. But
to have his old man breathing down his neck, giving fussy instructions.
. . . It was just too much. There comes a point when Pappy should step
clear, let youth stand on its own two feet.

"Tell you what, Kem," I said at breakfast a few dawns later. "I'll stick
around camp today, take care of Doc Speegle, get my notes up to date.
You take George and go get yourself a proper ram—by yourself."

Actually all this was window dressing. Doc Speegle, a Texas physician
who was in the party, had injured his knee a few days earlier, but he was
already hopping around. The fact was that after four days of following old
but tireless George and young and tireless Kem and his young and tireless
guide John up and down assorted rockslides, old man Page was pooped.

So Kem, George, and John rode off into the frosty morning, heading
toward Two-Basin Peak, and Russ Cutter, another member of the party,
set off with his guide in another direction. Doc and I turned to serious
duties, like testing sleeping bags for daytime use and watching a pair of
gophers steal horse feed for their winter larder. Tough day. The gophers
had lugged off a quart of oats and Doc and I were giving the sleeping
bags a second test when we heard horses. I stuck my head out of the tent.

"Hi," said Kem, as he swung wearily down off his pony. "Well, I got
one."

"Swell! Whereja go? How big is he? Was it a long shot? How manyja
see? Remember to take some pictures? Much of a climb?" Parents can be
like that. Kem didn't say a word—didn't have to. He just stood there,
quietly proud, while George unlashed the hindquarters and cape and head
of a very respectable ram. I quickly put a tape to it in the fast-fading light.
A good full curl, a scant yard around the curve and light, but fine for a
young man's first ram.

Kem's trophy hadn't come too easy, I gathered. He and the guides had
climbed blind, no sheep being visible above the last willows where the
horses were tethered. Two hours up on the ridge, they found sheep two
basins away—a long climb up and around. Worse yet, one young ram stood
high on a snow patch as a lookout, covering the only possible approach to
two better ones.

Halfway across, Kem and the guides were caught flatfooted on an open
rockslide by seven young rams that paraded out of a hidden gully at only
thirty yards. But eventually they started the final stalk on hands and knees.
After what seemed endless crawling they got within one hundred and fifty
yards unseen. George sidled up to Kem and signaled that the right-hand

ram was the trophy. No jitters this time. The boy's first shot dropped the ram in its tracks. Then Kem and the guides took some pictures.

The boy was his usual quiet self at supper until Doc Speegle startled him. "You like blondes or brunettes?" Doc asked.

"Huh?" grunted Kem, coloring but rallying quickly. "Season's closed on both up here," he said. "We going back to Whitehorse?"

"Doc means we saw a blonde this afternoon," I explained, "a straw-colored grizzly on the slope across the creek. Want a crack at it?"

"Only if the rest of you aren't interested," he said. "*I* didn't find the bear." That was the right answer, thank heaven.

But the cards were stacked against us. Fog and cloud sogged down off the mountains next day, sending the blueberry slopes into misty obscurity. That hurt, for I knew that Kem yearned for the great moment when he'd confront his first grizzly at, say, fifty yards.

But meanwhile, Doc Speegle and his guide Paul had been making hay. The spotting scope had located a grizzly for them four or five miles downcreek, and the bruin had been kind enough to stay put while they saddled up and made the ride and stalk through his pet blueberry patch into easy .300 Weatherby range. And just to wrap matters up, on the way back they'd found one bull moose feeding in a pond, and decided to immortalize him on 16 mm. film. But while they were waving their arms at him to induce action, a much better bull reared up out of the willows. So we had moose backstrap for supper that night.

Russ's ram gave us another change of diet but a big letdown to Russ. The sheep had been one of a half dozen that, for some reason, had fed down off their normal high basins to slopes opposite our base camp. For their pursuit by Russ and his guide we had front-row seats behind the spotting scope. In fact, by frantic gesturing with a sleeping bag liner we were able to signal Russ of the ram's movements. Only the final shooting was out of our sight. Russ returned disconsolate.

"It was a pretty long shot," he recounted, "because one ram had spotted us and started the bunch running. Maybe three hundred, and I just couldn't believe the 6.5-.270 would shoot so flat, so I held over. First bullet hit over, too. Then just as I let loose the second this darned little three-quarter curl stepped in front of the big ram and took the bullet square in his neck."

The tender chops off the hapless ram didn't alter the fact that Russ had filled his sheep license. I was the only sheep hunter left—still hadn't picked a ram from any of the bunches I looked over every day. Better get at it, since we expected to move on into caribou country when we filled on sheep. Then, too, I wanted a moose and a grizzly for Kem.

The moose seemed easy. From a patch of spruce timber perhaps sixty minutes' ride downcreek, four bull moose had occasionally moved up onto the willow slopes for brief feeding periods. The heavy timber in which they were hanging out was impossible to hunt—too thick and noisy with underbrush still in leaf. But they couldn't stay in cover forever.

"You and John Bob spend a few hours each day in the slide rock above that timber," I advised Kem. "One of these days those moose will feed out where a stalk will be a lead-pipe cinch. Make it early and late—during midday they'll be holed up in the thick timber. The best of those bulls is at least a sixty-incher. Your job is to be patient, wait, and keep out of the timber and the risk of spooking 'em."

"What are you going to do, Pop?" Kem asked.

"I'll keep on chasing white rams that look like Boone and Crockett material," I answered. "The moose and any bear that happens by are all yours."

George and I had a line on a small bunch of rams nobody had looked over. The horse wrangler had seen white dots high in a basin west of the peak we'd come to call Black Rock Mountain. Without binoculars he could only guess they were rams, but it was a new area, worth a climb.

It held sheep all right. Six rams. One looked very good, seemed wide and dark in the horn—but at a mile we couldn't be certain of the head's quality even with the 20X spotting. Between us and their bedding ground, high under the rim of the open basin there was not a patch of cover.

"We go up and around," decided George, folding the spotter tripod and slipping it into his pack. "Get onto the hogback behind them."

He made it sound very casual, but "up" meant straight up to the peak of Black Rock Mountain, with slide and broken rock all the way. "Around" meant toenailing and cliff-hanging around the back side of the final hundred-foot pinnacle itself, in order to get behind an edge of hogback that ran from the next westerly mountain clear to the tip of Black Rock.

Four hours anyway, I thought, after we'd slogged the first few hundred yards up through the black shale. *Four hours, and the sheep could move halfway to Alaska and we'd never know it. Old man Page, you're nuts to bet on this deal.* But whoever said a sheep hunter is a purely rational being?

It didn't take four hours; it took five. The climb was all right, just a long, lung-busting process, and we made it around the pinnacle easily on a sheep track smooth as a garden path. But the back side of the hogback spelled real trouble. It rimmed up. Unable to walk down toward the sheep basin hidden behind the ridge, we had to climb like Himalayan Sherpas, then drop off the rim and traverse nearly half a mile of really steep slide rock. Not shale and small stuff—nothing to them. This was a teetering treachery of frost-cracked boulders from the size of a football to that of a grand piano, all balanced precariously.

But we tiptoed across the slide without calamity and finally bellied over the hogback toward where the rams should be—if they hadn't moved. Crawl a few yards and peek. Crawl a few more and peek. And they hadn't moved. They were up, feeding, in much the same area.

But we were flat behind the last bit of cover. The rams would have to feed up into range. George was sweating a little beside me. Not from the climb, I figured; more likely because the fluky afternoon breeze might switch, as it does late in the day, and carry our scent down to the sheep. To complicate things, a line squall was moving in.

"Nothing to do but wait, George," I whispered.

And the waiting game finally paid off. A young ram, fed up even with us, and a couple more began some butting games only a hundred yards out. Only then did the old one move into a position I could reach with certainty. The rifle had been steadied over a rock for long minutes, waiting for him to step clear and turn broadside. We could hear the roar and swoosh of the oncoming squall as I let off the shot and the big ram buck-jumped, then crumpled. The other rams stood in confusion for a few seconds, then bounced off toward the curtain of rain.

The usually impassive George unbent for a moment as we walked in on the ram. "Dandy horns—oh, dandy horns!" He chortled. "Easy forty—and so thick!"

The head *was* oddly thick at the horn bases, I thought, but a full forty inches long? Maybe yes, maybe no. It might make the record listings, at that, and the Dall did, though just barely.

It was still raining hard and our packs were getting heavier every step when we dropped down off the ridge toward the horses. Horses? They weren't there. Strange, since George had knotted his pony to a wind-twisted brush and mine would stand ground-tied all day. Had the squall driven them off the mountain?

Rain-bleared binoculars gave us an answer. Sashaying across the slope a thousand yards below us was a grizzly, light and blondish even in the fading light. This was the waddle-gaited character whose scent had spooked our horses, and probably the same bear we'd allotted to Kem a week or more earlier. So I had two scores to settle with him.

"Let's go, George," I shouted as I dropped everything but the rifle and sprinted down the mountain.

"He's a big bear—shoot him good!" said the guide.

The bear stopped in a berry patch long enough for me to catch up with him, an easy hundred-yard shot below us. The one-hundred-and-sixty-grain Nosler slammed between his shoulder blades in a puff of spray, and the bear flattened, then slowly rolled onto his back. He'd spook no more horses. The grizzly was in surprisingly good pelt for so early in the season, and that compensated for the dirty work ahead.

Hiking off toward camp in dark and drizzle, with George battling half a sheep lashed to his pack and the soaked bearskin draped over my shoulders like a slimy furpiece, was misery. Fortunately it was lightened when we found the horses halfway in, stopped by a rain-swollen creek. We reached the cook tent near midnight, only to hear that Kem and John Bob had gambled on a hunt to the timber and lost their moose by spooking them in the thickets. That let my spirits down considerably. But not for long. As I crawled wearily into my own bedroll, a voice came from the one next to it.

"We lost out on the moose, Pop," Kem said. "But how about coming up next year so I can get another crack at one, and maybe get my own bear?"

I grunted an assent, then mentally began measuring the walls of Kem's room at home. Trophies take up a lot of space.

Antipodes

19 : Over the Top for Tahr

I had to shout to make myself heard above the roaring waters of the Ahuriri River. "Harry," I said, "I'd like to take one more crack at the tahr. Think it's possible?"

Harry nodded agreeably, although anyone else would have thought it a bit goofy to consider leaving a New Zealand river where you've just raised a brownie as big as your thigh in order to break your neck climbing mountains after goat. But a Himalayan tahr is no ordinary goat. He is something over three hundred pounds of agility and long hair, a beast native to the ten-thousand- to fourteen-thousand-foot level of the central Himalayas, but brought into New Zealand seventy years ago. Bull tahr grow no great shakes in the horn—anything over a foot is of record quality—but they come handsomely haired with a golden mane running over neck and forequarters. Above all—which is where the tahr lives, up on top of everything —he's a sharp-eyed and hard-to-get character, strictly game for the trophy-minded rifleman.

Life is like that in New Zealand. The hunter can turn fisherman one day, drop rod for rifle the next. That's the real charm of the two-island country, the reason why last March I had skipping-stoned across the blue Pacific, San Francisco to Hawaii to Fiji to Auckland.

New Zealand packs infinite sport into a small space. From where Harry Wigley and I were floating dry flies over big brown trout in a stream even more beautiful than Wyoming's Shoshone, it was only a few hours by car (a matter of minutes in one of the Auster or Piper planes of the Mount Cook Tourist Company) to the rearing peaks of the snowy Southern Alps, glaciated ridges where play chamois from Austria and tahr from the Himalayan ridgepole of the world.

"I think it can be arranged," Harry decided as he stowed his tackle in the Land Rover. I wasn't surprised at his reaction, because New Zealanders have a happy faculty of being able to arrange almost anything. "Jack Gibson told me that there were some big bull tahr up behind his Dusky Sheep Station in the Ben Ohau Range, not too far back. His herders spotted them while mustering sheep. But what about your dates in Wellington and the flight back to the States?"

"No problem if the airline has space out of Auckland. After I've eaten my share of one of these trout we'll get on the horn, ring them up, and arrange with Gibson for a day back of Dusky. Right?"

And right it was, no problem to squeeze out an extra day for the tahr. Now, the Himalayan tahr is ordinarily not a beast to be treated on a one-day basis, not if you want a trophy bull. In New Zealand, to which his breed was introduced as recently as 1904 by the Duke of Bedford, he steeplejacks along cliffs, far above the five-thousand-foot mark, and in New Zealand you start climbing a mountain not halfway up but at the bottom. Highly gregarious when the love light burns in their eagle-sharp eyes, the biggest bulls otherwise hang around alone. Usually they perch in some aerie above the slides, where they can scratch a spot of feed, always near some hidey-hole in the cliffs into which they can squeeze a bulk considerably greater than that of our Rocky Mountain goat, a body clothed save for lower legs and head with long hair shading from near-black to near-gold.

Decorated with a pair of heavy but short and sharply recurved horns, each with a battering-ram ridge along its front surface, the head of a tahr comes with its own crash helmet. Inside the outer skull, and separated from it by webbed reinforcements of bone, is another skull or brain cage. Presumably this is to prevent the bulls from braining each other in the shocks of rutting combat. Having chased the beasts in the alpine ranges fanning off 12,350-foot Mount Cook, it is my private opinion that this double-walled skull construction is to prevent the tahr from getting a fatal headache if he tumbles down a cliff. After all, tahr live up where chamois are afraid they'll fall off.

These Himalayan acrobats had been giving us a rough go. For several days before the fishing expedition on the Ahuriri, I had prowled rain-swept ridges between the Hermitage and Mount Cook. With Charlie Ollerenshaw, a guide, and long-legged John Rundie, a mountaineer by instinct but photographer for the occasion, I had scrambled up the Hooker River and over the upper Sealy Range. The tahr we'd spotted turned out to be nannies and kids or were located so high on cliff walls that there wasn't daylight left for a climb.

The chamois had come much easier. We had merely slogged up into the Hooker Valley four or five miles to where the frozen Mueller chasm, with its great curtains of glacial ice and pressure-racked snow, opened on the left. There I'd been lucky enough to spot chamois feeding low down. They were on the next to the last slide of the lower Mueller in a spot which Charlie figured we could reach by an hour's scramble behind the crest of a glacial moraine. When I finally pushed the rifle muzzle over the last rock, it was a lead-pipe cinch and I had me a fine buck chamois for the trophy-room wall.

But no such luck on the tahr. Hence the plans with Harry for a last-ditch try. No matter how fine the fare had been on Jap deer, axis deer, wild pigs, fallow deer, great red deer, stags or even Taupo trout—and the New Zealand sporting menu is a rich one—I didn't want to go home without those tahr horns.

"Everything is laid on," said Harry, finally untangling his six-feet-plus from the phone booth at Ohau Lodge that evening. "Gibson is sure the tahr are still there. At first light in the morning I'll fly you and John in the Auster around the range to Dusky Station. Gibson has a landing strip we use in flying rabbit poison and fence posts into his high pastures."

That and past experience with Harry and his flying machines gave me all the clue needed. "Fine and dandy—but none of those Wigley detours. I don't mind flying low and pulling up over every bush. I didn't lose my breakfast kiting around on the peaks and landing up on the snow of the Tasman Glacier. But none of this business of swooping into basins and trying to knock tahr off cliffs with your wingtip. Right?"

"Bloody well right," smiled Harry, and so indeed it was.

But next dawn, when we skimmed sedately around the range in the Auster, which is something like a Piper Cub with no roof and most of its innards showing, I knew that driving an aerial bus was a strain for him. Not for nothing had Harry spent sinful years as a hot-rock fighter pilot when the lifeline of New Zealand was threatened, bucketing around over Jap-infested Pacific Islands in everything from P-40's to F4U's. But this morning we traveled straight and level—at about fifteen feet above the grass—and landed at Dusky on a ranch strip that probably doubles as a ski slope when they have snow.

Sheepman Gibson indeed had "everything laid on." Waiting were a couple of his herders who had seen the tahr during mustering and horses for everybody save Harry, who demurred at the prospect of climbing so high. As a local guide we had Andy Ross, a professional rabbit exterminator who knew all the back country and, crippled by polio, had taken his saddle horse into areas few men reach on foot.

"About two hours above this ridge," he said, pointing beyond the border hills of the Tasman Valley, "we'll have to leave your horses and hike. The musterers saw tahr in a basin another five or six miles up, when they were trying to bring in some sheep that had gone hermit. Mind walking a few miles?"

That was a foolish question, after six weeks in the New Zealand mountains where all trails go uphill. But the horses made the early going easy. By 10 o'clock we were picking our way back and forth across the little stream that drained the upper basin, and within another hour were halfway up a slide, ready to glass a great rock-strewn basin that opened back into the main range.

Actually we faced a series of basins between peaks that marched back in two jagged lines to an ultimate snow-splashed cup at the backbone of the range. We had seen a few red deer in the lower valleys before we left the horses, but up here nothing moved. Perhaps the cullers (government hunters) had been through this country, as they had in areas near Mount Cook, cutting down the tahr in the constant warfare they wage against all fast-multiplying forms of mountain game. Or perhaps it was a bum steer.

But Gibson had been positive, and the 7 X 35 glasses proved him right. High on the left-hand palisades, brown rocks took on leggy contours, moved slowly across a snow patch. This was a fair-sized bunch, a small "mob," as New Zealanders have it, and so was probably made up of females and young stuff.

Further up, where a rockfall had left a chimneylike crevice, there seemed to be a dark body resting in the shade, with a bit of sun glint showing on hair, but it was too far off to be identified with binoculars. From our position on the slide we could see only into the upper slopes of the top basin, but it seemed to be empty. It was so like the highest basins in British Columbia that I half expected to see a grizzly prospecting it for varmints.

Slowly I worked the glasses around, patiently trying to force my eyes past cliff corners and into the darker sides of gullies where tahr might be resting in the shade. Minute after minute passed in slow study of the right-hand peaks. And finally, something over a mile from us, an object that looked like a black fly crawled slowly up a near-vertical face. That had to be a bull tahr.

Andy's horse could go no farther along the slide; so I sent him and one of the herders back down to the valley bottom to wait, figuring that man and horse down there would spook no tahr but might decoy any sharp eyes from us as we sweated across the loose rock, slipping down two feet for every three we climbed. But even so, when we had gained another five hundred feet of altitude and worked within perhaps fifteen hundred yards of the tahr, he began to move with seeming purpose.

From this range I could make out legs beneath the stocky body, even catch the horns against light-colored rock, could see him stop to crop clean the kerchief-sized patches of grass that clung to the steeps. We had to sit and wait in the cover of rocks overhanging our slide, letting him make his move, with no surety that he had not spotted us and started to climb out over the range. Angling up, jumping from boulder to pinnacle to boulder with ease disheartening to men burdened with rifle and cameras, the tahr finally reached the base of a vertical slab perhaps fifty feet high and some two hundred and fifty feet below the absolute peak of his mountain. There he disappeared.

For fifteen minutes, twenty, we sat and waited, binoculars steady on that spot. Nothing.

"John," I said, "there may be a gully we can't see behind that face, and he may be feeding in it. Or maybe he has somehow sneaked up over the saw edge. But I don't think so—I think he's got a hideout up there somewhere and has crawled into it the same way the markhor do in Baluchistan. What's your idea?"

No hunter, Rundle had, as a mountaineer, set his ice ax and crampons on most of the South Island peaks, and had often watched tahr. "I doubt he topped out," he said. "And we have no choice—every other animal we've spotted in this basin is too far for us to reach and get back to Dusky before sunset."

That settled matters. Assuming the bull was still hidden near that vertical face, we couldn't hope to approach from below without spooking him completely. We'd be in the open, our scent carried straight uphill by the late-morning wind drift. Somehow we had to work around the secondary basin that opened farther to our right, climb out of it onto the back side of the bull's mountain, all on the chance that he was feeding or lying doggo somewhere under that slab of reddish rock. A gamble. But there was one thing we could do to copper our bet—leave one of the herders at this final vantage point to watch for the tahr and us, and to signal in the event the goat moved.

The basin ran back farther than we expected. It was slow going, with deceptively loose rock and slick patches where semishaded drifts of snow had melted and refrozen. I blessed again the foresight that had provided for this alpine hunt a pair of boots cleated with the Vibram soles used by Italian mountaineers. It was two hours of lung-searing work before we were ready for the last hundred feet of finger-and-toe scramble that would bring us to the saw-edged crest of the tahr's mountain. He might still be there below us, or he might not.

Steadily, leaving John well below to keep noise at a minimum, I edged up the slope, infinitely careful to test every chunk of frost-rotten rock. There were two nicks in the saw edge above. The tahr, if I was lucky enough to see him at all, should be below one of them, but which? The right-hand one was nearer, easier to reach. Only a few feet more; so I beckoned John to start up behind me. I thought we might catch the tahr in a position for photographs.

But as Rundle worked his way over a difficult place the strap of his kit bag parted. The pack containing the cameras went rolling down the mountain, thumping and bouncing off rocks like a costly football, and fetched up in snow a hundred yards below. This could be an expensive tahr hunt.

No time to worry about Contax and Rolleiflex repairs, however. John still had his Leica safe under his shirt; so I moved up the last scraping yard to peer over with neck-straining slowness. I had drawn a blank—couldn't even see the vertical rock face. Dropping back behind the stony cornice, I eased along toward the left-hand notch. Perhaps that would give me a different slant down into the tangle of chimneys and teetering rock that made up the tahr's side of the mountain.

There he was, just over a hundred yards almost straight below, lying in a bathtub-sized crevice between the red-rock face and a chunk of stone that slanted away from its base. He rested secure in a hideout from which he could see the entire mountainside and valley below, secure from everything save a bomb—or a rifle bullet—from above.

The bull tahr may have been asleep—now and again bits of loose rock slipped and rattled down the chute between us without rousing him—or he may have been watching our rabbiter friend's horse as it grazed quietly a thousand yards below. It made little difference as long as the tahr remained motionless while I eased the 7 mm. Mashburn magnum from its position slung over the hogback to align its scope cross hairs on his spine. They finally settled just behind the taupe-colored cape that marked his withers.

The shot blasted and echoed endlessly among the crags, but there was no movement save for the pattering of a few stones jarred loose by the concussion. When I spotted the rifle scope on the tahr, I could see that his head had dropped. He never knew what had hit him.

We had a bull tahr, and in the glasses I could make out enough of the heavy-based horns to know that it was a fine bull. But then again, perhaps we didn't have a trophy. "Not a chance of getting down there without ropes," said John. "This whole face is rotten rock, shaled off by frost. That stuff you're leaning on would let go without much of a push."

I hastily pulled back from the edge, offering no argument. John should know dangerous rock. Furthermore, every few minutes we could hear loose shale sliding somewhere on the face. To use the one remaining camera and to get the horns for a trophy we needed wings.

"But after coming halfway around the world for this big Himalayan goat we can't quit here. I don't like the looks of that rock either, but to get at least pictures I'm willing to play the human fly," I said.

"Or we can drop back down to slide level and work around the mountain underneath him," John suggested.

"And then climb back up the gully again, more or less the same way he came this morning," I finished. "Let's go."

But we were running out of time. It was a long way back to Dusky Station, and even from above it looked to be a tough climb up to where the tahr lay. For almost an hour we struggled around the mountain shoulder on loose talus just under the cliffs. Even then came a problem, since from below we could not see the vertical red slab that marked the right gully to choose for the climb. The rabbiter came to the rescue. We saw him waving his shirt, and faintly heard his cry, "Left!" Back up the mountain again, only five or six hundred yards this time, but almost straight up. The last hundred feet were across slabbed faces whose cracks served as finger holes and where we had to prod every knob and test every foothold. But we got to the tahr's last hideout and took the pictures in failing light. Then we cut out the skull, removing its lower jaw to save carrying weight on the risky climb down. Finally I took a light steel tape from my watch pocket and measured the horns.

Nothing like the fifty-odd inches of a top kudu or a good elk, or even the two twisty feet of a domestic billy goat's headpiece. Only just a quarter over thirteen inches of ridged and rock-battered horn. But that put my tahr well into the record class for these Himalayan rarities. What matter a few millimeters of length anyway? This was a trophy for which I'd had to climb the same mountain twice in one day, and that the very last day of forty among the New Zealand peaks.

20 : Deer on the Dart

The icy Dart River water, milky with glacial dust, crested high on my thighs before we were halfway across, and the stout horse under me struggled for footing on the rolling rocks of the riverbed. The strengthening current was roiling in a bow wave off his shoulder, steadily sagging us downstream toward a roaring rapid. Better to turn back now and try again higher in the riffle—or go tumbling helplessly downriver. The major streams of New Zealand's Southern Alps are not to be fooled with—not when their normal race has been tripled and tripled again by unexpectedly heavy rains.

We made it on the second try, staggering ashore through a backwater to where Lloyd Veint, his son Jim, young Richie Bryant and my photographer friend John Rundle were working in the downpour, refastening soggy packs and twisted saddle gear. If the bedrolls and cameras were dry, we'd make out all right. Once out of the glacier-fed river it wasn't cold, just wet.

Lloyd looked at me cheerfully as I swung down off the tired horse. Before going into the outfitting game from his Arcadia Lodge on the lower Dart he had hunted all this country for hides, backpacking in for months at a time when the price of raw buckskin had made red deer a profitable crop in New Zealand. Weather and swollen rivers were no new problems to him.

"Must be those hydrogen bombs," he grinned. "Never saw anything like this past summer on South Island—flood after flood. We're grounded now, anyway. Next crossing we'd have to swim the horses and might not make it even then. Do you mind backpacking the rest of the way to Cattle Flats?"

It wasn't a question of minding. Either we carried ourselves and gear up the footpath on our side of the Dart, under the ledges of frowning Mount Earnslaw, or we sat under a beech tree, perhaps for days, waiting for the river to drop.

Cattle Flats was still a long way off, over twelve miles. The midvalley mountaineering cabin, where we could boil the kettle for nooning and pasture the horses, was a mile above this last crossing. On the first leg of our move into the heart of the New Zealand red-deer country we'd already had one layover, at a comfortable tent city Lloyd had established for less-adventurous hunters just below Chinaman's Flat. This we nicknamed Camp Luxury for its cots and kitchen, and at it we had waited a night for the flood to ease. This time we'd make Cattle Flats and the habitat of deer by the thousand, or bust a gasket trying.

We'd already seen incredible numbers of deer. In fact, I had been hunting and seeing deer—Jap deer and axis deer and English fallow deer and Indian sambar and American whitetail and the European red deer, or *hirsch*—clear down across New Zealand from the northerly point of North Island. Deer in variety and quantity unknown back home in the States. A deerstalker's paradise. New Zealand. Quite aside from such pleasant folderols as striped marlin in the Bay of Islands and rainbow trout in Taupo, it was the prospect of hunting such a profusion of antlered game that had led me to take off from San Francisco for the flight to the islands down under the equator.

There were red deer all along the Dart. Families and herds of from four to forty fed on every grassflat we crossed on the way up. Out of the herds on Mount Alfred, right behind Lloyd's Arcadia Lodge, I had already picked up two very fine stags, one a twelve-pointer. Coming from Invercargill in the Grumman amphibian that Arthur Hamilton's office had arranged for us, pilot Jim Monk had sideslipped Rundle and me through the steep-sided Greenstone Valley so that we could watch hundreds of fallow deer stream away beneath the plane's shadow. Plenty of deer—but it was still a long way to Cattle Flats, where we'd base for a try at the really big stags.

We didn't make it that night. Dark caught us—for sunset in early April in New Zealand comes at the same time it does in September at home—still several miles short. We were overloaded with duffel, and in spots the river had raged against steep bluffs to gouge away all semblance of trail. But Lloyd had the answer, a bivouac in a jumble of overhanging boulders. Camp Misery, we called it, that cramped half cave under a house-sized rock, with water dripping off the moss only inches from our beds. But our bellies were full of strong tea and Mrs. Veint's rich bread, and the sleeping bags were dry.

The sun broke through in the morning as we hiked the last few miles into the Cattle Flats opening. It burned the mist from the valley.

Across the Dart, below the Curzon Glacier, we could see the snow ridge of O'Leary's Pass, one entrance into the nearly impenetrable Arawata Valley. There Arawata Bill O'Leary and his mare Bloody Mary had worked out their lives in search for a bootful of raw gold that had been hidden in these mountain fastnesses by Australian bushrangers, so the story goes. Big country, to delight the soul of any lover of the world's high places.

And then we broke out onto Cattle Flats. Five miles of lush-grassed valley floor pinched between the mountains, acres of green. The sun-bright hides of grazing red deer seemed to glint on every acre. Never in a lifetime of hunting antlered game, from Kuiu to the Kaibab, Maine to India's Madhya Pradesh, had I seen so many deer together.

This was it, one of the great concentrations of red deer that have sprung up in New Zealand from plantings of English and Scottish stags over the last hundred years. The imported deer exploded in numbers and range to such an extent that in 1930 all New Zealand's planted game species were declared noxious animals, vermin. So great are the herds that a force of government-paid professional hunters trim them out at the rate of sixty thousand to a hundred thousand "tails" a year. This is the richness of game that makes possible no-season, no-license, no-limit hunting. Hard not to find trophy heads here!

Deer fled the gullies into the dense beech timber or bush as we trekked up the flats. Hinds and young stags turned and stared, then trotted away far ahead of us. Pairs of paradise ducks, the harlequin-feathered fowl, actually geese, that are completely protected down under, flushed to alarm the herds with their ringing cries. There were still deer in sight when we turned into the timber toward camp.

Camp was another cave, another overhanging rock—a tremendous chunk of schist that had in some forgotten day broken off from the mountain. Under its base there was a room fifteen feet deep and twice as wide, dry and sheltered. Lloyd had used this "bivvy" for years, had built bunks and a fireplace, even box cupboards for the stowage of food and gear.

"What'll we call this one?" asked John. "Cozier than a snow cave, what?"

I had already picked the spot for my sleeping bag. "We can't use Camp Luxury again; let's say this is Camp Content. Certainly no misery in this rock palace."

And there wasn't, not with the tea billy steaming beside the fire. By nightfall fresh cutlets of young red deer were sizzling over glowing coals. Solid comfort, and again evidence that game meat is sweet and tender if cooked immediately after the kill, but not top eating again until after it has been properly aged. With shelter and an inexhaustible grub supply we had it made—if the weather held.

But when Lloyd shook my sleeping bag next morning and waved a mug of strong, sweet tea under my nose, I knew the rain clouds had returned. Steady drizzle soaked the forest around us, and the cave opened onto a world of mist.

"It started again at midnight," said Lloyd, "and with this wind, fog will lie in the valley all day. No sense in waking you earlier." Then I realized that my watch hands stood at 10 o'clock—thirteen solid hours of ear-pounding.

There was no point in climbing to the tops that day, no sense in rising at dawn to slog for two hours up through the beech brush to reach the snow-grass grazing area under the peaks. Driving rain and cloud would have us blind beyond a hundred yards, and the deer probably would stay shacked up in protected timber corners. We hunted the edges of the flat in a desultory fashion, squidging through soaked brush over bunches of hinds and fawns and the odd six- to ten-point stag that would perhaps be a fair trophy in Scotland or Central Europe but was no great shakes by New Zealand standards. No amount of glassing through the rain curtains could turn up a real trophy on the flats.

"Not this early," said Lloyd. "The old herd stags may come down into the valley three weeks from now, but early in the rut they stay on the tops, very high. Plenty of hinds up there now for them to roar about. But there's one thing in our favor. The snow and cold above the five-thousand-foot level have slowed the glacier melting and by tomorrow the river will be down enough for Jim and Richie to bring up the horses."

"You mean so we can cross the Dart and get into the O'Leary Pass country? Where some of those whopper Arawata stags may have worked over?"

"Right," he agreed. "We can also hunt the Blue Duck Basin on that side. Not a hunter in this whole valley for months, and nobody in there for years."

"What if it's clear tomorrow?" I asked.

"Then we'll climb on this side and work the tops two or three miles upstream."

The dawn wasn't actually clear, but the clouds were high, blowing hard in the fair-weather direction; so we made the two-hour climb, Lloyd and John and I, the photographer swinging up through the bush with an ease born of years of climbing in the New Zealand mountains, the style of alpine work that produced Sir Edmund Hillary. No patent-leather shoes on this Rundle fellow—heavy hobs and a Trapper Nelson packboard.

"There's a picture for you!" whispered Lloyd when we were catching our wind beyond the timber and two thousand feet above camp.

Beyond his pointing finger a stag stood in silhouette against the skyline. Another and another came up onto the snow-grass edge, their antlers showing first, then shag-haired necks and russet bodies, a parade of deer until six fine stags stood watching us curiously. They showed no fear, only curiosity, until a fluke of wind sent them scurrying off. Just as well—none of them carried the massive weight of antler we looked for, or the coronet of at least three daggers in each top that means twelve points and a potential trophy.

We climbed higher and out onto a point below the snow-patched rocks of the upper peaks in order to glass more of the Mount Earnslaw slopes. There were deer all along the tops, but even as we strained through binoculars for the darker body and rack of a notable trophy we heard stags roaring straight below us. Their guttural, coughing bawls echoed from a point only a hundred yards from where we had slogged up out of the timber.

John had the glasses. "I see five stags and three or four hinds. Regular family squabble going on. You look." And he handed me the 7 X 35's.

The lesser stags, eight- and ten-pointers, were just feeling out their muscles, shoving each other around. To the right I could see, half hidden in the japonica brush, a real whopper. He'd run those youngsters off as soon as he felt the real roaring, rutting urge. He was hard to see against the brush, and too far away to shoot. But he looked like a fourteen-pointer.

So back down we went, driving hobs and cleated Vibram mountaineering soles into the grass-slick snow-grass clumps, wasting foot after foot of precious altitude. The deer weren't there. Perhaps we'd rolled a rock, or the wind had switched, or they'd just wandered down into the deep timber on their own business. Hard luck.

And hard going back up again, but worth it. As we worked slowly up under rocky cliffs a thousand feet higher we spotted bunches of piebald goats—domestic goats gone wild. The few scattered black ones were obviously the offspring of a tremendous jet-hued billy that climbed up onto a pinnacle and dared us to knock him off his private mountain. Red-coated hinds barked at us and broke away as we topped each gully edge. As far as we could see the slopes and slides were dotted with the brown-red of *hirsch*. Never the stag I wanted, though, not on this side.

By 4 o'clock, oncoming dark and the threat of a weather change drove us off the slopes, down through the timber to the flats to pick up a tender-looking joey for supper steaks. We had glassed between seventy-five and a hundred adult male red deer, and yet there was no trophy, only ample reassurance that another frosty night or two would set the big stags wandering and roaring. Among these thousands we'd certainly find some trophy candidates.

The horses were ready next morning, standing placidly out on the flats waiting for the first rays of sun to warm their backs. We had eaten, saddled up, and were already across the waning flow of the Dart, now only just belly deep, before ordinary mortals were out of their beds. With the horses tied beside a deer trail leading upslope, it would be shanks' mare from here on out, but this was going to be the day. With only puffs of cloud fleecing

across the peaks, and brilliant sunshine slanting through the passes, it had
to be.

The wind was upvalley; so exploring the Blue Duck Basin was out. Our
moving in that direction would only set the deer fleeing man-scent, as they
had the day before. Once clear of the bush line, we'd move southerly, along
under the blue-ice loom of the Curzon Glacier and the deceptively easy-
looking saddle that marked O'Leary's Pass.

No trouble to find deer. A ten-pointer racked away as we clambered up
out of the beech forest; it moved in the red-deer run that is unlike the leaps
of our whitetail or the rubber-ball bouncing of the muley, more like the gait
of a light-footed horse. Across the first gully young stags were fencing
while an old-timer, heavy but with only a fair head, ruminated over the
need of chasing the young bucks away from their hinds. Higher up, still
another stag roared somewhere out of sight.

"He'll be a good one," said Lloyd. "Now, Warren, I know how you
Americans feel about shooting, with your limits and buck laws and all, but
if these Dart deer aren't kept trimmed back the government cullers will be
sent in here to slash the herd; so don't hold your fire. With any luck at all
you'll see five hundred deer today. Shooting half a dozen big stags won't
hurt a bit. Right now, with so little hunting in here, it'll help."

"What about rifle noise? What I'm interested in is a trophy, not a kill
record."

"With the roar starting, it won't bother deer beyond a few furlongs
unless we're scented," replied the outfitter. "Remember that back in the
hide-hunting days we took a thousand head a year out of here, and if you
American hunters and the Deerstalkers Association members don't keep the
herds down, the cullers will. Jim will get the racks and hides packed down
to camp."

A pity to waste the meat, I thought, but an old red stag in the rut, or
roar, is no culinary delight, and getting out game meat is neither expected
in New Zealand nor, in many areas, practicable. So we looked over stags.

The first one fooled us; it was an eleven-pointer that looked like a full
twelve, and I dropped it at two hundred yards with the one-hundred-and-
seventy-five-grain Nosler bullet from the 7 mm. Mashburn magnum. Then
across a tremendous rock-strewn ravine littered with chunks of ice and
glacial detritus, we spotted another shag-necked big one, not yet with hinds.
He counted thirteen points on a heavy rack over forty inches on the beam,
a fine trophy—and a three-hundred-yard shot.

Even as we were eating lunch, another batch of four hinds and a smallish stag crossed the skyline above us, then spooked off into a ravine. The big-
bodied bull that followed was a monster, one foolish enough to pause just

long enough for me to roll into a hasty prone position and cartwheel him over the edge. This was a real Arawata bull, at least five hundred pounds, with a mane of neck hair as shaggy an any bull elk's. His twelve-point rack went forty-two inches on the beam and just a shade less in width. A trophy with lunch.

And so it went during the early afternoon as we worked along under the snow line of O'Leary's Pass, circling atop basin after basin, bellying up over ridges to glass deer feeding on the broken snow-grass slopes. Another brace of heavy-headed red deer were picked out of roaring-season herds to give the younger stags a breeding chance, a pair of coroneted twelve-pointers. From their body size, upwards of two hundred kilos, these, too, must somehow have made it over the bluffs in circling the secret Arawata Valley.

The sun was low when an impassable gorge opened before us to bar any further climbing to the southeast. A glider might have dropped us down to camp in minutes, but Lloyd knew that working down to the river crossing would take upwards of an hour, even if we found a good deer trail through the beech timber. We must turn back—but not without one last glassing of the area below.

"Shift around so the light is in your face," requested John, fiddling with his Rolleiflex.

"In a minute," I grunted. "Right now I can see three bunches, each with a good stag—and that one doing all the bellowing is a real corker. We'll work on him. Now what about your picture?"

While John was finishing his camera job Lloyd had the stalk all planned. It wouldn't be too easy.

"We're exposed up here," he began, "but if we can hump along down and get in line with those boulders we'll be out of sight of the hinds. Then move fast to keep ahead of the breeze, and you'll be in range. Don't worry too much about the stag—watch his hinds and move only when they're all feeding."

The jumpy females never did drop their heads all at once, but an unexpected gully gave us cover as far as the boulders; then we scuttled another hundred yards to the last bulge of the snow grass, crawling fast up to the ridge. The gentle afternoon breeze was slow, very slow, but the air was moving ahead of us and there was no time for a final point count, no chance when my head and rifle scope lifted clear of the grass for real evaluation of the stag as a trophy. The suspicious hinds had already been frightened by man-scent into bounding flight, leaving the great stag alone on a little point, a majestic symbol of the Dart and its crags.

Even as he broke into motion the cross hairs settled and I swung them ahead of his shoulder point for the final trigger squeeze. Seventy-three grains of powder lashed the mountain stillness into echoes, and we could all hear the bullet smack into the stag's ribs. He staggered, dropped, then slid a few feet on the slick grass as we piled down the slope toward him.

And he was the king of the mountain, a fitting climax to the day on the steeps of the Dart Valley. Fourteen points, forty-four inches along the great beams and forty inches across the spread—the kind of red deer that devoted New Zealand deerstalkers seek for weeks on end, with hobs on their boots and seventy pounds of camp gear on their backs.

We'd done it the easy way, with fast airplanes across the Pacific and even up to the mouth of the Dart, with stout horses to cross the river and carry our gear to base camp. We'd done it the way any other American can hunt the roaring red stags beyond the Wakatipu. We'd done it cheaply, too, by North American standards of outfitting cost—though there can be nothing cheap about such a rich experience. Sometime, if my knees hold out, I'm going back up the Dart with hobs on my boots and a pack on my back, perhaps even over into the Arawata if we can find the trace left by Bill O'Leary and his mare. Not for the gold O'Leary sought, but for another go among the riches of red New Zealand deer.

---

21 : Notes on New Zealand

It is a sad fact of modern life that the hunter voyaging to the Antipodes in expectation of game populations such as are suggested by the preceding chapters, which were based on 1956 experiences, is doomed to brutal disappointment. New Zealand still has red deer, whitetail, wapiti, tahr, chamois, and several Asiatic deer types, but in nothing like the profusion of two decades or so ago, in fact only in huntable but disappointing quantity and quality.

This may represent political triumph, but it is certainly a disaster from both the point of view of economics and conservation. It derives, in essence, from the hard truth that New Zealand politics are in large part controlled by the sheep-raising and cattle or dairying industries, all, of course, dependent on grass. Hence any measure which really, or even hopefully, would lessen the competition between wild and domesticated species for that grass will be passed; all others will be defeated. We have had, usually in localized fashion, ample parallel examples in the history of our own grazing states.

With no predators to exercise natural controls, the game herds in lush New Zealand did indeed grow out of bounds, but the declaration that such beasts were vermin, in 1938 as I recall, is hard to justify, and there can be no justification whatever for the slowness of New Zealand's government to realize that constant slaughter, beyond all concerns of licensing or seasons or limits, with government-paid "cullers" operating on the herds year round, would have sorry results.

That the government's attempt to poison out the fallow deer inhabiting one valley, an idyllic area off Lake Wakatipu which a single sheepman craved for his flocks, came to a disastrous finale was as much joke as tragedy. The story reveals a sad mishmash of attitudes, however. To protect the sheepman, the officials decided to sow the region with pellets dosed in 1080, a multiple-generation killer long damned in this country even when used against coyotes, to eliminate the deer. A training process was used, employing aircraft-sown pellets of untreated feed, presumably to set up the animals at the proper time; then they were given the "hot-pellet" treatment, despite screams of outrage from true conservationists and Bambi-lovers alike. When investigators later prowled the valley they found somewhat over twenty dead deer. That kill could have been accounted for, in that valley, by any reasonable rifleman in a single day of execution for the price of a box of .303's. The poisoning schemes were dropped, thank heaven, but I suspect the sheepherder now enjoys his valley all alone. A sad commentary, the whole tale.

The ultimate payoff, of course, one of great joy to the grazing industry, came when it was finally realized that a market existed for the venison accruing from the kill—meat which had for years been left in the bush to rot. Systems were evolved with roadside coolers and refrigerator trucks so that even the local weekend hunter's account might be credited with one or two deer butchered and eventually routed to the tables of Germany or the United States. Meat hunting has now been perfected, with teams of pilot, skinner, and shooter using FN semiautomatic rifles and Hiller or Alouette helicopters to murder deer and chamois alike in the steep southwestern fiord country. They may kill as many as one hundred and fifty-seven animals a day, at thirty-five pounds a head—over three million dollars worth in 1969.

No animal anywhere has ever been able to stand, without quick threat of extinction, the pressures of being hunted for money.

New Zealand's first efforts to publicize any national sport-hunting opportunity were made during the days of the propeller-driven airplane, when a journey to Christchurch from Detroit, say, was a trip indeed. By the time of the jet and the growth of the international attitude that distances were unimportant, to be measured only in hours or dollars rather than days or weeks, the cream of the Antipodes hunting had been skimmed.

The residue is chiefly a pale skim-milk blue, despite the sincere efforts of outfits like the New Zealand Deerstalkers Association under chaps like John Henderson, to set up management controls on game that show real balance and rationality, make of the New Zealand game species a major asset to the country rather than a menace to the sheep-raiser's bank account. That day may yet come, but I cannot think it likely as long as New Zealand is on a grass-based economy.

Australia never has had much real hunting, unless you can call the slaughter of kangaroos or wallabies, again in the interest of the grazing outfits, a form of hunting. In the tropical far north, however, at least one outfitter, based in Darwin to penetrate the wilderness of Van Diemen's land, is demonstrating both skill and responsibility in handling safarists interested in sea-going crocodiles and more particularly in Asiatic water buffalo. These herds of evil-tempered black beasts, the thriving end-product of a fruitless rice-growing attempt, are now much desired as trophies since the original wild buffalo areas of the Indian subcontinent are largely closed.

Europe

22 : An Elk Is a Moose

In Scandinavia an elk is a moose. That is, an *alg* is not a cream-colored, spiky-antlered deer like our own elk, which should properly be called a wapiti anyway. He's a bigger beast—long-legged, nearly black topside, and carrying palmated antlers. In short, he's the same eight hundred to one thousand pounds of walking beefsteak we know as the moose of eastern Canada. The *alg*, pronounced "aylg," is a moose with a Swedish accent.

Hunting him is prime sport for both Norwegians and Swedes. In the Swedish timberlands a quarter-million license holders set out annually, taking some thirty-five thousand head; bull or dry cow makes no difference in the Scandinavian scheme of things. But the northland *alg* acts more like a deer than an ordinarily stupid moose.

He is hunted in three ways. Mass driving to standers we tried—"we" being Frank Forsberg, publisher of *Field & Stream*, and I—on the multi-million-acre timber holdings of the great papermakers of Sweden. These were ceremony-filled hunts that ended in multicourse dinners and aquavit-inspired song. Still-hunting and smaller drives are used by the farmers and smaller landowners. These we also tried during a two-day blizzard. But best of all, the moose are hunted with the Norwegian elkhound, trained for generations to locate and hold the flat-horned bulls.

The grizzly-coated elkhound is a businesslike dog. Not for him any crazy dashing about, like a pointer unleashed. Cast off in the timber slopes and swampy lowlands of the Scandinavian moose country, he sets silently to work, quartering off from the hunters as they edge the muskegs and slant through lanes of carefully maintained timber. Four to five hundred yards either side of the trail, he hunts quietly, nose down and tight-curled tail aloft, checking back every quarter hour or so. No sound when he strikes the hot trail of moose printing deep into the forest mold, no sound at all until he locates the moose. Then he barks.

No baying to spook the cows or bulls into frantic flight, no raving outburst, no snarling battle at close quarters with the bull—just occasional signal barks as he circles thirty to fifty yards around his quarry, holding it, or them, for the hunters.

The gunners may dash madly toward the first faint barks, but since Scandinavian moose are as touchy—as aware of men with rifles—as any whitetailed deer, the last hundred yards is a slow, quiet, careful stalk to see the bull first. The moose of Sweden and Norway are smaller than those of Canada; forty-five inches of spread and a dozen and a half points rate trophy quality. But they are always smarter; the best bull we saw proved himself a real trophy only as he drifted away, too far ahead of the hunters, into a tangle of popple that would stop a bulldozer.

The Norwegian hunt pictured in the photo insert is typical—a mixture of timber hunting with dogs and glassing the upland graze and high valleys of Gudbrandsdal. This is a national-forest area, set apart for grazing since time immemorial. From June to September farm women and their daughters herd the milk cows, sheep, and goats there at imminent risk of capture by the lusty trolls who, so 'tis said, haunt the timbered glens. As the leaves frost, the cattle are driven down into the valleys and the rich cheese of summer is trucked down to the markets of Lillehammer. Then the land is left to the moose—and to the hunters.

In Norway a moose hunter need not be a rich man, or in Sweden either, for that matter. Amund Enger of Norma Projectilfabrik had arranged for our shoot with three typical devotees of the *alg* hunt—farmers Johan Jensen and Oystein Roen and Nils Froisland, a long-legged road contractor who can give a Yukon Territory Indian cards and little casino when it comes to galloping over ridges.

These three annually lease from the forest rangers eighty thousand *mol*, roughly twenty thousand acres—an area some twelve miles by four. Their 1960 lease permitted the taking of six moose, each bid in at thirteen hundred kroner. That's one hundred and eighty dollars apiece, twice the cost per moose of a Quebec license. Expensive, yes—but the slain moose becomes the property of the leasing hunter, and he may sell it in the market at the equivalent of forty cents per pound. That makes the hunt less costly than the cheapest trip to Canada. Under careful ranger regulation there's always a proper supply of game.

We lived in a *seter*, a herder's cottage built when George Washington was chopping down cherry trees, where Forsberg and I bumped six-foot heads on age-smoked beams and our photographer, Bob de Zanger, outraged the white-scrubbed table by placing on it his non-Norwegian concoction of spaghetti and tomato sauce à la Thirty-fifth Street and Lexington Avenue. But the *seter* was warm and dry, and from the timbered ridge beyond, the black grouse and the capercaillie, or *tjader*, were saluting the dawn when we hiked forth each morning.

And there were moose. No great trophies in the four days we hunted Gudbrandsdal, but Nils outmaneuvered the first, a young bull, then I outlucked one that ran the wrong way in dense timber into a .358 Norma slug from my Husqvarna sporter. Roen and Jensen, with Johan's wise old elkhound, Tagg, hung a third on the meat poles before we left. So there are plenty of moose in Norway—even if they are called elk!

---

23 : The Herds of Hardangervidda

Reindeer? Does that word mean to you Dasher and Prancer and Donder and Blitzen making a frightful clatter dragging Santa Claus along your rooftree? Or perhaps you think of Rudolph, the red-nosed one?

Not I, friends. From here on out reindeer to me means European caribou, one of the spookiest critters going, dwelling in a chunk of country the good Lord blessed only with rugged beauty. Sure, there are tame reindeer. They are herded and milked by the Lapps, even used to pull sleighs, but those of Norway's Hardanger Plateau are different beasts indeed. Try milking one, if you can catch it, and it will boot you clear to Sweden. The European caribou is one of the sportiest of game animals.

We got our first inkling as to how sporty, my goose-hunting buddy Phil Williamson and I, when the Oslo police in granting our rifle licenses saw to it that our pet bolt actions were blocked off so as to work only as single-shots. And we got the second when our chartered Cessna swooped us down onto Ugletjern, the lake where nests the great snowy owl. There we saw the hunting cabin of our Norwegian host, G. A. Treschow, better known as Mike when he's wearing his hunting pants. Ugletjern rippled blue in the middle of a vast valley. Around it timeworn mountains rolled off into dim distance. This would be big-country hunting, and we would have to do every inch of it on foot.

The Hardangervidda, a rolling emptiness of tundra and glaciated rocks, actually a ground-down mountain range, is rich in history. Timberless, in winter covered by snow several meters deep, it is a cruel place. The Vikings wore footpaths across it, traveling from west-coast harbors to Oslofjord, and they left behind crude stone shelters, half underground. During the late war, it was the hangout for those ski-borne heroes of the Norwegian Resistance who raided the Telemark heavy-water plant, and kept the Nazis from having atomic firecrackers before our side did. Canisters left from the British air drops of guns and grub still litter the hills. Until quite recently the Hardangervidda held wolves and bears, and its tundra has always fed European caribou. There were only one hundred and fifty back in 1930 but now its moss feeds the most thriving herd count in Norway, between thirty thousand and thirty-five thousand head.

Mike Treschow, whose family estates go back to 1541, owns a small chunk of the Hardangervidda, twenty thousand hectares, or roughly fifty thousand acres. No great shakes by Texas measurements, perhaps, but that's still enough so you can hike all day behind a long-legged Norwegian and never hit a boundary marker. And to keep the overall caribou herd healthy, in 1965 Mike had to crop one hundred and seventy off his section.

Phil and I were going to help on that job. We would be permitted to take up to ten trophy stags apiece. And other American sportsmen will be able to hunt European caribou with Mike and his men in the future too, at only seven hundred dollars for a full week of it, all in a package once the airline drops them in Oslo.

Not that the caribou were necessarily on Mike's own land. Constantly drifting upwind, feeding on the move, individual herds of from five hundred to five thousand wandered from one range of hills to the next. They were here today, miles away tomorrow. Seldom were there small bunches you could easily stalk. The prime stags always showed their snow-white capes in the rear third of the biggest possible mobs. And when you sprawl on the moss, flat as a bug behind a boulder, trying from two hundred yards to pick the best stag from a milling tangle of white capes and waving antlers, there are always literally thousands of eyes to see if you push your fanny up too high, hundreds of noses sniffing if you misgauge the wind. And should one caribou run, they'd all run, spooking each other clear over the mountain.

The European caribou is closest to our woodland caribou of Labrador and Newfoundland in coloring, but his rack is slim, more like that of the Barren Ground type. A good stag will dress out at one hundred and fifty pounds, occasionally a bit more, so the average weight is less than for our North American stags, but mix a few European bulls into a Labrador herd and only naturalists could tell them apart.

Yet there is one great difference. Wave a handkerchief at our caribou, and, like as not, the stag will head your way in curiosity. Wave anything at all on the Hardangervidda, and the whole country becomes as empty as Yankee Stadium in February. These beasts are superspooky.

And why not? Men were hunting caribou throughout Europe long before they did in North America. The earliest of cavemen depended on caribou for meat, for warmth, and for primitive tools as our much-later Plains Indians came to depend on the buffalo. One of the earliest items of human art is the scratching or drawing of a fine stag, etched on a flat bit of reindeer antler, that was found in a Swiss cave and dates back ten thousand years.

Modern Norwegians, hardly a race of rocking-chair sitters, figure to meet the problem of wandering herds head on. They simply hunt farther, twenty-five or thirty miles a day, moving from one high glassing point to another. You hike from Ugletjern to Glaeimane to Besanuten and back, quickly learning that anything on the map labeled *"nuten"* is a mountain with no downhill sides whatever.

At noonday you hunch on the dry side of a rock cairn such as the one Knut Rom built to work off excess energy after only a twenty-mile hunt. You gnaw on Dagwood-style sandwiches of heavy dark bread laced with goat cheese and smoked salmon and sardines and dried reindeer tender-loin. Lots of protein to rebuild your walking muscles. If you want tea, you tote it in a thermos, because in this whole Arctic upland no bush can grow big enough for firewood.

It's good hunting and good healthy living. The cabin is comfortable, the featherbed warm, and the hunting stories are the same in Norway as they are in British Columbia. Only the accent is different.

On the Hardangervidda there is no other rifle game than caribou, but ptarmigan of both the rock and willow types make a shotgun handy, and the area is splashed with ice-water lakes, the deeper ones loaded with two- to four-pound brown trout. During the September caribou season these trout disdain flies, prefer flashy metal, but being practical men we set a net one night and came up with *truite bleue* for the whole crowd!

And now and again from some mist-blown peak you spot the white sterns of cows or the nylon-glistening capes of bulls, and you make a mile-long stalk, finally ending up at the magic two-hundred-yard point, trying to figure out just which stag merits the one bullet which is all you're going to get to fire into that bunch. As often as not, you back off, because there is just then no right shot at the precisely right stag.

It is challenging hunting. Phil told me he got as much charge out of picking from one herd a pure-white bull caribou as he did from nailing a world record Hunter's antelope in Kenya's NFD. I certainly felt that our own caribou hunting was a lead-pipe cinch as compared to that on the Hardangervidda.

And there's something to be said for that one-cartridge-only bit, too. The Norwegians wrote that limit into their game laws to prevent meat hunters from wasteful slaughter, from "browning" the herd and so wounding unnecessarily. But there's another side. Of the sixteen stags we took between us in a full week's hunting only one could move after the shot.

That's understandable, I suppose. Once you have crawled half a mile and then have lain for twenty minutes listening to the distant grunts of the herd and to the strange clicking noise made within their hoofs, once you've finally picked out your master stag and made sure that he is clear, with no cow ahead or behind to intercept the bullet, you make that one shot perfect or you slack off the trigger squeeze. The whole sporting atmosphere makes a man wonder just how badly—in trophy hunting at least—we really do need repeaters for our own antlered game. Maybe the Norwegians and Daniel Boone were right.

---

24 : The Call of the Cuckoo

Birdcalls you seldom hear at thirty-six thousand feet and six hundred miles an hour. Yet even as I happily chewed *coq au vin* on the jet I could've sworn I heard the two-toned song of a cuckoo. Not sensible at all. But the mission that had me rushing across the Atlantic to Amsterdam and thence down to Madrid wasn't very sensible anyway. Most trophy hunts have a certain irrationality about them, and most trophy hunters, like those prizefighters whose heads constantly ring with bells, hear the call of the cuckoo now and then. Even in comfort aboard a high-flying jet.

For those who are not members of the Audubon Society, the cuckoo is a bird slightly bigger than a robin, fairly common in Europe. There he makes a noise precisely like the hourly announcements of those fancy clocks the Bavarians whittle out for tourists. He has a few American relations, but their song varies harshly from the ventriloquial "cooook-cooo" of the old-country version. The European bird sits on a tree in the mountains, echoing his call off the opposite slopes. From these occasionally comes a real response, from some other cuckoo, so that fantasy and reality can get mixed up and the man who would chase a cuckoo by his song wears himself to the knees in short order. Much, I thought, as I sopped up the last bits of chicken and wine sauce, as does a trophy hunter.

And this particular trophy hunt, I remember thinking when our plane's wheels eventually locked down for the Madrid landing, certainly proved me a cuckoo chaser. I'd already been thoroughly licked at it once.

The ibex of Spain is hardly a rarity, and thanks to the interest of confirmed hunters is not likely to be announced by the *New York Times* as an endangered species. Yet it is a trophy owned by few from these United States, surely fewer than a dozen. My first pass on Capra Hispanica, in April of 1969, had been an utter strikeout. For the three days of my hard-won permit the rain and fog lay so heavy in the Sierra de Cazorla a man couldn't see his riding mule's ears, much less spot ibex on the peaks. During that trip, the few watersoaked love calls by the resident cuckoos had sounded like derisive hoots. A more intelligent man would have given up the whole business.

But the ibex of Spain has unique qualities. For one thing, it had become virtually extinct until King Alfonso XIII, himself an ardent hunter, moved to reestablish a true game species as hunters so often do. In 1914 the King used his royal prerogatives to establish a set of three reserve areas in the mountain regions of Spain. At first the *macho monte* or stud of the mountains was under total protection. Then as the ibex bred up, limited hunting became possible, under controlled permits.

Today, there are more ibex than in Spain's known history, just as we now have more whitetail than when the Pilgrims landed, due to such hunter-inspired management. Nicolas Franco, my host in Spain and a trophy hunter of world note, gave me as his guess a total ibex population of at least eight thousand head, scattered in various of Spain's twenty-eight national parks and hunting reserves among the six mountainous regions proper for ibex. The desert-dry Gredos range, only one hundred and fifty miles west of Madrid, has given up fine heads on permits issued through the Tourist Department; the more remote Sierra de Cazorla y Segura section of the great southern Sierra Nevada range probably has more animals, but permits from the Ministry of Agriculture are harder to come by. As of now, ibex continue a steady increase under such sensible biological controls.

As a matter of fact, under present government methods, game everywhere in Spain seems to be improving in quantity and quality. For example, back in 1950 an Exposicion Nacional de Trofeos de Caza had displayed game heads of gold, silver, and bronze medal quality—about like our Boone and Crockett Club contest winners—of the ten types of big game found in Spain. These are the red, fallow, and roe deer, boar, chamois, mouflon, ibex, lynx, and very surprisingly, bear and wolf. There were only four hundred and thirteen specimens in that show of twenty years ago. But in 1970 the exposition I visited had on display over twenty-eight thousand *record-quality* trophies! This from a country twice the size of Wyoming but with ten times the population, a land of which much is either desert or under heavy cultivation.

"Very encouraging," I had said to Nicolas as we drove southward over the high tablelands of central Spain. "But the remarkable accomplishments of the government people or of fanatical hunter groups like your *Club des Monteros* won't mean a cussed thing if we hit weather like last year's at this time."

But no hint of rain darkened the moon when we passed the barrier into the national park in which we'd hunt—the Spanish see no point in having the inevitable natural increase of protected game shot off by wardens or rangers—and the lights of the *parador* or inn set high in the mountains gleamed bright and clear. The sky was still clear at 5:30 next morning when, a full hour's drive by Land Rover from our wake-up potion of lye-strong coffee, we climbed onto mules for the next lap upwards.

Since it is a national park, open to the public, the Coto de la Cazorla has graveled roads winding precariously around most of its valley sidehills, so that much of its roughly seven hundred and fifty square miles of mountain scenery and some of its game can be seen by tourists, but so far the Spanish parks have not been discovered by the weekending thousands that are beginning to swarm onto Spanish highways in their buzzing seats. Unlike some of ours, their parks have not been turned into unfenced zoos with parking lots and Hershey bar wrappers. Once we turned off the road onto steep slopes dotted with Spanish pines we saw no soul save our own party.

Nor much in the way of ibex. For some puzzling reason, they were not, as they normally would be, scattered along the rocky spines of the Cazorla peaks. Early we located a sizable band placidly feeding in a grassy saddle, with no approach possible but as we watched, looking for a billy of size, they wandered over the cliff edge that looked down onto the red-tiled roofs and the ruined castle of Cazorla, a mile or so down. But when we looked over, the ibex had somehow vanished. During the day we looked at perhaps forty animals, counting nannies and kids. Since that was perhaps half the usual number, my guides, one of whom had aided Generalissimo Franco in the taking of a colossal trophy red deer, the modern record for Spain, were abnormally quiet as we rattled back through evening darkness toward the warmth and food of the *parador*. I had the awful feeling that the lousy luck of the preceding spring was due to repeat itself.

But the men who listen to cuckoos are, if nothing else, ever hopeful, and by full light next morning I was crouching behind a boulder, glasses on a ten-acre pocket high in the Cazorla, estimating horn length on a full-grown male ibex. Beyond him the light browns and tans of at least forty ibex showed against morning grass, a few of them with the darker body markings, near-black pantaloons, and chinwhiskers that distinguish the proper *macho montes*, but I could take this flare-horned billy easily. He was at less than two hundred yards. Question. Was he good enough?

I looked at Nicolas. Pursed lips and an upward move of the eyebrows made his meaning clear. "Your problem, *amigo*."

I looked at the chief guide. He smiled. I asked, *"Bueno?"* He smiled some more and raised his hands, palm upward and flat. I'd seen that before. The ibex, if it could raise no more enthusiasm from either friend or warden, had to be mediocre. "No," Nicolas said afterward when we'd slid back around the ledge away from the band of ibex, "he might make sixty centimeters, or even sixty-two, but was no trophy. No reason to shoot."

By nightfall that "average" billy had proved the best we could approach all day, and when we headed for shelter ahead of a black cloud fat with rainwater I gloomily predicted, "Another washout. Precisely like last year."

Friends who had hunted in the Gredos had enjoyed no such floods or fogouts. The lush Cazorla ridges, removed from the Mediterranean by one even higher range and so benefited by a moisture fallout like that of the Olympic Peninsula, might have more ibex but they were certainly harder to come by.

Since Nicolas had business in Madrid the third hunting day, and since for that try I was scheduled to switch to a new set of guides and a new area, to practice my eleven-cents-worth of New Mexico Spanish on total strangers, the pressure really came on. We had already worn out the mules and looked holes through my binoculars, had climbed everything in sight in a cleat-booted scramble around on rocky spines that only a goat critter could love. The weather wasn't really improving, and on that last day I was scheduled to head north shortly after noon.

The gentry who met me in the dark morning were professionally optimistic, however, and before it became light enough to turn off the Land Rover headlights it was evident that we were heading into a radically different sort of country. Theoretically ibex are creatures of the highest bare ridges, steepest cliffs, and rock outcrops. The tableland we were moving into, a sort of pass, was high enough perhaps, but everywhere garmented in timber, save for little rock buttes and canyons. It reminded me of mule-deer country in the Jemez section of New Mexico, where the piñons and junipers give way to long-leaf pines.

When the Land Rover wheels ran out of track, a mile from what could've been a ranch house outside the park line, we set off on foot across this forested terrain. No sense in my discussing matters with my guides since we couldn't understand each other and their chief gesture had been to put finger across lips for silence. Screwy sort of ibex hunt, I thought.

It seemed even screwier when I came to realize that we were moving as cautiously as deer hunters, and when we came to a canyon edge the pause was as much to listen as to look. Why listen? Cuckoos, maybe?

Then I remembered. Young male ibex, being full of masculine beans and later scheduled for knockdown battles with the old billies, spend much of their time in rough horn sparring. It is only partly play. When they slam together and wrestle their horns for an opening the impact and rattle can be heard for half a mile. The dense atmosphere, still wet, although the rains had for the moment quit, would give that sound full carry.

We saw them first, though. On the opposite canyon slope, in pine timber, a band of ibex. Sex unknown and unidentifiable through the growth. Then we heard the banging of horns. A few males, anyway.

The stalk down our side of the three-hundred-foot gully was easy enough but in the bottom we ran onto a family of *jabali*, a wild sow and her dozen striped piglets rooting happily. A bucolic scene, and if there'd been a really big boar it would make a sight sought by every Spanish hunter, since to them a pig with eight or ten inches of ivory is a proper trophy; but the danger was we'd spook the family. They could run up through the ibex and blow the whole operation.

The fatter of my two silent guides solved that problem. He sneaked off upcanyon and deliberately gave the pigs his wind from an angle that made them flee away from the ibex. Score one for our side.

And in fifteen minutes of gumshoeing up the slope we were ready to score two, or even perhaps win the game, except that we couldn't see the ibex well enough to pick a trophy head. It was like guessing a whitetail deer in a thicket. Horns we could see, but which set was good and which indifferent? To make matters worse, there seemed to be two bunches of ibex shifting around, and if one batch of nannies and young males moved a hundred yards downslope they'd wind us for sure.

For fifteen minutes that grew into half an hour we sat there frozen. No way to move closer and we were still two hundred yards from the senior males. No way to pick out the best one of them. Who ever said that ibex were to be hunted in timber like deer, anyway? The whole idea was cuckoo, like that idiot bird.

The group of five or six billies were sporting on a rock projection I could see through the pine branches. All full grown, but one looked darker. Then he momentarily climbed up onto the top rock and posed. Could be no doubt about the trophy proportions of those horns! The two guides still could not see him, but when I lifted up the rifle and poked it through, my left hand resting on a springy pine bough, I could make him out in the scope and square the cross hairs on the shoulder. Good enough.

For an instant after the rifle sets back into your shoulder there's always that nervous leap of question—was it right? If the answer is a solidly reassuring bullet thump, the rest is anticlimax.

And so here. From the moment the long-horned ibex collapsed on the rocks until the park's director of hunting gave me a printed slip announcing that my ibex rated trophy classification in the bronze medal class— and so an extra fee of sixteen thousand pesetas—little happened. Events, yes, like our own rough taping of eighty-five centimeters and enthusiasms from the guides, and the job of getting a pack animal to move the ibex to the Land Rover track. But only one happening of consequence. As we waited for the packer, the sun broke through, and a cuckoo saluted it from somewhere higher on the mountain. No derision in that sound. A welcome, and a challenge, perhaps. But for the time I was through chasing cuckoos.

25 : Weidmannsdank!

"*Nicht schiessen!*" came the hoarse whisper from Nicholas, and the jaeger plucked at my sleeve. "Don't shoot!" repeated the guide. The cross hairs of my scope had already settled into surety just behind the shoulder of the great stag, and he was as good as dead, but Hochsteiner's anxiety was wasted. I didn't intend to fire, indeed had lifted the bolt handle of the Steyr-Mannlicher halfway to make impossible any accidental letoff. I knew full well that a *"Kapital"* stag with twelve massive bone-white points like this one was not for me. As far as deer were concerned, my invitation extended only to a pair of Class II *hirsch,* not the real royalty of the red-deer family which are so carefully kept whole through prime breeding age. But it was a thrill just to make believe taking so fine a trophy, with his characteristic three-pronged coronets whitely visible atop each antler in the half-light of dawn.

Not shooting is what the American hunter must get used to in Europe —and he may well learn to abide by it on our own North American continent before too many generations. Here we generally bust the best bull or buck we can find, on the democratic principle of every man for himself, I suppose. And while we will gaily pay thousands for the services of a fine stud horse or a pedigreed bull to improve our domestic breeds, generally we let herd improvement of wild animals happen as it will. Not so on European big-game herds. On any well-run *Jagdrevier,* or hunting lease, they are managed with great care to produce on a given acreage the highest possible number of head of the best possible quality that can be assured by selective shooting. And when the jaeger, or professional guide—and my friend Nicholas after thirty-odd years in the Donnersbachwald was near professional perfection—says do not shoot, you simply do not shoot. So that morning I had to pass up the monster and content myself with an eight-pointer that with four hinds crossed the alpine basin a few minutes later. He stood fatally still just too long at what Hochsteiner assured me was *"zwei hundert metres,"* precisely the yardage at which the newest model Mannlicher in 7 X 64 was zeroed. And that was the last really easy shot I had in Austria.

Characteristically, Nicholas made much of it. First, as we approached the stag he unleashed from his pack his trailing hound, a red-brown dog of a breed called *Bayerischer Gebirgsschweisshund,* used by jaegers solely for trailing up wounded game. Normally the hound trots tied to that pack all day, never makes a sound, stays quiet when his hunters are glassing or stalking. Dogs like these could almost eliminate the hit-and-lost percentage that wastes so many of our own deer.

Nicholas let him wool the stag a bit as a sort of reward, then reclipped the leash and bent to snip with his knife two branches of ground spruce. One, the *letzer bissen* or last supper, went into the stag's mouth, essentially a last-meal symbol of respect from the hunters whose interest—and money —had in the final analysis made life possible for the deer. The other was dipped in blood, and this *schuetzenbruch* was laid across Hochsteiner's hat and offered to me with the traditional salute: *"Weidmannsheil!"* To that I replied with the formal *"Weidmannsdank,"* or hunter's thanks—as much for the opportunity of hunting as for the luck of the chase—which closed our little ceremony.

We could, I suspect, over here do with a bit more of such attitudes toward our own game. Formality is foreign to American customs, by and large, but if a small formality helps increase respect for the animal we hunt and finally kill, I'm all for it.

Widespread among American hunters is the idea that Europeans who pursue deer and boar are pantywaists in green knickers who shoot on barbered reserves that are overloaded with half-tame game. This may have been true on some "royal" areas—I cannot envision Hermann Goering, for example, hoisting his poundage very far after chamois—but today the facts are quite the contrary. European hunters wear knickers because long pants are a blasted nuisance in steep climbing. They prefer green because it's good camouflage where the timber is largely conifers, so it has become the hunter's traditional color. For reasons of training and licensing procedures the idiocy of shooting at noises in the brush, or odd-shaped lumps that might or might not be game, is less common among Europeans than it is here. Red or blaze orange is just simply not needed among the overseas big-game fraternity.

And if their hunting is easy, then my experiences in Norway, where twelve hours of foot-slogging after caribou or moose was our normal daily stint, or in Spain, where the gentry of the Corzala wore my legs off from the knee clambering around after ibex, or on half a dozen other European hunts, were not typical but exceptional. And chamois hunting has to be tough no matter how you cut it, unless you can find one tied to a tree close to the road. In that event the peak-loving chamois would probably pass away from too little altitude or too much air pressure!

The Donnersbachwald would be no cinch, I learned early. It was too beautiful an alpine area, and where you have fancy scenery you have steeps. Standard procedure for Nicholas and me from our dinky Glatthutte which clung below Donner or Thunder Basin, called for crawling out of the sack at 4. We shivered down tea and crusty bread, then started before 5, with flashlights, to climb above the timber line onto the grassy top levels favored by the red deer. An hour and a half of steady plodding upward would see us right—but we'd still be from one to two hours of hard climbing below the chamois peaks. Plenty of room to operate in. The revier jointly controlled by the Steyr-Mannlicher people and the Semperit Tire outfit totaled thirteen thousand hectares—that's roughly thirty-three thousand acres or fifty square miles—of timber, narrow valleys, and alpine peaks running up to six thousand five hundred feet or so. No Mont Blancs, but the day's hunt started at about three thousand five hundred, so the climbs were long.

The countryside is lumbered in the clean and selective European fashion which leaves no slash tangles, and the valley people run a few milk cows, feeding them hard-to-dry hay through the deep snows of winter. A *Forestmeister*, the bearded Herr Loschek, and his crews, which include seven jaegers like Nicholas, rule the operation. Its game production is phenomenal. From the Glatt region of some seven thousand five hundred near-vertical acres for which Nicholas is responsible, his hunters had last season taken twenty stag *hirsch*, forty hinds, ten roe deer, twenty-four chamois, without at all harming the population. Hence the entire revier, with its seven similar sections, is well worth the fifty thousand dollars annual lease fee shared by Steyr-Mannlicher and Semperit. In America, that would be charged off as a nontaxable business expense!

Observant hunters in this country are already noting similar approaches set up by individuals, companies, or by syndicates, as for example the New Hampshire Blue Mountain Reserve. Whether this trend is good or bad could be the topic for a future discourse.

As far as Nicholas and I were concerned, Donnersbachwald was a mountain hunter's heaven. While he gutted the *hirsch*—the Austrians do not attempt to split the pelvis of these heavy deer, but core around the anus and so take it in rather than out—I had already spotted moving dots up on a sawtoothed ridge. They had to be chamois.

The chamois, or *gams*—*gamsgeiss* for the female, *gamsbock* for the male—of Europe may be no close relation to our white mountain goat, but they share delight in the highest, rockiest ledges and scree slopes available, their chief defenses being altitude and eagle-sharp eyes. Rarely weighing outside the forty-to-sixty-pound range, the little *gams* is far fleeter than our goat on open slopes, and has balance and jumping ability to navigate ledges impassable for the larger animal. On one point of importance to hunters the chamois differs from our rather solitary-minded bearded billy—often they run in mixed groups that may count between five and fifty. As with the white goat, however, trophy estimation on a chamois is a real task, the difference between good, bad, and indifferent measurements of the dainty back-hooking horns being only a few centimeters.

On the Donnersbach schedule, as Nicholas finally got across to me in our communication mishmash of a little English, a little German, and a lot of gestures, the season, or *jagdzeit*, on male chamois is not open until November eleventh, beginning of the *gamsbrunft*, or rutting time. But as confirmed hunter Dr. Breitenfeld of the Steyr-Mannlicher staff had already told me, a really old and smart female grows longer horns than the average buck and is locally considered a better trophy. How big or how old or smart I had no clue from my earlier experience on the dainty goatlike climbers in New Zealand, since the aim down under had seemed to be more quantity than quality. In Austria my permit said two chamois and I reckoned to make at least one something special.

With the *hirsch* properly cleaned, rather surprisingly Nicholas produced from his rucksack a walkie-talkie, waited a few minutes for a precise 8 o'clock, and made contact with his home five or six miles down the valley. From our position in the high basin it was a straight shot, no radio interference. Porters to come up for that first stag were quickly arranged—I had been wondering just how the two of us were going to tote one hundred and fifty kilos off the mountain.

By midmorning I wondered how I was going to get myself off, since we had worked steadily upward across a major ridge and into a truly alpine area of cliffs and trickling snow water. We were surrounded by all manner of fine yodeling places. Up among the echoes is no spot for a man over fifty, even if he is cavorting around in boots handmade by a Viennese expert! But we had made operational contact with the chamois.

"Too many," I said to Nicholas as we peered up at the high basin or col opening beyond our final clump of brush. "*Zu viel.*" That exhausted my supply of German, but perhaps the situation wouldn't exhaust our ingenuity. About half of a mob of four dozen chamois we had seen earlier had fed up over the left ridge and settled down for a midday snooze. More had disappeared onto ledges in the shade of the peak proper. With careful study—the middle-European jaeger still swears by a three-foot extension telescope and his climbing staff instead of the modern spotter and tripod —we found more. Five had bedded farther to the right. The nearest ones were over a thousand yards from us, but once beyond that last bush we'd stand out like coal on a bed sheet.

"*Nicht gut,*" we agreed.

The pidgin-English–German began to flow again, this time aided by a stick and a little patch of smooth gravel. If we dropped back behind the lip, moved across the basin mouth under the shaded right-hand wall, which would keep us hidden from the far right group of chamois, perhaps we could use a glacial moraine to hide us from any eyes at center and left. There was no other possible stalk.

When it ended we were still in a poor position, at least three hundred meters below the little group, a long shot for game so small. The odds could be better either by bellying up through a gully floored in ice-water-soaked moss, or by working left along the crest of a breakneck dropoff. I dislike crawling among ice cubes, so we took the circling climb. Finally the end of our cover was still two hundred and fifty meters from the sleeping animals, but study with glasses showed the lowest one to boast creditable horns, so I wormed into a comfortable shooting position and was ready. Then it came again.

"*Nicht schiessen!*" hissed Nicholas.

"What now?"

As far as I could make out from Nicholas's words and gestures I must wait until the chamois woke up and stood, not so much that a standing target was better, as it is, as that it was simply not kosher, not sporting, old boy, to clobber the game while asleep. That waking-up process might take all day!

It didn't. Just as my arms were about to break off from holding the rifle, the chamois stirred and stood. Then it dropped instantly when a one-hundred-and-seventy-three-grain H-Mantel bullet whistled through its rib cage. Fine.

But Nicholas didn't seem to think so. He was violently urging me to get up, to sprint to a little ridge beyond which the other chamois had disappeared. From his muttering I gathered that one of them had, as they moved, showed a very distinctive length of horn.

Hitting a hundred-pound prong-horn antelope on the run is tough in the flat country of Wyoming. Expecting to hit a chamois of half that size which is leaping all over a tilted-up Austrian rockpile is downright ridiculous. But I bellied over a boulder and waited until the bouncing figure Nicholas pointed out finally stopped to look back. Pretty far, but a back-line hold might do it. It did.

The *Weidmannsheil* and *Weidmannsdank* ceremony over the first chamois was quick and simple. On the second, Nicholas put extra fervor into his handshake, said his *Heil* a bit louder and with a broader smile. And my thanks were even more fervent. As we studied the horns and teeth it was evident that this trophy, ten inches, or twenty-five centimeters, around the curve, was of extra quality, worth recording. As Nicholas pointed out, at eighteen years the animal was a real old-timer, surely past breeding usefulness. It was hard for me to believe that a fifty-pound animal could beat the deep alpine snows and howling blizzards for so long.

With the husky red deer, winter survival is easy to understand. I knew that at Donnersbachwald discreet feeding was practiced in hard winters, and perhaps more important, careful culling of the herd tended to eliminate less-desirable animals that would waste browse during the early snows yet couldn't make it through the crucial later months. Though it tends to concentrate the hunting privilege in the hands of a few, this management on a more intimate scale than we can apply on a state basis does have certain advantages.

We watched half a dozen stags the second day, for example. One was another heavy-antlered *"Kapital,"* untouchable, and none seemed quite right for my second stag. Interesting to me, the red-deer male, who in the rut does not bugle like our wapiti but rather roars with a sound like the combination of an angry bull and a seasick yachtsman, also continues to feed more or less normally while he is managing his harem. The elk I have watched in full rut have always seemed more concerned with breeding than with browsing. But perhaps the *hirsch* we glassed were close to the end of their roaring period.

I was close to the end of my hunting, anyway, since when Nicholas woke me at 4 of the last morning, I realized we had only until a couple of hours after sunup to find the proper stag.

Nicholas was humming as he stoked the breakfast fire, and his *"Guten Morgen"* was bright. I got the impression he had something up his sleeve. When we struck out in darkness cut only by flashlight glimmer, heading in a brand-new direction, down the valley rather than up, I finally figured out what he had in mind. Down that way at dawn and dusk of the preceding day we had heard the roaring call of a fully mature stag, one apparently anchored to a preferred spot with his hinds, probably halfway up the mountain, where timber gave way to grass.

As we crossed the creek to climb through the conifers we heard him sound off again. Much higher. And again, after thirty minutes, higher still. Nicholas was moving faster this morning and I had already puffed through both first and second wind. Perhaps the stag had roared from this next clearing, I thought hopefully?

But the jaeger stepped briskly across and headed upwards and there was nothing to do but follow. I could already see the timber opening onto higher slopes just ahead.

I hadn't realized we had come to a watching place until I stumbled into Nicholas and almost stepped onto his old *Gebirgsschweisshund,* trotting happily along unleashed as a special guest on this final hunt. At thirteen years of age, the dog was wheezing less than I was. We slipped in behind a big moss-topped boulder, across which we could see, beginning two hundred yards up through scattered larches, the yellow of a steep grass slope. Deer were already visible, and Nicholas had time for a telescopic peek at the darkest-necked stag before he fed in behind a treetop. I'd already had my 7 X 35's on the animal. It was good, perhaps too good. But Nicholas looked at me and nodded. *"Schiessen,"* he said quietly.

With the Steyr-Mannlicher laid over that mossy rock bulge the scope was steady, but the waiting tiring. Would the stag never move into the clear? A hind fed out first, then another. But the neck showing next was dark, shaggy, and I could see the flicker of polished antler tips. One step more.

Nicholas had already indicated that the range would be something like three hundred and fifty meters, and it seemed to me all of that. But I was shooting very steeply uphill, more than thirty degrees, enough so that the gravity effect would be lessened. A very scant backline hold should be about right, I guessed.

As the stag showed his whole forequarter and I laid the horizontal wire tight on the withers the rifle bucked. The *hirsch* collapsed into a sliding fall as we heard the bullet strike. The guess had been good.

When I finally clambered up to where the fallen *hirsch* lay, Nicholas looked rather odd. There was a touch of the "boy caught at the cookie jar" in his face. It wasn't hard to see why. This stag was indeed good, perhaps really too good. Not quite a twelve-pronged *"Kapital"* but no scrub either. It was heavy and the warty beading around the antler bases indicated it was a gentleman of some years.

Then Nicholas relaxed. What was done was done. This American's hunting holiday had certainly been rounded off to near-perfection. As the jaeger handed over the blooded sprig of evergreen and I received it with a heartfelt *"Weidmannsdank,"* we smiled at one another. In the strong and ancient brotherhood of sportsmen, whether on the Alps or the Rockies, the thrills and satisfactions of mountain hunting are always and essentially the same. That both Nicholas and I knew.

Asia

26 : Asian Opportunity

Asia is not the "newest" hunting ground. It was hunted by a handful even before the day of the self-contained rifle cartridge. It was, for example, hunted by such Americans as Roy Chapman Andrews, Colonel Morden and his chum James Clark, just after the First World War. A Springfield rifle was seized from Jim Clark, during his lifetime a good personal friend and a bulwark of New York's Museum of Natural History, by the Mongols he met in the Pamirs, in *Ovis poli* country. It is still displayed in my club, Campfire. Adventurer Morden lived six or eight houses down my road. Before these very real American hunters of Asia, of course, had come the British, most of them army officers who had infinite time off because their explorations might have military value to some future colonial activities. Men like Littledale, Maydon, and others had swarmed all over Asia in lands both high and low. Asia has not been discovered of late; rather it has been rediscovered, as political situations have opened up and Asiatic interest in the Yankee tourist dollar has heightened.

As a matter of fact, I was hunting such Asiatic sheep species as *gad* or urial, and the spiral-horned Kabul *markhor*, back in the early 1950s, in areas into which, as far as I know, no Caucasian nimrod had ventured since the days of the Khyber Pass battles. The Pakistan government sent me on a train from Karachi, unfortunately right past the desert mountains holding the Sind ibex, of which nobody then knew anything much, to Quetta in Baluchistan. From there, by truck and pack train we climbed into the mountains bordering Afghanistan, the Khalifat and Pil ranges, a section remarkably like New Mexico. Here for centuries the Baluchis had been potting at the Afghans, and they had been potting back, with the local wild sheep and *markhor* more or less caught in the middle. From a camp of at least fifty donkeys, as many men, a veritable city of tents, a Swiss photographer and I hunted. And I was expected to provide wild meat for the whole crew, not force this group of hawk-nosed and *djellaba'd* mountaineers to slaughter their domestic sheep. Those were a measure of wealth.

How they rated on the money scale I found out only late in the hunt. One Rahmatullah, a blue-eyed six-footer who possessed greater abilities as a shikari or hunting guide than any of the eight or ten others working as such, had one day demonstrated his skill by finding for me an excellent specimen of a Kabul *markhor* after his colleagues had produced only two-year-olds. That night, as we listened to the men chanting around a huge bonfire, apparently some ritual for the Moslem time of Ramadan, he stepped up and through our interpreter offered to come to the United States "to be my personal bearer and go with me on all shikaris." As a clincher he showed his Pakistan driving license. With a mental vision of Rahmatullah wheeling my family Buick up New York's West Side Highway, on the wrong or British side, I explained that my country was very cold, very distant, I was a poor man, and he'd anyway be missing the second wife which, I had been told, he had recently taken on.

Five minutes later back he came with a request to see my rifle—actually the Mashburn-made Old Betsy #1 in 7 mm. magnum which has been with me on a hundred hunts. This was understandable, since to the Baluchis any rifle was a thing of great interest, and one with a scope which could hit and kill surely at three and four hundred yards was a cause for outright awe. After peering through the scope for a bit and admiring the walnut and hefting the piece in his strong brown hands he turned to me, obviously wanting to trade for the sporter. When I yanked my head back in the world-recognizable query, what'll you give me, we needed no interpreter; but that functionary properly intervened when, after a moment of thought, the tall Moslem offered his thoughtful reply.

"For this fine rifle," he said, "I would give thee fifty fat-tailed sheep—and my second wife."

The fat-tailed sheep I was familiar with, since some were visible in the camp. The wife I couldn't imagine, since Baluchi women are kept in strictist purdah, invisible to men and certainly to Christian men. But I had at the time been hunting for well over a month, and purdah or no this sounded like an interesting proposition. Yet Rahmatullah, I considered, after only a month or so of marriage must have found something very wrong with #2 if he wanted to swap her for a rifle, even for a custom rifle, and furthermore I had only seven cartridges left for the wildcat caliber. That was hardly enough to make it a fair trade for Rahmatullah, and one must above all be fair. So now I still only know about the fat-tailed sheep. They are ugly as sin.

For the more-handsome sheep of Asia, the *Ovis poli* found up beyond Hunza, or in the appendixlike Wakan corridor running northwest out of Afghanistan, or on the Russian-held Pamirs; and for the great *Ovis Ammon* types of western Mongolia and the Tien Shan, there has in recent years developed hunting opportunity. In fact, it is now almost as easy to hunt Ammon and various forms of ibex as it is to book an Alaskan trip, and the prices are not so very different. A bit nearer home, the forest and mountain varieties of Iran, so intelligently conserved by the Shah and his brother Prince Abdorreza, can be hunted on a system of reserves and stone lodges almost luxurious, and certainly a triumph of game management. It is this opening up of various Asiatic hinterlands which is new, and it is a source of regret to me that *Ovis poli*, for example, became a real possibility only after the idea of gallivanting around at eighteen thousand feet—which has already killed one seemingly healthy American hunter—seemed a bit beyond my years. But the Ammon country, or at least the middle and southerly sections of it, are nothing like that high, really no more demanding then a Wyoming elk hunt, so who knows?

Americans hunting in any part of Asia, be it the low country of India or the Malay Peninsula, or the bare slopes up on the eaves of the world in Central Asia, face one problem, that of communication. The Asian may well speak our language in quite intelligible fashion. He may seem at least as understandable as a Maine Yankee does to a Georgia Cracker, for example, but that does not mean he either understands us perfectly or says what we think he does. There is always some degree of communication breakdown. The Asian, for one thing, is generally more polite than we are. He tends to say what he thinks we want to hear— which may or may not be the hard truth we actually crave—and that can lead to misunderstanding.

I recall asking an Indian shikari, Khan Sahib Jamshed Butt, about the sloth-bear possibilities on a Chanda hill visible from our dak bungalow. He assured me that they were excellent, that if we hunted over there, the snap-tempered and wire-furred bear would undoubtedly appear and get himself thoroughly shot. That there hadn't been a sloth bear in that region since Noah's flood, that the terrain was in fact quite wrong for that brand of bear in every way, did not appear until after we had wasted a day covering the little range of hills.

Since Americans aren't likely to learn Mongol or Pushtu dialects, and are hardly raised with the Asian's ideas or values, only patience and gentle insistence on absolute clarity of understanding—by both parties—can solve the problem. There are, I might say, even some U.S. outfitters with whom we don't communicate well, either. The backwoodsman, for example, can hardly be expected to make sense of the importance of minutes and hours, even of days, to men whose entire lives have been regulated by clock-timed appointments.

---

27 : Pigs in the Garden of Eden

The rumble of the big plane's four engines eased to a mutter when we started the letdown for landing at Basra, first stop on a hunt that would take in Iraq, India, and Baluchistan. I put aside the guidebook. For two hours, flying across the sand plains and wadis of Saudi Arabia, I'd studied that booklet. But the only fact that stuck in my travel-drowsy mind was that just north of Basra lay, so it was believed, the true site of the Garden of Eden, where Eve slipped Adam a thornapple and started all our human troubles.

Funny place to come for a boar hunt, the Garden of Eden, and a long way from home. But Bob Angorley, Keeper of Iraq's Royal Game Preserves, had said the big *khanzir* were there, and he should know. What I didn't know when we eased onto the runway was that Eve had also fed the grandpappy of all the Asiatic wild pigs a few apples from the Tree of Good and Evil. She must have, judging from the ability of his bull-shouldered descendants to create tusky trouble.

The first boar, true, raised no real ruction, but did give me some idea of what to expect of a four-hundred-pound *kibbir khanzir* in terms of vitality and general plug-ugliness. He took a one-hundred-and-seventy-five-grain 7 mm. magnum slug behind his shoulder and still had steam enough to sprint a hundred yards through the camel-thorn with a second shot tucked in just abaft the first hole, before plowing his tushes into the clay. But the second—what a rumpus that button-eyed swamp devil caused! He and a couple of his cousins. It all happened like this. . . .

But first let's understand there are three ways of hunting the boars of Iraq. These big pigs hang out in huge marshes that flank the Tigris and Euphrates rivers in their courses down the Iraqui flood plains to Querna. There at the site of the Tree of Good and Evil, the rivers join to form the navigable Shatt al Arab and flow into the Persian Gulf. Islands in the marshes give the hogs resting and breeding places but little feed; so morning and night they visit the fields to raise general hell among the wheat and rice plantings, the truck gardens of the local Arabs. They, being Moslem, are by their religion forbidden to eat pig; if they are fully orthodox, even to touch the porky pests. Hence the boars and sows have a field day until some obliging *ajnebny*, or foreigner, turns up with a rifle.

He can chase hogs through the six-foot marsh reeds in a shallow-draft *belem*, poled along by a couple of turbaned gondoliers, and get shots at close range. That style of swamp shenanigan we tried once, and just once. Or the boars can be driven out of such brush patches and date groves as exist in this land of few trees. Or they can be picked off at the marsh edge as they leave the sheltering *burdy* and *gassab* reeds for a rooting good time in Abdullah's melon patch. All these schemes ultimately involve a small army of gabbling Arabs, more excitement than the day the circus tent caught fire in Emporia, and some quick shooting if you don't want the *khanzir's* tusks in the seat of your new khaki pants.

Iraqi boars are big. Four- and five-hundred pounders are by no means record weights, and grizzled old soakers of six hundredweight show up now and again. Ten times the size of the javelina of our southwestern states, they show the same single-minded truculence. Never bothered by the marsh Arabs, they'd as soon chase men as *pi* dogs any day. Rather, mebbe. And the cutting tusks either side of a boar *khanzir's* snout will measure over ten inches around the curve.

It had been high noon when our little caravan, Angorley's pickup and a Chevy we borrowed from TWA, rolled to a stop on the bank of the Tigris. Opposite snoozed the village of Shaik Jassim, just a cluster of mud and reed huts between the *shaik's* brick house and the small blue-domed mosque which gave the settlement its name, Abdullah Ibn Ali. Blue sky, the murmuring river, and buzzing quiet.

"Peaceful place, isn't it?" I ventured to Angorley and Jules Gindroux, the airline agent who'd come along in the hope of seeing edible pork laid out in windrows.

But just then our driver, Ali, leaned against the pickup's horn.

That got the same reaction as the noon whistle down at the pickle works. Over the river every hut disgorged Arab men, barelegged kids and *pi* dogs. The country peace was cracked by shouted greetings of *"Shlonak! Shlonak!"* and a pair of king-sized *belems*, high-prowed pushboats, slid out to ferry us and our duffel trans-Tigris.

Fresh in a Moslem land, I thought we'd sally forth pronto for pigs. But first came the ceremonial greetings from Shaik Jassim and his village ministers, with touchings of foreheads and mutterings of *"Allah b'il khair"* and *"Shlon kafek."* Then there was a ceremonial sitting about in the sheik's house while we made no sense in three languages and drank dead-sweet tea; and finally, after the scope sights on the *Amerikani's* rifles had been inspected by the village elders, a ceremonial hand washing before *koozy* or lunch. No ritual there, not after the *shaik* had ripped off the first chunks of lamb and presented them to the visiting firemen. From there on out it was every man for himself.

The post-*koozy* coffee, a mud-thick brew spiced with cardamon seeds, strong as lye and twice as bitter, only increased my yen to have at the pigs. Eventually we straggled across the fields, with twenty-odd villagers traipsing along like kids at Coney Island.

Half a mile out that first boar raised his ugly head from a barley patch. Angorley restrained the gabbling villagers while an *abba'*d and *agal'*d gent named Ali and I sneaked into shooting range. And such a muchness of pig he was when the one-hundred-and-seventy-five-grain pills rolled him over. Better than a solid four hundredweight, bristles along the back and mud all over the underside, longer than my rifle from withers to trotters, a two-foot snout carrying paired self-sharpening tushes that knifed out six inches either side. No gent to meet in a dark alley!

When the Arabs ran out of wind over the first boar, Angorley tapped me and said in his pure Oxonian English—he was educated in India and talks like Anthony Eden—"That island in the marsh—could that be a pig atop it?"

So it was, fast asleep, with six hundred acres of six-foot papyrus reeds and swamp water between. Soon down the marsh edge came a *belem*, a gondola-prowed dugout the length of a canoe, with little freeboard even when only the bow and stern polers weighted it down. Hospitable Shaik Jassim had lined the *belem* with soft Persian rugs. "Nothing too good for us luxury lovers," I muttered to Bob as I teetered into the craft. "Let's go."

The pig was still there when we broke through the reeds into open water, all right, but our self-tipping ark was pointed dead at him. To hit the pig I'd have had to shoot one leg off the bow poler—not a good idea in a country where personal injury means a blood feud on a strict "tooth for tooth" basis. So the pig splashed off into the papyrus, pork gone to freedom, for all of me.

But not for our Charon and his assistant. They swung the *belem* into the greenery along the faint trail of bubbles left by the swimming boar and in a dozen pole shoves drove within yards of the pig. We could hear him splashing and blowing along, but I couldn't see any pig for the papyrus. Yet I knew where the porker should be, and cut loose a bullet toward the center of grunting activity in the *gassab*.

A gout of water like a depth-bomb explosion made it clear I hadn't hurt the pig much, yet he was either tickled by the bullet or maybe he took a dim view of being splashed. Before we could even slow the *belem* old razor-snout switched ends and headed for the boat.

"*Irrmy! Irrmy! Cigga ul gowad! Gaa-al belem!*" screeched the bowman. That means just what you think it does.

At that point, with his choppers clicking, the boar burst through the reeds amidships. There seemed to be no place for four or five hundred pounds of pig in that boat. He'd have muddied up those Persian rugs. Come to think of it, if he did much rooting around with his tushes in that little *belem*, something, including me, might spring a leak; so I swung the 7 mm. onto him like a shotgun and poked a slug through his stubby neck. That permanently finished the *khanzir's* boating aspirations.

And that was the end of any further yachting expeditions into the papyrus. Once in the marsh—and the *Hor-al-Howiza* stretches a couple of hundred miles—any further boars were home free. But that evening we picked up half a dozen more when they trotted out to plow up the Arab garden patches, discreetly taking them at rifle ranges, not at four or five feet, believe you me.

Next morning a call to the airline's weatherman brought bad news. From his talk of fronts and isobars I gathered we were in for heavy thundershowers. Rain on the dusty roads of Iraq means greasy gumbo, rim-deep and practically impassable. A fine thing, to come to a country largely desert to find it swept by devastating floods in the north, travel-clogging mud in the south.

We had no pigeons to send out as Noah did during his flood, but phone lines were still up. When the roads were clear one hundred and forty-five miles upriver, off went the pig hunters for a different style of hunt.

"Any of these *khanzir* stay on dry land, Bob?" I asked. "Must be some that would rather run than swim."

"Oh, yes. In the high lands below Amara we'll have some forest pig shooting. Very different. Drives and all that. Many very large boars, old chap."

"Fine; then I'll tote the .375 Weatherby—give me a good chance to sharpen up on short-range quickies before tackling the tigers over in India, no?"

"I suspect you'll have some close-range shooting," said Bob quietly.

The high land turned out to be only two feet higher than the Tigris River, and the forest was just a string of date groves thick-grown with thorny brush; but we certainly got the close shooting.

Fifteen miles south of Amara, we headed off toward the river. The car bounced over low bunds squaring the irrigated *aarib hinta*, or wheat fields, and growled through shallow ditches toward the palms. Trailing this time was a big six-wheel truck, surplus British military equipment. This trip there'd be a *load* of pigs.

Before we'd uncased my rifle we had plenty of beaters—they materialized from behind every *shoack*, or camel-thorn, most of them dressed in the flowing *abba*, with the desert headdress, called *chafayieh*, bound around their dark heads by glossy black wool ropes, all eager to turn a few cash *fils* by helping the *ajnebny* slay pigs. I foresaw problems of shooting pigs without potting Abdul or his cousin Mohammed, too.

The disorganized mob of beaters hadn't scratched through more than a hundred yards of palm-spaced brush when boars began to show, first a sow, a *bagoora* with three squealing piglets. Then a bunch of six or eight grown animals peeled off across the flats to my left, heading in a big loop that would carry them back into the dense growth behind us.

"Hi! A veritable sounder of swine," shouted Bob Angorley in that British accent of his. Ali snatched up the skirts of his black *abba* and we hightailed for the open country.

At the brush edge I slid into a sitting position on some handy thorns. Four of the bunch were still in the clear, the last one a tub-bellied boar that lacked sprint speed. But he was no slowpoke, because at two hundred yards half a pig length of lead wasn't enough. The slug plowed up clay under his curly tail. A second round, with the 2½X scope showing four feet of daylight beyond his snout, caught him square in the shoulder. His tusks plowed dirt and flipped him on his back, trotters waving feebly in the air.

One down and three to go, but one sprinter had already ducked into a field of wheat. No shot. My three-hundred-grain slug socked into the rib cage of the next to flatten him on the clay. Where was number four? Ali tapped my arm and pointed—that smart pig had diagonaled through a clump of thorn and was digging out for Persia. A long shot; so I held higher and squeezed carefully. When the scope settled back from recoil the last porker wambled around in a shaky circle and collapsed. More hot-barrel fun than I'd had in years.

From there on it wasn't a question of finding pigs; it was a question of pushing them into the open for a possible shot. They crashed through the brush ahead of us like short-coupled tanks, leaving behind only grunts and a musky smell. One old soaker slammed straight through a group of Arabs to scatter them like chickens ahead of a runaway truck, *abbas* flying in all directions. Pigs squirted out of the brush like seeds from an Elks' picnic watermelon, offering enough shots so that I was whacking only the biggest ones that crossed the path. Angorley would yell, "Tally-ho! There he goes, Mr. Page!" in his formal fashion and my rifle barrel would heat up another ten degrees.

By midafternoon Bob and I were ready for a break. As I chewed some cold lamb kabob and swizzled tea strong enough to revive Meschach, Shadrach, and Abednego, our crew of self-appointed assistants dragged the porkers to the big truck. That took directions in turn by Bob's man Ali and every other grown male in the party. In the Arabic lands every job of work requires fourteen loud arguments and a junior-sized Geneva Conference.

"You know, Bob," said I when the last few hundredweights of hog had gone onto the pile, "we've relieved the local Arabs of a lot of nuisances, and I suspect the ships docked in Basra will appreciate fresh meat—but there's still one boar I'd like to feed a bullet."

"Why bother? You'll see pigs in India, though they won't be nearly as large as these." Angorley was anxious to show us a few coveys of Iraq's famous black partridge.

"Just one more—that *kibbir khanzir* that rampaged back through the beat. I think he's holed up in that thorn jungle we didn't work out."

Ever accommodating, even if I wanted to stick my fool neck out, Bob hailed a few of the *abba*'d gentry and off we went to the thicket. They spread around at the far end. I poked into the edge nearest the river, looking for an opening the boar might cross.

There wasn't any opening. I have no idea what brand of sticker-bush grew in that thicket, but it matted in solid walls of thorn, cut only by belt-high trails the pigs had worn. In spots I could see thirty or forty feet, in others five or ten. When heavy bodies crashed invisibly off to my right, I decided the tangle might be a fine refuge for pigs, but was no place for Page.

Just then Bob and the boys set up a hullabaloo at the far end. But nothing was coming my way, or was it? I swung my scope over in its mount to leave the open sights clear—in that tangle shooting would be largely a shotgunning proposition—and shoved off the safety.

Brown bulk blotted out openings in the thorns ahead; then I could hear surly grunts and the tusk-chopping of an angry boar. If that snouty gent was coming down my path, which was the main drag through the briers, I'd either stop him or he'd run me over. I certainly couldn't dodge him. The *khanzir* grunted a few cuss words; then there was silence. He was coming or he wasn't. I dropped to one knee to get a clear shot up the trail.

With a rush and a snort he rounded the corner, bristles up and tusks clacking in pig-headed fury.

I've never faced a charging Alaskan brown bear and I don't want to, but I doubt he'd be any madder than an Iraqi boar—just bigger. I've heard a lot of guff about how a man relives part of his life during a charge, but I doubt that. The only thing I remember was an impression of yellow ivory and the maddest-looking steam engine of a pig that ever was. I don't even recall aiming the rifle. Yet it must have been instinctively pointed right. Ten feet in from the trail corner and twenty feet from me two and a half tons of high-speed bullet energy smashed into the boar's neck and spine. He collapsed like a wet paper sack.

So did I. I just sat there in the trail with the .375 Weatherby lined on that *kibbir khanzir*, watching for a wiggle.

That's pig's bones are still in the thorn thicket, unless the hyenas have spread them around. He was too heavy to tote and too old to eat. But we axed out the tusks and I'm keeping them as a reminder to stay out of thorn thickets too dense to dodge pigs in—and as a reminder of life in the Garden of Eden.

---

28 : The Rams of Iran

A fellow going to Iran to hunt ibex and urial and such really should like caviar. Fancy sturgeon eggs may not be absolutely necessary to hunting the peaks of the Elburz, but they add a final touch to one of the world's great hunts, especially if like me you're kooky over the real McCoy of the caviar world. After all, the fish eggs of Iran are not the black-dyed oversalted gook we call caviar at home, but a fresh pearl-gray delicacy so good the Iranians gather it and the Russians claim it.

The caviar treatment actually started aboard an Alitalia jet heading eastward for Tehran. The steward ladled out a double spoonful from his pushcart of predinner goodies and later renewed that dosage, Alitalia being most considerate of their passengers' gustatory welfare. It kept right on next day, when hunting friend Phil Williamson and I foregathered over lunch with David Laylin and Tari Farmanfarmaian, the heap big bazoos of Iran Safaris Ltd., to plan our hunt. The waiter globbed onto our plates more of the pearl-gray eggs, about the size of No. 6 shot, and decorated the pile with a dab of minced onion. You don't like caviar? Well, chum, perhaps you've never really had any, and you certainly rate my sympathy.

When we rattled and rocked up to the stone hunting lodge in the Almeh reserve section of Mohammed Shah Reza Park, however, I had to figure the caviar period was but definitely over. We had rolled out of Tehran before dawn, geared and swayed over the successive ridges of the Elburz Mountains that cut between the deserts and the Caspian Sea, our Land Rover panting over passes two-thirds the height of eighteen-thousand-foot Mount Demavend.

Then we'd turned eastward in the lush semitropics below the Caspian, rushing past Turkoman herders whose whole families rode to market on one stick-legged donkey. North lay Russia. We headed southeast, back up into the mountains, on a road that makes the Belgian-block section of the General Motors testing track look like a pool table and is five hundred times as dangerous as the Los Angeles freeway. Iranian bus drivers, hastening their loads of pilgrims toward the holy city of Mashhad, regularly pass each other on its blind curves. Obviously they feel that the pilgrims are somehow protected by the Moslem equivalent of St. Christopher. No caviar on that journey, just cold sweat!

In Iran, the history of hunting goes far back behind the day when whiskery chieftains chased Asiatic lions in chariots. It has always been, in the Iranian or Persian tradition, largely a sport of the upper classes and royalty. Most recently, however, Iran's fabulous mountain-country hunting got a big boost, about a decade back, when Prince Abdorreza invited various American friends and functionaries to try for ibex and urial and their adventures were duly reported. Then there began a period of commercial outfitting. This started with a company that did not meet the expectations of the Prince, whose devotion to the cause of conservation via controlled hunting is absolute, so it is now handled by Iran Safaris, Laylin's outfit, which has His Highness's unique and full approval. Asiatic lions are of course long gone, but the programs now burgeoning under the leadership of this tough, world-known hunter, 1962 winner of the Weatherby Big Game trophy, will see to it that the mountain species will be with us for the foreseeable future. Phil and I were in Iran primarily to see how that modern approach, and the new safari firm, were working out.

We had some answers before noon the first day. Domestic sheep and goats have since before the Crucifixion eaten the Middle East down to bald rock. But in the Almeh, grazing has been forbidden. Within a few years, despite the fact that the Bojnourd area is almost as arid as Arizona, these slopes have come back with a rich cover of mountain grasses, food for thousands of head of native wild game. Obviously firm taboos on domestic animals in the game reserve areas pays off. The urial of the area had already so prospered on the rich feed that in a morning of riding we had seen at least two hundred sheep, the higher bunches almost entirely bearded rams. Modern ideas of control and ecology were working to perfection. The sheep were there.

Yet it would be the same old story. Sheep hunting anywhere means huff and puff, sweat and strain, stare and spot, over and again, before you get to the good parts, the stalk and the shot. The Elburz or the Brooks Range—the only difference is in the climate.

It had seemed for a moment that Phil would shortcut all that, early the first day. I had flubbed a long try at a fair ram from a skylined bunch. We had been caught in the open, and' my steeply uphill shot, the rifle across Ishmael's back, had gone somewhere into space. One of us had jiggled. So it was Phil's turn when Dave Laylin, peering restlessly over the ledge where we had shaded up for lunch, spotted a ram in the gully. The horns bulging back and up, but not sweeping forward, in the characteristic flattened urial curve, it was a big ram. When Phil managed to miss it, shooting over its back by not allowing enough for the steep downhill angle, it suddenly became a bigger ram. And as I now look back on it, this was the biggest ram that ever lived. For all the richness of sheep, this hunt was obviously going to be no picnic, not with two misses as a starter.

"But it can be a gourmet's delight," I chortled when we approached the dinner table that night. David's cook had used as a centerpiece a kilo can of pearl-gray fish eggs, discreetly surrounded by bits of toast.

The Kopet Dagh urial we were hunting in the half-million-acre reserve around the Almeh represents only one of the Iranian sheep. According to Clark there are six, with considerable overlap in the eastern Elburz. In practice, however, most Iranian hunters talk about four, with the small sheep of the isolated Laristan area a question mark. Under Prince Abdorreza, game department records are kept on the basis of three, the red sheep (*Ovis orientalis*), the western red sheep (*Ovis gmelini urmiana* or *ispahanica*), and the northeastern or Kopet Dagh urial (*Ovis vignei arkal*). In this last-named type, the record ram, shot by Alex Firouz in 1966, boasted horns over forty-four and forty-one inches around the curve, so it was comparable in length to any first-quality North American ram, though somewhat lighter, and a very different horn shape.

"Then, according to licensing laws, David," I said over the coffee cup, "my Maryland friend Williamson and I can take up to two urial in our six-day reservation here in the Almeh, at sixty dollars for the first, one hundred and twenty dollars for the second."

"Right," he agreed, "and you get one each on all the other species available here."

My first ram was an example of a classic sheep-hunting blooper. Hunting together, with both Laylin and leather-legged Ishmael Malek doing the guiding, we had spotted a bunch of rams containing one good head. They were feeding slowly around the bulges of the opposite mountain. To cross the open valley we had to let them work out of sight. Thereafter a climbing stalk along their trail was risky, because at any moment we might pop over a ridge smack into the middle of them, or worse yet, onto inferior rams that would spook their still-hidden brothers. On the wash-wrinkled desert mountain that's exactly what happened.

Two rams were at no more than ten yards when we peeked over an escarpment. Six pairs of eyes bugged. The rams, their horns looming huge at that distance, recovered first, spurted into a run. I recall asking David which he considered larger, but doubt that he ever had time to answer. The upsweep and swing of my 7 mm., virtually shotgun style, and the slam of a one-hundred-and-seventy-five-grain slug into the shoulder of the nearer ram occurred without, alas, conscious thought.

There's a moral to the story, one I've long known but must've forgotten in the hot excitement of the moment. He who looks for trophies must never rely on snap judgments. They're too likely to be wrong. This one was. The wrong ram. Just an honest five- or six-year-old, mediocre on any score. I had shot better Asiatic sheep back in 1954 in hunting the *gad* or *cycloceros* type of urial in the Pil and Khalifat ranges of Baluchistan.

Phil had far better luck on his first urial score. He and Ishmael, faced with an almost impossible approach, bellied uphill over smooth ground to reach two gullies that linked and twisted until they were in possible range. Possible, but not easy. Perhaps four hundred, certainly three hundred and fifty. Two good rams, twins, stood very close together. Phil pulled down on the right one and waited endlessly, but when they did not separate he finally squeezed off the round. But it was the left-hand ram that staggered as he ran, dropped after a second hit. Perhaps the wind had been heavier than Phil had thought. At any rate, this was a good urial, eighty-eight centimeters or a strong thirty-four inches around the curve, a foot around the bases, which is about as heavy as these urial run. Caviar for that one.

That luck continued for Phil. He and David, leaving Ishmael and me to work further on the southerly and easterly urial ridges, switched to the ibex and forest game that favored the steeper, wetter sides of the range facing toward the Caspian. On ground that was a mixture of spit-a-mile cliffs and forested slopes, he first tried for ibex.

The Iranian ibex (*Capra hircus aegagrus*) is a smallish goat below ten thousand feet, grows more body bulk, though not much bigger horns, at higher altitudes. The billies of Bojnourd rarely weigh over one hundred and twenty-five pounds, usually less. Skittering across the cliff faces that would scare the average British Columbia goat into hysterics, in bands up to forty or so, they make difficult targets. At least Phil found 'em that way. He had to shoot up a storm to stop his ibex, but the high ammunition cost was small potatoes compared to the pleasure of taping one of the best heads taken in the Almeh in a generation, one hundred and ten centimeters, or over forty-three inches.

Nailing my ibex a day later took less shooting, only one round, but completely wore out a pair of pants. We found two bands each of two to three dozen animals, one headed by an excellent male. Near midday, with no evident intention of ever feeding nearer our cliff-edge hide, they bedded down. A stalk into practical range meant crawling, sliding, and creeping down two hundred yards of near-vertical face, agonizingly slow, hard on britches, but possible on ibex because, like most goats, they don't fear danger from above.

"Nice shot," offered Mohammed Hussein Rahimi, the head warden of the Almeh who had accompanied David and me for the ibex. "Not the biggest ibex ever, but a quick kill."

I was looking back up the cliff. "If he were any bigger we'd never haul him out of here, and over a yard of goat horn suits me just fine."

All of which wasn't getting me any nearer to a reasonable urial. Phil had announced his intention of looking into the *maral* or red deer that fed on the northerly or forested edges of our mountain, when I set out into ram country for a last try with Ishmael and a couple of "horsemen." The horsemen walk while the hunters ride, tend to pop over skylines at the wrong moment, theoretically earn their keep by holding the horses during stalks. But we couldn't use the horses very far that day—too many sheep.

It was perfectly evident that the ram bunches—the females were in great mobs in lower country—had shifted onto a round-topped range bald of cover. Walking and crawling would be the order of the day and the great problem, once a good ram was located, would be to stay out of sight of other bands and lesser sheep, because spooking one bunch of urial may well clean a whole mountain as if with a vacuum cleaner.

The best-looking ram we could locate in an hour of careful spotting fed just our side of the ridge top. Below him was a boulder jumble left by an old slide.

"We get those rock," said Ishmael, "is good."

That was ungrammatical, but perfectly clear. The nitty-gritty part would be in sneaking around two other clusters of sheep, one already acting anxious, that fed in the mile between. And we didn't make it.

In the first four hundred yards, as we eased up over a little butte, we were spotted by four rams we had never seen. Feeding in a little valley fold, they stared at us in amazement. None were shootable.

Pulling our heads back down so the strange lumps would disappear with sheep-mystifying slowness was agony; but when we could scuttle around the base of the butte and peer up at them again they were still staring at where our noggins had been.

Safely out of their sight, and trying to work down around the mountain toward a gully that ran up almost to the crest and the big ram, we paused to rest where the rocks of a ravine edge helped break human outline. Across the wash, perhaps two hundred yards, grew a few clumps of cedarlike trees. We were about to cross into their shade when seven rams trotted out onto that edge, in full view, not spooked, just moving off from feeding to bed grounds. While we stayed rooted on the sharp rocks they inspected the tree clumps, began to move in, move unconcernedly. Of the seven, one ram was the choice, showing a horn structure not common among the urial, a full curl rather than their usual out-and-in flare.

Ishmael and I had worked out a simple system of communicating opinion about the best ram of any bunch. If our ground was sand, we made scratch marks; if pebbles or shale were handy we used rocks, simply laying down one after another to indicate the left-to-right count to the biggest ram. Moving very cautiously, he put down five stones. I counted across with the binocular. Yes, No. 5 was good, probably the best, particularly with that full curl. But No. 5 was also back in under the trees, lying down, shoulders too obscured for a sure shot. Problem—how to get him out of there without blowing the whole deal.

That problem solved itself. Sitting in reasonable comfort, Ishmael could stay still forever. But when the rams first appeared I had wormed around into a slantwise prone position, with well-sharpened rocks prodding all the tender spots, so that pain added to the shudders of muscle tension that built up whenever I tried to steady even binoculars on the sheep. This would never do. I moved. So did the sheep. Not much, either of us. But enough. The rams were suddenly standing outside the tree shade, staring at the odd-colored rocks with hats on, but I had twisted around into a reasonable firing position, with only one stone edge gouging into my hide.

For an instant, as the 7 mm. magnum set back solidly and the bearded sheep bucked and ran, I thought I'd missed. But the bullet plunk had been unmistakable, and Ishmael was already pounding my back in the victory signal. The ram lost his steam and folded up on the third jump, making one last futile kick as if to drive himself after the sheep skittering off down the mountain. The slug had gone precisely true, and I had a Kopet Dagh urial of very respectable dimension.

We were back at the stone lodge well ahead of David and Phil, but even as we swung off the horses we spotted their little caravan winding down into our protecting canyon. On an extra horse rode lumpy objects, and waving atop his back as he lurched down the steeps I could see the ivory-tipped prongs of a sizable deer rack. Phil had his *maral*.

Now our cook in the Almeh did not speak English. But he understood perfectly what I was shouting toward his end of the lodge. "Caviar! Tonight all us lucky fellers eat caviar!" That means the same thing in both English and Persian, particularly if you repeat it in obvious celebration and at the same time open the cold-box door. Iranian cooks know the proper food for sheep hunters.

29 : Tigers Are Real

At eight o'clock the central India sun merely flickered in mild foretaste of its one-hundred-and-twenty-degree noon blaze, and the morning air was still cool on the dark bungalow porch. Cool enough for a man to think comfortably about tigers, even feel detached about the business of shooting one—a spectator at the play and not one of the actors. Nothing much was happening in Somanpalli. Near the village, dust rose in a lazy stir where a brown boy importantly switched his father's cattle to their morning slosh in the river. It was best to sit quietly and think slowly about tigers.

And tigers are a lot to think about. The striped cats you and I have seen padding behind bars at the zoo may suggest menace from whiskers to twitching tail tip. But they're not real, those zoo beasts—just illusions of fanged and clawed power for people to gape at. We were waiting for news of a tiger that would be real. Tigers were brutal fact to that boy and to his buffaloes and humped cattle. When a hungry cat killed from his father's tiny herd, life became leaner for a family already starvation-poor. And only the evening before the young Methodist preacher from Sironcha had jeeped over to visit our camp in Somanpalli and told us of a very real tiger, one that had stalked and eaten a teenage girl, leaving of her only one foot and an ear.

Tigers are real in India, but it was beginning to look as if I'd never see the big cat I'd come nine thousand miles to hunt. For three mornings straight a procession of forest people, *Gonds*, had trotted into camp. Their reports had been sadly consistent—the eleven bullock baits they had staked out before sunset each evening and brought in for feed and water each sunrise were still untouched. Half the runners were already in from the jungle this morning, and it was beginning to look like another fizzle.

Then sandals scuffed fast around the corner of the porch, and before me stood a slender tribesman. The sweat on him and the roll in his eye told me the drama was about to begin. But the Telegu he spouted at me called for an interpreter.

"Khan Sahib! What's the fellow talking about? I think we've got a kill!"

Even my impatience didn't hurry the head shikari, Khan Sahib Jamshed Butt. He walked solidly over from the shed where he had been salting the cape of a great-horned sladang, trophy of the day before. Then, while the scout sputtered, Khan gravely smoothed his mustache and listened with the dignity of a shikari who had himself slain one hundred and fifty-three tigers and attended the passing of perhaps four hundred more.

"*Sherne bailko sagonke darakth kepas pakri hei! Bara bheri sher hei!*" the *Gond* repeated and flapped his arms toward the west.

Khan Sahib, with his thumb, pointed more calmly. Then back and forth they tossed more unintelligible Telegu. Interruption wouldn't help; so I waited until the shikari, satisfied, turned to me. "Sar, a tiger has killed in the teak forest twenty furlongs west from this place, a very large tiger, this man says. We will make a beat and surely this tiger must come before you."

The play's overture was finished, the curtain up. And shooting a Bengal tiger—the royal striped cat of India, whether he prowls the grass jungles of Assam or hunts the teak forests of Chanda, where we sought him—is something of a production. Up in the grass country or south in the tangles behind Mysore, it is a hippodrome spectacle, with enough elephants to satisfy Billy Rose, along with pageantry and ritual lacking only a ballet troupe. In the Madhya Pradesh, India's Central Provinces, there are no elephants or mass game drives; but even so, dethroning the king of the jungle with a bullet calls for the most skillful staging.

Khan Sahib, then top shikari for the outfitting firm of Allwyn Cooper, Ltd., knew the directions. Before I could fetch my .375 Weatherby and a handful of cartridges, he had ordered runners to our village and to the hamlet of Aserali, several miles closer to the Indravati River, to recruit the beaters we'd need. Already leaning against the hunting jeep was a cord-sprung *chapei*, the short wheel-based cot common all over India. It would be lashed into a tree with jungle vines as a *machan*, eight or ten feet above the jungle brush. Perched on it, we'd perhaps see the tiger move ahead of the beaters. Camera, jug of water boiled free of dysentery bugs— the stage props were ready.

The tiger goes by the name of *sher* in Madhya Pradesh and is called *bagh* or *sela-vagh* in the other provinces, but everywhere he is a creature of habit. Otherwise few tigers would be killed except by accident. When, in his private circuit of fifteen or twenty miles, a tiger has snapped the neck of a domestic bullock or buffalo or perhaps a sambar, the elk-size deer that is natural food, his needs are two: water and dense cover in which to sleep off a hundred-pound bellyful. Nine times out of ten he'll drag his kill deep into that cover to conceal it from the ever-circling vultures and the impertinent jackals that act as jungle morticians. To the forest people, the primitive *Gonds* who know every *nullah* pool and bamboo hide in their territory, the line of this drag points to the lying-up spot where the tiger will snooze all day after his gorging.

And we were lucky on this fellow. A quick search at the bullock stake-out revealed the six-inch pug marks of a heavy male. He'd go ten feet, perhaps five hundred pounds, in Khan Sahib's smiling opinion. The drag trail aimed almost due west, but there was no cause to follow it and risk disturbing the tiger, since the village headman and Moto Singh, the local forest guard, were positive he had moved the bullock to the head of a certain bamboo tangle. Just north of it a drought-shrunken pool was the only water for several miles. And luckier yet, the ground of our beat was fenced on the north and west by the open firebreaks that checkerboard India's managed teak forests, on the east by grassy *maidans* no sensible tiger would cross at midday.

"If he's in there, do we try to drive him south?" I asked as the shikari scratched out a map in the sand.

"Yes, sahib, we will put the *machan* here, and the stops here, and the forest people will march toward us. Then the tiger must appear from the bamboo where he is resting."

We were still mapping strategy when the chorus of beaters began to arrive, drifting out of the jungle paths in family groups of three and four. Old men and young in quick-wrapped *dhotis*, the oldsters with turbans, most with water gourds slung off one shoulder. Some carried the ax of the jungle people, long-handled but with a soft-iron tomahawk head sized about right for a Cub Scout.

There were boys among the one hundred and forty-odd recruits, per-haps that same youngster I'd seen herding his father's cattle. Teenagers

NORTH AMERICA

In the world of big-game hunting every area has its own sights and scents and
sounds, and in North America these are always associated with packhouse camps,
with tents against a lake or a mountain, with the mixed scents of sweaty horses
and the cooking fire, the jingle of a lead mare's bell and the squeak of saddle leather.

Moving out from main camp with a light outfit to a
spike camp right up under the sheep basins in
British Columbia carries with it a truly unique blend
of hope and excitement, because it means
going into the heart of things.

Left: The stone sheep ranges of British Columbia's Kechika region produced for me a ram of record size after a stalk clear along that left-hand ridge.

Facing page: The log buildings of Rainy Pass Lodge, Bud Branham's base situated 150 air miles from Anchorage, Alaska, will always symbolize a blend of human warmth and wild remoteness *(top left)*. It was from there that Bud and I followed a huge grizzly's tracks, snowshoeing after him up a ridge above the Skwentna, and caught him napping at the top fringe of alders *(bottom left)*.

The grizzly weighed less than half the heft of the huge moose we packed out of one Rainy Pass side valley. That one was a 72-incher and I suspect that in his prime, just as the fall rut began, he scaled close to a ton—the antlers alone must have gone a hundred pounds *(top right)*.
We ran out of grub at the Wrangell Range spike camp and ended up eating the grizzly whose hide is being worked on by the outfitter *(bottom right)*. Sliced thin and pounded hard with an axe, it fried up tasty and not much tougher than the sole of a Russian boot!

At Palo Duro Canyon, outside Amarillo, Texas, we found a fine specimen of the aoudad or Barbary sheep *(top left)*. This goatlike beast has been introduced into New Mexico, California, and Texas, and deserves high rank among our game animals. *Top right:* Checked out by a Texas warden, the aoudad went 285 dressed and boasted 30 inches of horn.

Bottom left: Shooting at long range is always questionable procedure, but in this Wyoming scene I had a solid rest, a potent rifle whose trajectory I knew by the inch, and I bagged the elk with one 175-grain Nosler from 425 yards, first shot— a 6-point bull which didn't miss the Boone and Crockett list by much.

ANTIPODES

Politics and economics have prevented New Zealand from realizing its potential as a hunting paradise, with game animals once considered legal vermin subject to legal extinction because of grazing and dairying interests. Today the error is being realized, but when I hunted there in 1956, the upper valley of the Dart River held literally thousands of European red deer.

The stag *(directly below)* made the New Zealand trophy list. *Bottom:* This comfortable cave served as lodging when we hunted the grassy tops, up between the timber and glaciers.

1

2

3

4

5

6

7

8

9

10

Trophies are not dead animals but living memories. This 1954 Madhya Pradesh tiger (1) ate a little girl the week he died. The Alaskan grizzly (2), who never ate a salmon, was ruled a brownie. In 1963 this British Honduras jaguar (3) was a respected trophy, not a woman's coat. The bearded urial of 1968 (4) makes a handsome trophy in Persian or any other tongue, and the polar bear (5) taken in 1966 at 47° below was no picnic as non-hunters think, nor do hunters endanger them. In much of Africa, elephant like this Zambian 75-pound bull (6) and Cape buffalo (7) are common. Mountain caribou for the record list (8) are tough even in British Columbia, and so are stone sheep like this buster (9), though its country is easier than the Iranian Alburz's ibex (10).

EUROPE

Thousands of European caribou, or "reindeer," roam on the Hardangervidda in mid-Norway, always in big herds of up to 5000, and hunting them on trackless tundra wastes with only one round in your rifle, as required by law, is a sporting challenge. Yet the herds must be cut back each fall lest they multiply into starvation or illness.

Top: Always moving, the herd will vanish at a slight disturbance; glassing for caribou *(bottom left)*; tundra campsite *(bottom right)*. The Norwegians have a knack for making the hunt comfortable, with tight cabins built from lumber sledded in during the winter, since no local growth exceeds ankle height.

Picking out the one stag caribou from a herd of thousands can make for a difficult stalk. To make this one shot, we had maneuvered for three hours after locating the herd.

In contrast to Norway and Sweden, Denmark is a neat, small country and hunting on it is likely to be on a small acreage, like the thousand acres owned by Hans Larsen. Through the careful husbandry of his gamekeeper, Larsen's hunting lease was alive with pheasants, roebuck, huge European hare, and migrating ducks during the fall. Rifle builder Larsen with the author in the gamekeeper's comfortable home.

Feathered game in Europe is largely driven, as a practical means of harvesting for market the birds that are raised on *revier*, estate, or *finca*. Bum shots are not welcome on the firing line. And shooters dress up a bit, like the author shooting French pheasants in the Norwegian outfit at left. *Bottom left:* A Portuguese "secretario" or bird-finder and all-around assistant. *Bottom right:* The trap champion of Portugal clicking off driven red-legged partridges as they zip in and over.

ASIA

When the author first hunted Asian sheep in 1954, there were reserves and no outfitters for the remote ranges. Today, even the great-horned *Ovis Poli* and *Ammon* types can be hunted with proper outfitting. One part of Asia has become a model of conservation. Under the Shah and Prince Abdorreza, Iran now boasts thousands of four types of sheep, as well as ibex, forest game, and boar. By closing off large mountain areas to domestic sheep and goats they have created richly grassed reserves that support great herds of game. Both the villages and towns seem to benefit, and poaching is virtually unknown. The lesson to us lies in the closure of game lands to the damage done by sheep and goats.

AFRICA

So many people have spent so much time in Africa and written so many words and taken so many pictures about it that the author prefers to recall not the lions lounging in the sun or the giraffes sticking up through the acacias or the other "standard" sights that are available in any Kenya Park—and today some in New Jersey or Florida—but more intimate and more real things. It's the offbeat memories of Africa that are sharp, like Jackson, the monkey that ate aspirin and tsetse flies and pointed out the great cats, or the fuss of setting up a new safari camp with its promise of fresh adventure.

In no African park do you march into steamy jungles for a bongo camp near the Pygmy villages, and only a few years back the couple at the fishing lodge on Lake Rudolf were murdered in their beds. Yet today the Danakil and the Pygmies are becoming willing photo models. But the crocodile hasn't changed. He still eats people, and it's not very smart when you've shot a 16-footer and blood leaks into the current, to wade the river. Big brother just might be lurking.

In Zambia, the $1400 game license permits you one croc so there's no problem ahead for them except over-breeding. An old buster like this, armor-plated his whole length, won't make much of a suitcase, but he could have made a fast meal out of any Zambian woman washing her clothes at the river.

Hippo are bad medicine when caught ashore, surprisingly nimble on their stubby legs.

Elephant are forever photogenic, either when parading on the river bed or contemplating a charge, like this bull interrupted as he lunched. The Western bongo posing with the author and a Pygmy friend was the second bull shot by an American, Kermit Roosevelt having taken the first just before World War I.

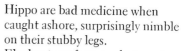

Ethiopia has always been the abode of mystery, and that mystery is not lessened by the power and personality of the Emperor, H. I. H. Haile Selassie. The author has been lucky enough to meet the Emperor twice, before and after a hunt for walia ibex, the first since they were made royal game in 1928. His Imperial Highness granted both permit and assistance on an expedition into the Semien. There, at 12,000 feet, we made camp where Maydon had stopped over a generation before.

and patriarchs, ready to march through bamboo tangles with a junior-size hatchet and faith in my rifle as their defense against a quarter ton of cat. All in the hope of earning one rupee—which is worth twenty-two cents. They'd get only eight annas—half a rupee, the price of a swig of palm toddy or a glass-bead bracelet—if the tiger did not appear before me or if he clawed his way back through the lines of half-naked beaters.

Fifteen or twenty stayed behind when the tribesmen filtered off toward the head of the mile-long jungle patch they were to beat. These were men of standing, courage proved in earlier hunts, who were to serve as stops. Spread twenty or thirty yards apart on a line either side of our *machan*, they were to climb trees and remain stone-silent unless the tiger threatened to break through their stop line. In that case they'd speak to the tiger or clap their hands or tap gently on their tree, in order to turn him gently, back toward the center of the beat and the *machan*. They were safe enough because tigers don't climb trees. Not ordinarily, that is—though shikaris have been pulled from *machans* ten feet up and stops have been clawed down from tree forks half again as high.

In minutes the acrobatic *Gonds* had lashed three poles into the lowest fork of a tree by the *nullah*, or dry wash, that paralleled the tiger's bamboo hideout. Our cord-sprung cot was hauled up and lashed flat to the poles with bark twists as tough as rawhide. Vidyha Shukla, the brilliant young Brahmin who, as Allwyn Cooper, Ltd., had outfitted a month of Indian hunting for me, was to take pictures of the tiger if he came before us; so the boys rigged another *machan* fifty yards to the right. Uncomfortable, unstable, just high enough to be in the flying range of every jungle bug, the *machan* is still not a bad place to shoot from, and it's fine to see from.

In the scheme of Indian hunting, the *machan* is not stuck up in a tree to eliminate danger to the sportsman. In the teak and sal jungles, even when the blistering sun has burned the brush clear of leaves, the growth is still so thick that you must get above it just to see a tiger, let alone get a clear shot at him. If the hunter flubs his try and wounds the cat, whether he shoots first from the ground, from an elephant *howdah*, or from a *machan*, he's headed for bloody trouble. Further, though a tiger has such poor scenting powers that he'd find difficulty in distinguishing a man from a chunk of strong cheese, his ears and eyes are fantastically sensitive to any man-sound or movement. Yet, unlike a panther or Indian leopard, seldom will he look up. Hence you wait for him a few feet off the ground.

And you wait hard. We had squirmed onto the *machan*, and with a final admonishment to keep quiet the shikari had sent the stops to their posts. The jungle lay silent before us, not with the dead silence of a desert but with the furtive rustlings that betrayed teeming life in the thickets. I snicked open the bolt of my rifle to be sure of the cartridge in its chamber, and tried a quick peep through the scope.

When we had planned the spot for the *machan*, Khan Sahib, with all the supreme confidence of a man who had slain many tigers and fought off the panther that had scarred his right forearm, had pronounced exactly where the tiger would leave the thinning bamboo and show in the open. A branch of our tree loomed square across that spot, and I risked a creak or two from the *machan* lashings to get a clearer field of fire. If *sher* slipped out farther up the cover or crossed the *nullah*, I'd have to shoot awkwardly. But the shikari had been right a week earlier as to how a record wild water buffalo would travel, and I trusted his judgment. Still the jungle was quiet, though by now a cloud of little insects like Quebec black flies minus the bite were trying water landings on my forehead and making power dives into my ears.

Quiet. Then, faint as an echo, came the dull thumps of the beaters' drums and a thin crying. The drama's third act had begun. The rifle was easy in my hands, though already the checkering on the grip seemed sweat-slippery. I wanted to smoke, but although I knew the tiger would never smell tobacco, he might see the movement of puffing a cigarette. Furthermore, I'd have to shift my seat to get at the lighter. Better just wait while those little black gnats put on their airshow under the brim of my helmet.

Brush cracked between us and the oncoming hullabaloo of the beaters. Tiger? Couldn't be—too much racket for a cat. Three sambar deer—two does and an elk-size bull—smashed through the line of stops in heedless flight. Deep in the bamboo a *cuk-cuk-cuk* alarm signal told me what to expect next, and in a few minutes a peacock pattered out of the thicket and beat his way into the air. Like an eight-foot pheasant, he zoomed out through the treetops. We could hear the beaters clearly now, hoots and shoutings. A family of frightened langur monkeys swung past through the trees. The beater noise built up in a steady crescendo.

Thumps and shouts, the beating of my blood for another minute, then Khan Sahib touched my shoulder lightly. There was the tiger!

Silent as smoke, he was easing through the bamboo, stripes and yellow hide blurring behind the clustered stems. He was moving toward the edge of the *nullah*, almost exactly where we'd hoped he might cross. As the bamboo thinned out, the tiger broke into a characteristic bumpy cat-trot and disappeared for a moment to dip over the ravine edge down onto the sand. Now was the critical moment—if he made one leap across the clearing, up out of the *nullah*, he'd again be half hidden by the thicket. There he would offer a poor chance for a shot, even a dangerous one with so much scrub to deflect a bullet. We'd gambled that he'd pause on the *nullah* bed, even turn our way for a few steps.

My sights were on the cat's shoulder. All thought of slick hands or a shaky shooting platform was forgotten when he stepped into the clear. He was still well out, ninety paces, we found later—beyond the scatter-gun range common when tigers are driven. We hoped he'd come closer, not because of any limitations of the rifle but because he'd have to pad at least twenty yards straight down the open *nullah* to show properly for the camera. But the tiger stopped and stood solid in the sunlight.

I don't believe that animals think the way humans do, but either instinct or logic made this tom tiger feel that even a small open space was no place for him, and the whiskered head swung toward the sheltering bamboo belt. Certainly it was not conscious thought that put the last few ounces of squeeze into my trigger finger. The rifle crashed once. As recoil blotted my sight picture I knew the slug had hit him square between the muscle-spread stripes of his left shoulder. That tiger was dead. He had to be.

And so he was. As the noise of the shot ripped through the jungle, all other sounds ceased, the beaters instantly went silent. The tiger, shoulder and spine smashed by three hundred grains of lead, hadn't the life even for a final leap. That I knew before Khan Sahib could pound my shoulders and shout in congratulation.

"Yes, he is dead, Sahib," he said. "But you must shoot again. Shoot once more to let the beaters know, for they will not believe that so large a tiger has died after one firing."

So I drove another slug into the *nullah* bank, where it sprayed harmless sand over the tiger, thinking, I remember, it would satisfy their fear without injuring the striped hide that had drawn me so far.

We were hardly down out of the *machan* and over to the trophy when the stops and the first of the beaters clustered around us, jabbering their good will and relief at being rid of another possible killer of their cattle, thrusting forward individually to make the sign of greeting with palms together, forefinger tips to forehead. But I was impatient of congratulations —more concerned with the muscle power in the forequarters of the tiger, his full ruff, and the ear that had been slit in some jungle ruckus. Water still dripped off his hindquarters and belly hair from the pool where he had been lying to escape the noon heat. But he was dead, all five hundred-odd pounds of him.

One of the beaters popped up with the flight bag I had stuffed with camera clutter that morning. There was a steel tape in it, and we quickly had the cat stretched straight-spined on the sand. Khan Sahib's guess had been conservative. From nose to tail-tip the tiger was just a hair-tuft under ten feet, but he was a whopping male and we were all proud.

The cot from the *machan* did double duty as a bier to carry the tiger out of the jungle to the jeep. On the triumphal trip back to our dak bungalow the younger beaters jogged alongside, grinning, while the wiser ancients took shortcuts through the teak. My palms were dry on the rifle now, and cigarettes tasted real again. Then Khan Sahib paid the ultimate compliment: "Sahib, the buffalo, the gaur, and now the tiger all have appeared before you. You have fired and they died. No longer when we hunt together will I carry my rifle. It is no need."

But that sort of bouquet after the final curtain wasn't needed. The big prize was the shine in the eyes of the cattle-tending boy who raced up when we came into camp with the tiger. Then he dared twiddle the whiskers and poke at the fangs of *sher*, perhaps the same *bheri sher* that had eaten the little brown-skinned girl. He knew what a dead tiger really meant.

---

30 : Taurenga Giant

He was a bull of great age, they said, with black horns that spanned more than the height of a tall man. His hide was scarred by many battles, and he was huge, even as the great trucks that brought the camp things for the sahibs. His great hoofs cut deep the banks of jungle pools, and he was wise, for had he not been hunted these many years and yet not been bagged by any shikari? So spoke the *Gonds* of the village of Taurenga. I found they spoke the truth. And I was lucky in the finding. Any man must be to travel ten thousand miles to hunt one buffalo, shoot him, and tape ponderous horns one hundred and two inches from tip to worn tip. Very lucky.

Before I left New York, I had read of this one buffalo in letters from Vidya Shukla. Before we left Nagpur for the train and jeep trip into the Raipur hill country, I had a full biography on him from the shikaris of Shukla's outfitting firm, Allwyn Cooper, Ltd. My special license allowed any water buffalo, but only the Taurenga bull rated that permit.

There'd been water buffalo before. They plowed the paddies of Iraq and jammed traffic in every Indian village, but these were tame animals, meek, sag-horned, and decrepit. Even domestic buffalo, I was told, had the stark courage to face a tiger, but there stopped every resemblance to the wild beast. For a wild water buffalo bull, of the few left in the Indian hills, stands over six feet, weighs better than a ton. He's canny enough to avoid the forest people from whose herds he entices droop-horned cows, yet would charge a Patton tank.

That first cool dawn, neither the whispered "Sahib!" of the bearer nor the squabbling of a family of langur monkeys was needed to rouse me. Dream buffalo had charged through the mosquito bar all night. When photographer Scheidegger and I jeeped miles to the bank of a rocky *nullah* and I hand-spanned bucket-sized hoofprints sharp in the sand, a great day really began. As we planned strategy a muntjac buck, his antlers sprouting from hairy pedestals, crossed in range, but casual shooting was taboo in the haunts of the Taurenga bull.

The big wheel that first morning was not to be our own shikari Khan Sahib Jamshed Butt. The local politico ran the show. He led, we followed, since we needed his village people for beaters. Already his scout units had jogged in to report a young bull sloshing in a *nullah* pool, dubious tracks over the hill, and finally a sighting of the master buffalo himself. The local big wheel laid out our first drive. But drive is the wrong word. You don't drive a water buffalo. Beaters try to nudge him, and you hope. The three of us climbed boulders edging the riverbed so that I could shoot over the jungle grass.

The buff moved, all right, but not out into my handsomely open field of fire, any more than a whitetail buck will cross a hayfield at high noon. One flash of a blue-black tank shape barreled through the brush two hundred yards in, a hullabaloo rose from the beaters when the big bull smashed their line, and that was all.

"This deal," I said to Khan Sahib as hoof thuds faded into the jungle, "this deal is for the birds, not for a bull. No buffalo wise enough to grow ancient will ever cross this wide-open *nullah*, or even show on its edges in daylight." And Khan Sahib agreed. On our next pass we'd lay out the tactics, set the *machan* back from the opening to give us a crack at the buff both coming and going.

Not afraid of small brown men in loincloths and Boy Scout-sized hatchets, the bull hadn't moved far. By afternoon next day trackers had doped his whereabouts for another push. The *machan*—built solely for vision in jungle cluttered by brush and head-high *ghas* grass—we spotted a full furlong in from the *nullah*, with only a couple of "stops" in trees on either side, since the bull would certainly turn if he neared the open stream bed.

A quick-starting sweat of anticipation made the rifle slick in my hands as we began the long wait in the *machan*. We'd see the big bull. I felt it in my bones.

Until the first faint cries and ax thumpings of the beaters began, the jungle was dead quiet. A few bugs buzzed. Occasionally crescendoed the yelping of a bird whose name sounds like "papaiya" and whose call sounds like a hysterical woman. Then, from the wrong side, where trees would never permit a shot, a frenzied yelling swirled among the beaters. Something had either busted through them or had turned back into the beat. The buffalo? Heavy hoofs thumped on hard ground and vague shapes rattled brush. Gaur! Four of 'em, a big bull sladang in the lead.

"*Nahin*, Sahib! Not fire!" The shikari had his hand on my shoulder. Then I remembered that down in the Chanda country where we'd hunt tiger there was an old buster of a gaur, up in the record class. And the tall-shouldered oxen rocked off into the jungle green.

Quiet, then more hoof thumps. This one's a bull buffalo. I can see him coming fast and reckless, so that he knocks his horns against the trees. He's coming in from the right angle for a shot. Little brown men are still howling far off when he stops a hundred-odd yards up and I have a chance to look him over carefully, and shift the rifle to bear on him, steady. His head is up, nostrils wide. When he pivots to look back toward the beater noises, the horns swing like massive twin gates. That's him!

The bull moves into an easy trot, straight for a ten-foot opening. The cross hairs sway just ahead of the swell of his shoulder, and I squeeze off the .375 Weatherby, driving a Kynoch solid into him with a two-thousand-eight-hundred-foot-second handload. That does it! But it doesn't. The bull stumbles, nearly down, but lurches into a three-legged drive through the brush. A clear spot, and a soft-point whacks into his chest behind the shoulder mass. He should drop. Even two thousand five hundred pounds of bull should drop. But it takes another solid before the master buffalo of Taurenga, like a storm-blown oak, crashes into the deep grass.

When we poke in on him, rifles ready, the buffalo is dead, a great slaty blue-black mound, almost hairless, little trickles of blood oozing from the mosquito-bite bullet holes in his inch-thick hide. All of them are angled through the vitals. A lot of life in such a big death.

The heavy neck was so ponderous that three men could hardly level the horns into position for pictures and the tape—one hundred and two inches, eight and one-half *feet*, from tip to tip, measured around the curve Indian-style. Over sixty-five inches of spread on the square, a foot more than any record African buffalo. Where can that barrel head be hung in any man's house? But it must go somewhere. The twenty-inch base of the left horn carried a bullet hole from a slug of years back, fired at him by some hunter less lucky than I, and his hide was scarred from battles he had won. But he'd lost the last. And I knew that the *Gonds* were muttering "Sahib" and pressing their hands in salute, not only to me as a shikari but even more to the great buffalo bull of Taurenga.

---

31 : Just Back of Tehran

It was still cold dark in the sheep mountains, but looking back from the foothills we could watch the lights of Tehran wink out as dawn crept across the plain. An airliner, possibly sister to the ship that had brought us to Iran a few mornings earlier, showed silvery as it lifted a wing to align on the runway lights. Only a few miles from the awakening world of men, a few minutes from the rumble of early Tehran traffic, we were riding in the harsher but cleaner world of the mountain sheep, specifically the red sheep.

In Yukon Territory, from the wildness of a Dall sheep range I remembered we had seen trucks pluming dust clouds on the Alcan Highway, but this offered even sharper contrast. The spurs of the lower Elburz which we were penetrating were perhaps insignificant compared to eighteen-thousand-foot Mount Demavend and the columns of two-mile peaks that march up to it, but these spurs were true mountains, akin to the rocky ranges of the Arizona desert, and they held large quantities of Asiatic sheep. Yet they rose from the plain only an easy Boy Scout hike from the teeming metropolis of Tehran. We could almost smell the morning cook fires that hazed the city below.

That superb sheep hunting exists in a part of the globe's face that had for centuries been eaten clean of its graze, stripped of much of its forest, is a kind of testimonial to the practical conservation being exercised in Iran under the impulse of Prince Abdorreza, himself a Weatherby Trophy winner and one of the world's greatest mountain hunters. How else could total wilderness and totally wild sheep exist almost within rifleshot of the bustling capital?

There are two ways of hunting the highly adaptable red sheep of Iran. One is tough, a sport for the muscleman, because it involves a long trek deep into ranges that hold sheep up between the ten-thousand- and twelve-thousand-foot levels; one is easier because the ridges are lower and the traveling less, much less. My Maryland hunting companion,

Phil Williamson, and I could exchange congratulations that by some miracle Iran Safaris had arranged for us the latter. The sheep were just as big, and certainly neither of us ever deliberately sought out the hard way!

Of course we couldn't be too sure. Tari Farmanfarmaian, partner in the safari outfit and our guide for the red-sheep operation, looked as muscular as an acrobat and clearly had as much nervous drive as the hot-blooded Arabian horses we rode. And the equerries, or guides and wardens, who rounded out our entourage, all looked rawhide lean, capable in the hills. We might well be in for a tough time. There was nothing to do but squinch our posteriors and our knees tight against the postage-stamp English saddles, completely ill adapted for the mountains, and see what these heights might bring. Our alternative: we'd cut it or we wouldn't.

The red sheep, one of the four Asiatic sheep inhabiting the ridges and peaks of Iran, is at one hundred and fifty or one hundred and seventy-five pounds slightly smaller than the trophy urial, but is much larger than his cousin of the Luristan desert, a midget type whose existence as a game animal has only recently been proven by Dave Laylin, Tari's partner in Iran Safaris. The red-sheep, or *Ovis orientalis*, rams carry much less beard or brisket ruff than do the urial, and their buff-tan-brown coloring, while hardly Ferrari crimson, is definitely on the reddish side.

"Much like this ground," I commented to Phil. "Lot redder gravel here than in the Almeh."

There had been more feed in the urial reserve two hundred miles farther northeast, too. These desert hills behind Tehran are blasted, burned, and grazed until even wire grass is a rarity. Maybe red sheep could exist on stones. They certainly must have to travel far for water unless they could get along on dew licked from the rocks.

But there was nothing wrong, vitamins or no, with their eyes or their agility. As our cavalcade wound up a canyon onto the first ridge a small band of young rams and ewes appeared at eight hundred to one thousand yards. They paused not to check our licenses or to stare in curiosity, but in seconds scrambled up over a leg-breaking ridge and out of sight. Spooky. This area might be carefully controlled, but its sheep certainly knew trouble when it rode up on a sorrel horse.

From the ridge crest, by carefully staying behind the edge, we located the same band joining up with others to sweep two slopes clean of sheep, but we could see the light rump patches of animals feeding undisturbed farther west, and by leading the horses along below a ridge comb we could get into glassing range. One bunch of six or eight were rams, all showing the light sweeping horns of *orientalis*.

"We must look more closely," said Tari.

"If there's a reasonably good head I'll have to try him," I added. "I climb aboard Alitalia westbound tomorrow morning, have only the one day on reds."

And Phil agreed that I should get first crack since he had a second day to hunt before taking off for home.

A two-day sheep hunt sounds easy, too easy, but it wasn't. For one thing, I missed the ram. We had slipped down into a valley and then behind a mountain shoulder and so into a very shallow gully that angled along below the sheep. From that point concealment meant belly-flat crawling for a hundred yards, over sharp gravel and sharper rocks, to a corner. Beyond its edge the sheep were in plain sight, but so were we, two hundred and fifty yards below them. I wormed out into position, spotted as the best ram the second of the bunch that had frozen to watch me. But shooting prone uphill, with the back slope of the little gully hoisting my feet higher than my head, meant it was impossible to bring the gun muzzle up to target level and still keep the butt firm against shoulder. Firing so awkwardly meant almost surely a scope cut over my right eyebrow, and chances of a hit seemed poor with so many muscles under strain. But there was no time to change into a sitting position or to crawl up onto the exposed slope. I might well get no other chance.

"The bullet snapped over the ram's back, off into the blue sky somewhere," I told Phil, wiping my brow with an already reddened handkerchief.

Since it was hardly fair that Williamson should not have a try for a ram after I had flubbed once, we decided to split for the rest of the morning and he headed off into an easterly range. I had a blood feud with the ram I'd missed, and Tari had told me that these sheep were not likely to travel clear out of the country when shot at, but were more likely to spring off over three or four ridge formations, then hole up on the rockiest slope they could find. We could probably locate them again, he suggested, and might well get another chance.

As long as the rams were running, their tracks showed clear enough, were easily distinguishable from the older tracks of wandering bands, but as they moved higher, slowed to a walk, their trace became indistinguishable from much older marks. In a country of no rain, only the wind removes those sharp edges that tell a new track, and apparently there had been only gentle breezes for days. We'd have to crawl up the last stages of every ridge and peek over, use the glasses constantly to locate the rams ahead before they spotted us. The country grew so rough that Tari and I left the horses to be trailed along behind us by the wardens. A higher peak, its face badly broken by slides and rocky crags, lay just ahead.

Son of a family once prominent in Persia's ruling class, athlete, linguist, firearms fan, darling of the ladies, Tari was above all things a sheep hunter. It was clear to him, as it was to me, that if we approached that face correctly, hiding ourselves, we would probably locate our rams. The best system seemed to be to toenail out under the crest of a bold jut of rock. Its end would give the right glassing point for the basin.

But we hadn't reckoned on finding the rams so soon and so close. Even as we whispered plans, we heard stones rattling down the slide just beyond the rocky point. The sheep must already be moving out.

I scrambled madly up the few feet of rotten rock to the edge. Perhaps warned off by the horses moving along a mile or so behind us, the rams were steadily walking away across the slide. As I popped into view, only fifty yards from them, the band whirled, broke into scattered singles making a mad dash, not up, but down, the rock slope.

Which was the best one? Even at that slingshot range, at first they all looked alike. Then there couldn't be any doubt. The ram farthest over carried the best head by far. At the bellow of the 7 mm. he pitched end over end and collapsed onto a rocky island in the shale.

"No doubt about that," said Tari, and there wasn't. The Nosler slug had ended things abruptly. The ram carried a solidly representative head, sixty-seven around the curve according to Tari's centimeter tape. He'd look fine on the wall alongside my urial. The earlier miss had been thoroughly wiped out.

Where we met Phil for lunch there was water and shade, both rare commodities in these stony desert mountains. The running water was only a trickle that sprang from rock and disappeared into the sand of a wash within a few yards, but it nourished a line of feathery-leaved trees like tamarisks, and some thoughtful soul had scratched out a catch basin that held muddy water for the horses. It was a fine place to eat and to snooze a bit.

After the nooning, it was Phil's turn. His late-morning travels had produced no bands of rams and the afternoon began to look like a repeat as we rode endlessly through ranges of bone-dry hills. The land was starkly empty, though from one crest we had a clear view out onto the plains, could see the smokes and window flashes in the desert mirage that meant Tehran. The sheep must have abandoned this section. But finally a distant ridge showed backs and horns where only rocks should be.

Those sheep were unapproachable. On our side of the ridge the slope was smooth for half a mile, so bare a grasshopper couldn't have hidden. Better to wait and let them move out of sight, then rush to the crest behind them. Tari, Phil, and I stood quietly, with just our heads over a gentle roll of ground, carefully holding our hands forward over the binocular lenses to cut any betraying flash from the late-afternoon sun.

But the care did no good. One of the horse holders got anxious, or curious, shoved his way too far forward. The sheep spotted him instantly, skipped off over the ridge, thoroughly spooked. Phil was out of luck, I figured.

And for one solid week I didn't realize how wrong that conclusion was. I had left Tehran at 5 the next morning, the witching hour when all the airlines seem to come and go from Iran's capital city, perhaps because landing in the high desert is easiest in the cool of dawn, and I had left full of worry lest the seeming bad luck hang on through Phil's second day. I was in the office answering *Field & Stream* mail when Phil called me from his Maryland home.

"I'm back," he said.

"What happened on the second day? Did you get a ram?"

"Well, yes," Phil answered. "It went like this. . . ."

The tale he told me was outrageous. Bad luck indeed! In the morning, on the range we had first hunted, he reported, they had seen a few bunches, mostly ewes and young stuff with no good rams. Rather than ride down to the trickle and shade at midday, they had lunched on a mountaintop, kept moving, until the hunt brought them into a patch so broken that the horses were useless, had to be sent back down off the range with two of the equerries. Even the rough ground seemed blank, but, reported Phil, his spirits got a tremendous boost when he picked up an eagle feather on the mountaintop.

"Always good luck for me," he explained. "I found one just before I shot the good ibex, and it has happened to me before in mountain hunting. With an eagle feather I was sure I'd find a good ram."

But the afternoon hours dragged by, Phil went on, and still they had spotted no huntable sheep, only ewes and young stuff. Finally Tari decided he'd better cut back to the jeep they'd driven out from Tehran, and would meet Phil and the one warden left with him down in the valley, where there was a road, or what passed for one. "I rested for a while," Phil said, "and then decided to take a look over just one more ridge."

As I listened on the phone, I was at that point dead certain of the end to Williamson's story.

"And on the other side, not very far, were five rams bedded down. One looked like a giant, as heavy as an Alberta bighorn. I got the rifle up over the ridge and the rams into the scope all right, but was scared to death the bullet would clip a bulge in the rocks right ahead of me. Fortunately it didn't. From the measurements, they say this old buster of a red sheep will go into the all-time eighth spot of the world records. Very massive and seventy-three centimeters on the curl."

"Wow! Congratulations and what a lucky fellow you are!" I said.

"Lucky? Oh, you mean because I found the eagle feather?" asked Phil innocently.

Now I ask you, how do you answer that one?

---

32 : Sour Notes on the Temple Bells

As of now, planning an Indian shikar is a very different matter than it was fifteen or more years ago. It was then perfectly possible to set up a hunt which would involve such bovine monsters as the gaur and the wild water buffalo, the whole range of lesser Indian types, plus both leopard and tiger on a generous basis. Common practice then called for allotting the shikarist two or even more tigers, and virtually unlimited leopard, according to the rather casually estimated game population of the shooting blocks assigned to him. On a 1952 hunt of some thirty days' duration, my own bag of both the great black bulls, two male tiger (with several opportunities on females or small males turned down), two leopard, plus all the lesser types, even including the black buck and the really rare Indian mouse deer, was by no means exceptional. If my head shikari had had his way, the take of fifteen head would have been higher, to the credit of neither of us. Fortunately for the future of hunting my own ideas have progressed. I only hope his have. In any event, times have changed in India.

At this writing virtually all of India, save a very few segments of the central Madhya Pradesh and the country of Nepal, is either closed to tiger or very soon will be closed. It seems likely that within two years the only tiger hunting on the Indian subcontinent will be for known rogues and declared man-eaters, with opportunities to be handed out to would-be tiger slayers in the order of cash deposits paid. The sporting is not the end, since cats that live on human flesh don't continue to exist by being stupid. Perhaps by then the Indian government will have lifted its momentary prohibition against shipping all tiger hides out of the country, even those legally taken under proper licenses, which has been their normal overreaction to the threat of extinction which has been claimed for the tiger and for the leopard as well. Conceivably, even our own government, likewise guilty of irrational overreaction in the matter, will have come to understand the distinction between the poacher or commercial murderer, and the sportsman-hunter.

The inability of governments, as well as of the staff of the *New York Times,* to understand that difference has long amazed me. It should be clear enough. The native trapper-poisoner who slays a beautifully marked cat so that its hide can eventually grace the frame of some wealthy female human—Gina Lollobrigida, when asked about her tigerskin coat, in all innocence defended her use of it on the grounds that the tigers were dead anyway, weren't they?—can perhaps hardly be blamed for fulfilling a commercial demand. But he is no more a hunter in the sporting sense than were the whiskery sharpshooters who slaughtered the American bison for their robes, or even their bones. He is a commercial killer.

And the professional cat killer, whether operating in Somalia, or Ethiopia, or India, or elsewhere, brings virtually nothing to the local economy. He is paid only trapper fees, perhaps 1 percent of the amount that any legal and easily controllable dude hunter will gladly give for the privilege of even trying for a tiger or leopard; and the profits up through the chain of fur smugglers, traders, and garment makers who process the furs from the jungle to the couturier shop enrich the economy of the cat's homeland only in relative nickels and dimes. What I'm getting at here is that the man who hunts for sport and the killer who slays for money are not in any sense the same persons any more than their contributions to the lives of men in the areas hunted are hardly of the same order.

India's cat hunting went to pot for two reasons, neither of them deriving from the gentleman from San Antonio or Detroit who craves a striped rug as trophy and welcomes the thrill of facing the world's toughest cats.

One is the world demand for handsomely marked hides for the glorification of woman. Often they are worn, even flaunted, by those most voluble in yammering about "conservation." The Canadian Tourist Bureau in New York City was picketed one spring by such self-styled conservationists, largely feminine, who were protesting what they termed the slaughter of the young fur seals from the St. Lawrence herd. That slaughter is actually a cropping that has been for years tightly controlled by the Canadians in reference to the readily established size of the herd each spring. The cropping is, of course, done solely to get skins useful in ladies' coats. To point up the irony even further, leading the sign-carriers was a handsome dame all dolled up in a leopardskin jacket! She completely failed to understand the anomaly she represented.

The other reason that has helped bring about the demise of India's cats has been strictly a home product. When those pukka sahibs, the British colonials, departed India they left behind them a tradition of manly expectations, *machismo* the Spanish might call it, a code under which any gentleman to be all man must have slain his tiger. Well-heeled Indians sternly adhered to that code, just as their military followed the British ideas of swagger sticks, exaggerated salutes, and such. And, after all, had not tiger hunting once been the sport of India's own royalty? Furthermore, in this age, the easiest and surest way of killing a tiger in India is by jeeping the back roads at night, cats of whatever sort obviously enjoying the ease of travel through cool dust. This has made tiger hunting cheap, open to all too many. Combine this with a human population that has continued to swell even more since the days of the pukka sahib and the tiger was in a tough spot. Understandably, the strongest cries for a rational policy of controls and enforcement came from the hunting out-fitters themselves. They didn't seem to rate much credence in Delhi, alas, probably because the Indian legislators, in a fashion reminiscent of our own solons, thought the outfitters were too concerned with their liveli-hood, and so not only neglected any intelligent controls on the easily controlled sportsman, but even further let the commercial trade in skins for the likes of Gina Lollobrigida flourish until the tiger is close to kaput.

Any memorial to the world's great cats with bodies either spotted or striped cannot be built on the hopes of hunters, but rather on the vanity of woman and the venality of the men who supply her.

---

33 : Charges Are the Bunk *

It makes me mad sometimes. In fact, it makes me mad almost every time. To hear those lurid accounts from returning hunters, to read in the public prints those dry-mouthed tales that are written by hairy-chested adventurers, in every one of which the hero is charged by some dangerous beast. Lions charge, grizzlies charge, leopards charge, moose charge, elephants and rhino charge, buffalo thunder in to drop only seven and one-half inches from the nimrod's left toe, even normally inoffensive beasties like elk or assorted brands of overseas antelope go on wild-eyed

* Reprinted from *The Gun Digest*, by permission.

rampages. They are halted only when the intrepid tale-teller fires his last remaining bullet at arm's-length range.

Or maybe intrepid is the wrong word. Perhaps the hoarse-voiced teller of tales should, in an overwhelming percentage of these instances, be tagged by some adjective more nearly meaning foolish than brave. To be sure, given certain sets of circumstances, game animals of the sorts labeled as dangerous will and do charge. It is my firm conviction, however, based on encounters during the past two decades with all but one or two of every species we call dangerous, that the vast majority of "charges" develop not from animal viciousness or man hatred, but from a major error of either tactics or technique by the man. In other words, the mighty hunter himself pulls some large, economy-size blooper that sets up the critter's attack. He asks for it.

A gentleman of politics from an Alaskan town, while out hunting blue grouse for the pot, met a brown bear along a stream. He didn't wait to check the bear's politics or intentions before slapping it with a charge of birdshot from twenty-odd yards. That bear must have been a Republican, rare in Alaska. He resented such treatment so strenuously that the politician no longer holds office unless it be in some Democratic precinct of Valhalla. He asked for what he got.

So does the nincompoop who knowingly puts himself between a sow grizzly and her last-winter's cubs, who tries to kidnap a tigress's young while the old lady is prowling the neighborhood, who starts feeding Yellowstone Park bruins Hershey bars and then holds out on 'em, who fiddles around with elephant or rhino trying to improve camera angles until the big beast finally gets fed up. This last stunt I tried once in Kenya. If the old bull, fed to his eighty-pound teeth by a couple of humans who persisted in poking a Bolex lens at him, had managed to stretch his trunk those last few feet we'd have gotten exactly what we'd been asking for.

But quite aside from such obvious nonsense, the hunter's own errors can set up a situation wherein the animal is almost dead certain to choose the most dangerous of the two alternatives open to any hunted animal, to run away or fight. And as I see it, those errors fall into two categories, mistakes of tactics and faults of technique.

It's an obvious goof of tactics—and technique as well—to gut shoot a grizzly bear from fifty or a hundred yards away, with you straight down the mountain from the animal. His fastest way out—and that is probably what he'll be looking for—is the straightest way downhill to you. Whether or not his run is a real charge, one meant to be pressed home on a man identified by the bear as a mortal enemy, or just a mad dash to get the hell out of there—and I know of one widely related bear-charge story on which the Alaska Game Commission, interested because there happened to be an extralegal bruin involved, inclined to the latter theory as did I— the hunter had knowingly put himself into the wrong tactical situation. He shot when and from where he shouldn't have shot.

A few years back a very famous young writing lady got involved in a Cape buffalo fracas which was essentially a tactical error by a professional hunter, though that ain't the way the young lady of the press told it in print. The hunter, who was a true professional and knew his stuff, as I can attest from having hunted with him, made an error of tactics, or judgment if you will. He let his client throw a slug into the midsection of a buffalo from a range that was just too great for her limited skill with a big rifle.

Ultimately that buff was killed, but it took a dozen or fourteen hits with banana-sized bullets, the attentions of two professional hunters, and a couple of their customers. In the melee—which makes a fine blood-and-thunder tale, believe you me—the original professional was slammed against a tree by the desperately fighting buffalo and so generally beat up that he spent a couple of weeks in the hospital. Charge, no doubt about it, a real charge, but what was its real cause? If there had been a rearrangement of tactics so that the young lady fired her shot, if at all, from a range dead-sure for her riflery, there'd have been no charging buffalo and no hospital bill.

This business of tactics with dangerous game, of getting into position for such shooting that the shot will be cold turkey—or as near to cold turkey as is possible for the individual hunter, for his particular level of jitteriness and his shooting ability—is an important matter for guides everywhere. It's doubly important for the gent who messes with the pugnacious beasts alone; it can make or break both the hunt and the hunter. A couple of bear stories exemplify the wrong and the right of it.

Harry Townshend and his guide Dick Johnston spotted an Alaskan brownie traveling the beach. They managed to get around him, waited behind a long right at the edge of timber so that if Harry's first hit was a bad one, unlikely with the log to give him a dead rest, they'd have the best opportunity of keeping the bear out of the brush. The devil's club thickets in that section of Admiralty Island are no place to go poking around after wounded brownies. In their hideout, unless the sea breeze shifted wildly, the bear would never scent them until after he reached the log. Bruin came shuffling along, Harry waited until he was at fifty or sixty yards and in the clear, then clobbered brownie with a .300 H&H pill placed to smash both shoulders and tie him down now for a clean kill.

Two other gentlemen, whom we'll identify only by initials M and G, because they're both bigger than I am and I don't crave to get into the wrong tactical position with either, were on another Alaskan beach with guide Hardy Trefzger. They also spotted a sand-walking brownie, a good one. The wind was in their favor, but instead of taking advantage of the brownie's mediocre eyesight and getting into sure position while he was still a furlong away, into a position where G—the hunter tagged for this trophy—could shoot surely and be surely able to keep the bear out of the high grass and willow brush, they flopped down on the spot. G started firing at roughly two hundred yards of range. He shot and he shot, chipping away at a thousand pounds of mad bear, poking him in the belly and tagging him in the foot, putting bruin into a spin of frenzied fury that ended when he lined out for cover. Now M got into the act with his rifle. Both of them whanged at the running brownie—Ralph Young and I, from a mile away, figured the Russians were advancing north from Yakutat—until their rifles were empty and the bear ran out of steam just short of the brush. That somebody wasn't forced to go into that brush after a wounded bear was as much good luck as sound tactical management, what?

There's a right and a wrong way every time we approach a big-game animal, whether it is one of the accredited dangerous types or not. It's the right way which produces the cleanly killed trophy every hunter is, we assume, working for.

Coming squarely down to it, of course, there are few of us who hunt actively who haven't pulled tactical bloopers. Nine times out of ten we err because we shoot when we are not absolutely sure *what* we're shooting at. That can be fatal. The basic maxim in working on major game is that we shoot only when we can surely place the slug either to kill on the spot or so smash up the beast that a follow-up finisher can be put in without fail. We shoot to kill or surely tie down, in short. Flouting that maxim means grief in big chunks, or certainly can.

I wanted a second Indian leopard quite some years back, and since in Nehru's land the law then permitted taking the cats under a light we spent odd evenings looking for one. They commonly use the tracks and roads, the spotted cats apparently liking the soft dust and easy going. One midnight we saw one in the jeep headlights. The cat was well ahead, but Pathak, the jeep driver, gave our buggy so much gas that we sprayed to a stop only feet short of the seven- or eight-foot panther, as the Indians call their leopard. Mr. Spots promptly leaped off the track into deep brush, though not far in, because we could hear him growling, cussing us out in cat language. I stepped ahead of the jeep into headlight glare, peering hard into the tangle of dark and tawny spots that bright light creates in leafy jungle brush—or on a leopard's hide.

Which was cat and which was bushes? Couldn't tell, couldn't tell. But finally, thirty-odd feet away from me, a pattern appeared which I was dead certain was not leaves but leopard hide. Must be. But I had no way of knowing whether the spots were on the front end, middle, or hind end of the big cat's body. Here goes nothing, thought I, and laid a three-hundred-grain Silvertip from the .375 Weatherby dead into the spot pattern.

This gentleman panther is decorating my living room today, but it's a wonder my hide isn't hanging among his trophies. With a caterwauling squawl two and a half yards of cat whipped out of the brush and into the center of the road a few feet from me. He was gathering his hind legs for a second jump right onto my shirt front as I managed to jack a second round into the rifle and shotgun it—no sighting, just pointing—in his direction. That did the business, driving straight into the spine behind his shoulders. This makes a good blood-and-thunder story, perhaps, or would with all the trappings, but it's a fine example of damfoolishness, too.

Sometimes, of course, we have sense enough to do things right, thereby avoid the wounded-animal charge and ruin a good story. In April of 1955 Alaskan outfitter Bud Branham and I were snowshoeing up a mountain beyond the Skwentna River, on the wallowing track of what was obviously a huge grizzly. In the top fringe of alders we spotted him, a great ball of silver-tipped fur, probably asleep. At seventy-odd yards the blob of bear would be easy enough to hit, but where was the X in that mass of hair? Furthermore, we were almost dead below more than a thousand pounds of bear, right in line for a downhill runaway or even a real all-out charge —and grizzlies can plow or swim through four feet of soft spring snow faster than a man can bust brush on snowshoes. So we quietly crunched around to a point nearly level with the bear, where he lay clearly visible through an alley in the alders. Bud grunted once, like an animal, not a man, so the bear got up more curious than alarmed. His shoulder stood out in the glass on my .35 Mashburn magnum—and his skull thereafter stood out in the record listings of the Boone and Crockett Club. That one we did absolutely right, both in tactics and technique.

When the hunter, and his guide, handle dangerous game correctly, there's only a small likelihood of a charge. Tactics form the larger part of that handling, perhaps; but so does technique, which in this instance I am using as a sort of catch-all word to signify the business of hitting the beast hard and in the right place. That may be a problem of caliber choice, of rifle-shooting ability, but it is also—and again—a matter of common sense. On dangerous game—and I repeat this deliberately—the first shot must be laid in either to kill instantaneously or to cripple completely. If it is so placed, any follow-ups are strictly frosting on the cake, not slapdash desperation efforts after trouble has started.

On truly dangerous species—lion, leopard, rhino, buffalo in the various African and Asiatic types, tiger, elephant, grizzly or brown bear, for example—being right with that first shot means smashing up a major bone or bones forward.

Major bone seldom means the head. Among the cats and bears the skull is itself a trophy, often needed for trophy registration in record lists, and so preferably not smashed up by rifle slugs. To speak more practically, the head is a small target, a moving target, and any of the cats or bears are left both hornet-mad and capable of turning a hunter into hamburger if the bullet misses brain, merely creases the skull or tears up jaw structure. The buffalo standing head on or quartering has his brain protected by a boss of super-tough horn, so rounded that a bullet from the average rifle is hardly likely to drive through into gray cortex tissue. Precisely where the nerve control area—we could hardly call it a think-tank—lies in a rhino's noggin is a matter for the anatomists, though logically, as with all animals, a bullet placed on the line between earhole and eye, a trifle nearer the former, should get into the fist-sized brain.

The head shot is most strongly touted for elephant. The great Karamojo Bell, we know, slew many hundreds of pachyderms with head shots, in effect punching in a knitting needle in the form of a 7 mm. bullet, and even 6.5 mm. full-jackets. Assorted other, and more modern, elephant slayers, hunting ivory or shooting for game control, have piled up similar counts with heavier and more modern calibers but similar bullet placement. But these were professionals. The average man, no matter how many hours he spends in the African Hall at some museum of natural history, no matter how many campfire bull sessions he goes through with his white hunter, when faced with his first or his second or even his third elephant finds it tough to locate the theoretically perfect spot and then to hold dead on it. Hitting a brain the size of a loaf of bread inside a head the size of an oil drum isn't easy. It particularly isn't easy when said elephant is looming over you in *mswaki* bush, thirty feet away, flapping his ears and winnowing the breeze for scent. His noggin doesn't look the same then as it was in the museum or around the campfire.

The loaf-of-bread brain is located at the rear of the skull, where a rod driven through both earholes will center it. Hence a solid into the earhole, on a perfectly broadside angle, will execute like lightning. If the head is slightly angled, hold a bit further forward in line with the eye. At a full quartering angle, when the brain is protected by the full mass of honeycombed bone that armors the elephantine nerve center, hold off until a better angle is present if possible. Head on, the point of aim to reach the brain is directly in line between the eyes, dead center to avoid breaking up a tusk root, or having the bullet deflected by the resilient ivory, and usually through the third wrinkle down from the top of the trunk. If the bull has lifted his head a bit, lower your point of aim to compensate for the slightly changed angle. There is no substitute for experience in such guesstimations.

The story of a recent elephant hunt in Zambia, told elsewhere in this book, exemplifies that perfectly. At the end of our stalk, I first saw the bull standing broadside, was about to dispatch him with a heart shot; but somehow alarmed, he spun to face me. Just as the sight settled onto his trunk root, he hiked his ears, raised his head a bit, and started into the charge. Dropping the point of aim a handspan was right, since the three-hundred-grain Hornady solid punched into brain for an instant kill, even as his right foreleg swung forward.

The neck shot has its drawbacks, primarily because the spinal column ahead of the shoulders is hard to hit surely. It lies in different planes in different animals, is practically nonexistent in an elephant, may be hidden by horn on the buffalo types and always sets lower under the massive neck muscles than most hunters realize.

Major bone, then, in the majority of circumstances, means the shoulder structure. Whether the slug smashes nigh or off shoulder, in either case probably cutting up the top section of the heart and its arterial complex as the bullet slants through, is immaterial, the only requirement being that the slug have ample weight, velocity, and jacket strength to drive well through. A grizzly with a badly smashed shoulder may not be killed on the spot, but he is for a time immobilized, time ample for a wrap-up shot. Buffalo, gaur, Indian or Asiatic water buffalo and the like, can move on three legs, in a most agile fashion if the leg alone is broken; but with smashed shoulder joints they are "available" for finishers. A rhino broken down in the upper forequarter goes nowhere except into a spin. Cats hit there and with one shoulder broken may react with typical feline speed by diving into cover, but seldom, if ever, can they consummate a charge from it.

You don't, of course, shoot an elephant in the shoulder proper with expectancy of accomplishing much. In the first place, his shoulder structure is much higher in the body mass than in other animals; in the second, the round bones may deflect even a solid metal bullet from its breaking job, even away from the heart and lung tissues behind. On tuskers, a solid jacket placed straight on or slightly angling into the top of the foreleg crease, as viewed from the side, will punch the heart, about the size of a five-gallon can; and while a heart-shot elephant may travel a considerable distance, with cannons like the .458, .470 or the .460 Weatherby, the beast's reaction is slow enough so that a second and third shot can be put in before many yards of movement. Of the nine elephants I have shot to date, none got twenty yards from the feeding spot on heart shots. The bull elephant banged in the head *without* definite brain injury, however, even stunned for five or ten seconds by the belt of some super-rifle like the .460, revives enough to charge, or to run off beyond likely recovery. Hence—and this again is advice often repeated—put that first one in where it does the most good most quickly.

Advice about what to do and where to shoot, once an animal of might has started a true man-destroying charge, gets to be pretty academic. It is true that slamming a heavy bullet into the front of a rampaging elephant's head, or into a shoulder, will turn him. Usually, that is. It is axiomatic that the buffalo tribe are best stopped, slowed, or deflected, by a breakdown of major bone; and there is basis to the point that a bear—which never stands up to attack, merely to survey a situation—carries his head, when he comes in like a leg-chewing watchdog, low enough so that his spine can be broken at the withers. It is reasonable that fast-moving leopards, hidden in the grass when they start to come, can be impaled by a bullet or a charge of buckshot during their last leap, much as Sasha Siemel used to do, sticking jaguars with a spear. Could be. But prescriptions for what to do in facing a charge can be written in several thousand words and still mean little more than the injunction: don't let the wounded-animal charge get started. Fix him *first*.

I, for one, wouldn't have the brass to write, as from personal experience, the dope on what to do when Leo or Bruin comes and means it. It would be as much a product of imagination and other people's experience as are 90 percent of the "There I stood" tales we read. I have never truly been charged by more than a few of the animals on the dangerous list, although red-eyed Asiatic boar, Iraqi pigs with foot-long tusks, tried it without any real provocation. A Bengal tiger kicked out his last at forty feet, only two jumps away from me, because I refused to shoot merely at his head but waited until his shoulder showed clear in the sight. Elephant, rhino, lion, African leopard—most if not all those met so far have not charged because they were either killed or so smashed up by a first shot carefully placed from the right tactical position that they had neither time nor energy to get into a charge. Twenty hundredweight of gaur or sladang made no menacing gesture because his spine, beforehand located by anatomical study of this oddly boned creature, was smashed to bone meal by a .375 solid. Of the rather considerable number of Cape buffalo I have taken, often shooting for ranchers on control work—and for my dough the buff is the toughest, the most dangerous beast to hunt on his chosen terrain—none has *yet* carried through into a charge. Sometime, if I keep on monkeying around with them as I did a year ago, hitting and following up wounded buff in jungles where the ranges on two kills were never beyond fifteen paces, at times as close as ten feet, the black bulls are going to give me trouble. But if they do, most of that trouble will be my *own* fault in some way.

As for bears—well, one day Alaskan Ralph Young and I were walking back down an Admiralty Island creek. I had already, on earlier hunts, taken several Alaskan brown bear, and none had been able to get out of his tracks. I complained bitterly to Young. "How do you expect me to write blood-and-guts stories about brownie hunting, the kind of stuff that has the readers all googly-eyed, if I never get charged? How about that? Something wrong with the brownies we meet?"

Ralph's answer was characteristically curt. "Listen here, Page. You just keep on busting any bears right smack in the shoulder like you've been doing and we won't have any charges. That's OK by me."

Young's philosophy seemed to me good then; it has remained sound over years of banging about the globe in close company with large-sized beasts of uncertain temper; and it rings true now. I just hope I'll continue to be able to carry it out in the future!

---

34 : Some Days You Can't Make a Dime

When I fell off the mule my knees gave way and I sat down hard on an assertive Bolivian cactus. Fifteen solid hours in a mule saddle had left my butt numb, but those cactus needles told me I still had it. I extracted them tenderly and profanely.

"What a day," groaned Dale Lee. "From 3 A.M. until suppertime in this danged jungle and we didn't see a *tigre* track fresher than stale bannock. Some days a man just can't make a dime."

He could have gone further. Some *trips* a man can't make a dime—for that matter, a plugged nickel. If you read the sporting prints regularly, you may get to believe that characters like me chase around the globe on a succession of hunting trips, every one of which automatically produces record hippogriffs and three-horned deer exactly as predicted. Would that it were so, friends. We scribblers who hunt for a living get stuck, skunked, and snafued just like you and Uncle Harry. Maybe not as often but just as painfully. Even more painfully, since we have considerably more than a vacation trip at stake.

The Bolivian thing was a classic. Dale, youngest of the Lee brothers of Arizona, is probably the greatest hunter of mountain lion and jaguar in the world, and he owns the best cat dogs on the American continents. But he couldn't find us even one big spotted *tigre* in the Gran Chaco. For a very simple reason: there just weren't any. Not there, anyway. Dale and the rest of us—Steve Lavoie of New Jersey who'd rather chase big cats than make electronic wizardry any day, L. W. Zimmermann and his grandson Dave, who have been making something of a career of hunting the world's tropical areas, and myself—we'd all been sold a bill of goods.

"I talked with that import-export guy for three hours," grumbled Lavoie, "and I was certainly convinced that this was a hunter's paradise."

The cactus spines were all out of my southern exposure by then but I was still smarting. "And *I* asked him two hundred questions. According to his tales, this Izozog country is broken by savannas, and not a thousand miles of machete-thick jungle, and it's lousy with pigs—three kinds— plenty of deer, and so many birds we should have brought down a case of shot shells. He said the jaguar were so thick the ranch *vaqueros* could buy new saddles every month just from selling their hides."

Zimmermann eased down on his private stump. "Far as I can see, few of them have saddles—they just throw a sheepskin over a saddletree and take off. The jaguar business must be poor even for them."

Only Dan Bush wasn't weary and sore. In his early twenties and a working lion hunter all year round, he wasn't bothered by a little thing like fifteen hours on a mule. Furthermore, he had in camp the solace of his guitar. It was a fine guitar, too. In it Dale and I had invested the magnificent sum of one hundred and forty-four thousand bolivianos, about twelve bucks, in the marketplace of our jump-off town.

Dan had already been a hit with "The Yellow Rose of Texas" back in the plaza at Santa Cruz, where, of an evening, the dark-eyed senoritas strolled around the square. So Dan didn't mind wall-dense bush, eleven million pepper ticks, or even the total absence of any game. Why should he, at twenty-odd and his guitar all tuned up?

But the rest of us, after two weeks of frustration and bad water with no game to bang at save a few birds for the pot, and the alligator we caught as the Parapeti River dried up, were more than slightly fed up. The airline had gone to a lot of trouble flying eight of Dale's superb hounds down to Bolivia in good shape, and its people had smartly eased us through the customs at Lima and La Paz. It was pretty clear that they hoped this *tigre* exploration into the Chaco would turn up something as attractive to sportsmen as the trout fishing over on the west side of the Andes, where Bolivia's Lake Titicaca grows rainbows as big as sharks. We'd all been misled by an informant who apparently didn't know fact from fancy. It happens that way sometimes.

"Can't say that roasted alligator tail wasn't good, though," Lavoie said optimistically. "A real experience in gastronomy!"

It had been edible at that—firm white meat that tasted either like fishy chicken or halibut that had been raised in a henyard. And if Lavoie considered roast alligator tail sufficient reward for getting stuck in the middle of trackless bush for two days and nights while his *vaquero* "guide" wandered in circles around a waterhole, that was all right too. When Lavoie finally had his fill of exploring the same chunk of Chaco thornbush and announced a desire to return to camp, the *vaquero* had thrown up his hands in pitiful despair and announced, *"No hay campo!"* He was teetotally lost in the green perdition that Bolivia and Paraguay once fought over. But the sound of three spaced rifle shots carries a long way in the Chaco. Otherwise Lavoie would still be living on alligator tails.

No one could blame Dale Lee. He had worn out three mules prospecting country far beyond our own hunting, poking 'way to the south, where the Yaniaguas, the bad Indians, have the two peculiar habits of running around stark-naked and potting with four-foot arrows any gentry lucky enough to have clothes.

"The natives in Africa give out misinformation the same way," volunteered Zimmermann on one of those last evenings before the Bolivian military picked us off the Izozog airstrip, the only practical link with Santa Cruz. "They'll tell you there are elephants where *tembo* hasn't been for six months."

"But they've got an angle," I replied. "If a Masai locates a lion for you he's in for some *shillingi*, no? If you don't find game, all they lose is time, and the Lord knows a Masai buck has plenty of that on his hands. Can't blame him, not really.

"Not that I haven't been fooled—and badly," I continued. "We had a Masai trotting into our camp on Kenya's Mara River every morning sputtering Swahili, bringing hot new dope on buffalo or elephant. He had more oil and ochre smeared on him and a longer spear than the *morani* who pose one-legged for those tourist pictures. A real savage! It took us three days to find out he spoke English as well as the average high-school principal and was staying at his father's *manyatta* as a vacation from clerking in some Nairobi wholesale house. That made him civilized enough to invent really good stories for the hard-working hunters. I'll bet the elephants he led us to one dawn were a big surprise to him."

Fumbling around on the basis of poor information is only one way of foozling a hunting trip. A man doesn't get hooked that way more than once, or maybe four times. There's also the business of running into tough luck, completely unpredictable bad fortune.

"Like Al Freeland," I said. "He came back from India without a tiger, the only one of dozens of hunters I've sent over to Allwyn Cooper, Ltd. But his partner shot three! Al was just fishing off the wrong side of the boat."

"Or you can smash yourself up by a fall or something early in the hunt," Lavoie suggested. "Dale, weren't you telling me about a fellow that backed into a skittish horse and got his leg busted or his ribs full of horseshoe nails?"

But Dale had disappeared into the jungle blackness to try once more to cozen a jaguar into answering the coughing roar he could produce with a rosined string and a five-gallon gourd, a call that had evoked all manner of responsive jungle music up in Nayarit and in Venezuela but hadn't so far raised even a grunt in Bolivia.

"Smart time to fall down is at the tail end of a hunt," I said to Lavoie. "Up in the Yakutat, on the Alaskan glacier bear hunt, I pitched off a log and chipped a bone in my ankle. Lay there laughing, and Ralph Young, my guide, rushed up all concerned. 'What are you laughing about?' said he. 'Hurt yourself badly, didn't you?' 'Sure,' said I, 'but this is the last day, we've already got the blue bear, and who cares if I have to crawl out of here? What if it had happened on the first day?' "

Ralph hadn't had any answer to that one, and neither had Lavoie now, but we kicked around the various misfortunes that can foul up a long-planned hunt until the fire burned low and Dan fell asleep over his twelve-dollar guitar.

"I'm not by way of being a superstitious man," said Zimmermann reflectively, watching the last coals flicker, "but when you come right down to it, there's a lot of luck in every successful hunt. Seems as if those little red gods of the Indians either smile or they don't smile. They must have been wearing a broad grin when that bongo walked out in front of you through the mist, eh?"

"Sure, any try for hard-to-get game is a calculated risk," I agreed, "and the aforementioned little red gods can turn grumpy even if you burn the finest Abercrombie and Fitch incense for 'em. Take my try for Abyssinian ibex, for example."

That had been a gem of frustration, one of the times when you know the game is there, when your try has the most powerful sort of backing, when you even get to see the game. Yet you can't get within miles of it— through circumstances beyond any human control. The gods had yanked the rug out from under me on that one by providing impossible weather.

It had been the rarest sort of opportunity. On the way south from Cairo toward Nairobi I had stepped off a plane in Addis Ababa, figuring to gab awhile with my friend Dan Reed and take the next plane for Kenya. The stop had evolved into an audience with his Imperial Highness Haile Selassie, the slight but steely eyed ruler of all Ethiopia, and from him I got an invitaiton—hitherto extended to no white man save a Chicago museum representative twenty years before—to hunt imperial game, the unique great-horned ibex of the Semien.

"But," I told the group at the fire, "we couldn't take the Emperor up on it until almost two months later, after I'd been on safari in Kenya and Tanganyika. There was too much arranging to do in Ethiopia—organizing the expedition and setting things up with the Governor of Begemdir Province and lining up mules and men and the local police for a guard into the high country and getting all the papers stamped. Things move slowly in Ethiopia anyway, so it was early August before we headed for the Semien and sixteen-thousand-foot Ras Dashan."

"What difference did August make?" asked Lavoie.

"It happens to be smack in the middle of the Ethiopian rainy season, and when it rains in Ethiopia it comes down in chunks. We knew that, Reed and I, but on the strength of the cloud-level reports he was getting from his airline pilots we decided to chance it. An Abyssinian ibex would be a trophy worth any calculated risk."

"So what happened?" queried Lavoie impatiently.

It was a long story. We'd started off on a note of minor frustration when the DC-3 flying us up to Gondar, the sixteenth-century capital of Ethiopia, got stuck in the mud at a way stop. We were able to take off again only after the local governor had ordered the entire male population of Debra Tabor to manhandle the tin bird back onto dry ground. Then we'd made an exploratory flight over the tremendous sweeping plateau of the Semien, a land gashed by mile-deep canyons that are more frighteningly scenic than the cuts of the Colorado, and run into thunderstorms so close to ground level that the clouds were full of rocks. Looked pretty bad, but still the try for an ibex with four feet of knobbed horn was a better long-shot gamble than the sure thing of hunting Kenya types of game in southern Ethiopia, which we knew was loaded with hunting possibilities.

Next, in a tired truck we'd rattled up the Italian-built road to a village called Davark, and there met the mules and the squad of police, with their captain, who were to escort us up into the mountain. Quite a mob. There was a Czech sportsman friend of Dan Reed's who had come along because he could speak Amharic, which I certainly couldn't. There was Lieutenant Mamo of the Imperial Guard, who had won the Ethiopian equivalent of our Congressional Medal of Honor by shooting up most of a battalion of Commies in Korea. He was on this shindig to represent His Imperial Highness. The tribal governor of the territory we were going to hunt came along with his retinue plus the police captain, a squad of eight, and an assortment of mule drivers. I cavorted at the tail end of the procession on a burro-size mule that had absolutely no understanding of Yankee profanity.

Two days we rode, in a howling downpour most of the time, up the steeps to the levels where giant heather grows, across canyons with torrents at the bottom, and finally ended up at twelve thousand feet at a hamlet called Ambarras. The people were hospitable at Ambarras, even though every adult male carried a rifle, usually a Mannlicher-Carcano that had been looted from a defunct Italian during Mussolini's dream of empire. When we got our two-midget tent set up and Lieutenant Mamo had a shelter half rigged to crawl into out of the near-constant rain, the villagers gathered round, sold us eggs at fifteen cents Ethiopian the dozen (about six cents U.S.), and offered all manner of other things free except firewood. Mamo had to buy that, since it had to be lugged up about five thousand feet by some villager's wife and was precious stuff. We had a home away from home, even if the police squad (which apparently had figured to live off the land) by the fourth day cleaned us out of canned goods and the lieutenant's precious bottle of brandy. So we were reduced to living on tea and boiled goat.

"Delightful," murmured Zimmermann. "But what about the ibex?"

The *walia* were there, I said, but we just couldn't reach them. The peculiarity of the rainy season at such altitudes in Ethiopia is that around midnight the skies clear and the stars come out. It stays clear, usually, until 8 or 9 o'clock in the morning. Then the sun, striking down into the incredible gorges where the Semien plateau breaks off, starts sucking up moisture. The clouds begin to rise out of the canyons to blank out everything in white sogginess. From then on you're in clouds, mixed with drizzles and bucket-heavy downpours, until after dark.

Only by starting before dawn could we climb another thousand feet or so to the lip of the plateau and get to work with binoculars from the points as the light strengthened. The second morning I found one bunch—too far to see horns, but they had to be ibex, because they were on a ledge, two thousand feet down and perhaps a mile to the west on the opposite side of a canyon, where nothing but some kind of goat could hang on anyway.

But we'd barely started the tortuous climb, toenailing along in their direction, when the fog and rain settled in so thick that it was hard to tell which way was up. An incautious step on the ledges could mean a man overboard. And in some places he'd have had time to recite the Gettysburg Address before he hit bottom.

Actually, I told the group at the campfire, we found three separate groups of the rare ibex, or *walia*, usually one old billy and three to six nannies and young ones. But there wasn't a hope—short of a miraculous cloud lift during the midday period, when we'd have time to climb down to their level and make a stalk by the human-fly method—of getting into rifle range. Major Maydon, back in the twenties, had hunted these same chasms of Geech and Bwahit during the dry season, and even then he had nearly broken his neck finding and shooting ibex. I still hope to pick up the Emperor's invitation for a try during the dry months, too. That would be a hunter's dream—a unique beast in a unique country.

But on this fogbound occasion, we had to climb by feel, and you can't shoot that way, not when the muggy, still air would magnify the sound of a rolling rock and carry it to amazing distance in the canyons.

"No chance at all, then," said Zimmermann.

"Not much," I answered. "We located a bunch one morning down off a point where the local natives said we couldn't possibly go, and climbed clear down there, about four hours down, in the faint hope that the clouds might just lift around noon and give us a few minutes of visibility. Seemed a possible chance because that had happened one day, complete with rainbows glowing underneath us, but the gamble didn't pan out this time. We sat for three hours in a rainstorm and couldn't see twenty-five feet. If my Ethiopian friends were doing any praying, as Coptic Christians, they probably made a better connection than I did with my mutterings to the little red gods, but nothing worked. The weather was just dead set against us and there was no payoff on our calculated risk.

"Matter of fact, just to add insult to injury, when we were climbing back out of the canyon a bunch of big Ethiopian baboons, the huge gold-maned fellows called hamadryads, got a mad on. They started rolling rocks down on us and chased us in under a waterfall. Better to get water down your neck than a ten-pound chunk of lava. That cooked it for me —I figured if both the weather and the baboons were against us, the try was a bust."

"Some days you just can't make a dime," said Lavoie.

Dale was still out somewhere in the jungle. We could hear the grunting roar of his gourd call as he again tried to tempt some wandering jaguar into answering. He wasn't making a dime either, because there wasn't any answer—not that night or the next or the next.

It happens that way sometimes.

The really ironic part of the Bolivia story didn't come until later, long after I'd flown back to the United States to get rifles and a fresh toothbrush for an African safari. Seems that Dale Lee continued his explorations and finally located on the Yapacani River an area infested with jaguar. Enough spotted cats so that three or four were answering his gourd call at a time, big enough cats so that one thoroughly clawed and chewed six of Dale's best hounds.

One night Dale sat on a Yapacani sandbar with his call and coaxed an evil-tempered tom jaguar up to twenty-foot range. The *tigre* roared and spat and wrung his tail until after daylight—but that was the night Dale's clients had elected to stay in camp. So it happens that way sometimes too. It can be raining gold pieces, but if it isn't your day you can't make a dime.

Africa

35 : Jackson Was a Lady

Jackson was long and skinny. Her amber eyes were set too close together and she had odd ideas about diet and personal sanitation, but Jackson was—and is—a lady. A lady monkey, that is, one of the Pallas, or Hussar, variety but above all a personage in her own right. Jackson owned a Land Rover, or certainly thought she did. She rode it with casual abandon, swinging from roof to seat back to gunrack like a nervous acrobat or settling down astride professional hunter John Northcote's shoulders only when a clear road demanded from her no supervision.

Jackson subsisted largely on a diet of crispy crunchy tsetse flies, dabbed out of the air with lightning swipes of her black paws. Bananas were acceptable but on her menu not to be compared with the zest of a stolen cigarette or the delicate flavor of a roll of Kodachrome film, preferably exposed. She chewed gently on her friends and bit savagely on her enemies, though not always did she make the distinction clear, and her ideas on property were basic—what's yours is mine. Jackson, in short, had neither ethics nor morality, but she did have a pair of game-spotting eyes sharper than the best binoculars ever hung around a hunter's neck. And thereby hangs a tale, largely Jackson's.

We—my son Kem, Mike Walker of Remington, Kem's Texas friend

Harry Koch, and I—first met Jackson outside the Kampala offices of Uganda Wildlife Development, Ltd., where we'd gone to settle safari plans with hunters Northcote and Nicky Blunt. Jackson was swinging on her chain from Northcote's hunting car, putting on for a dozen African kids a show that involved both gracious acceptance of the proffered bits of fruit and dead-serious attempts to gnaw off the hands that fed her. The same sort of vaudeville show went on in Mbarara, four hours west, when our safari cars and truck picked up last-minute supplies and the controlled-area permits for the Lake Mburo district. But we weren't much impressed. Vaudeville has been dead for decades, and we couldn't pick up a single shilling by passing the hat.

Furthermore, Jackson had by then located a loose carton of shotgun shells, had gnawed open the crimps of half a dozen, had eaten the wads and half the shot. Our feeling was that Jackson belonged in the monkey house.

"But actually, you know," John Northcote offered in her defense as we turned into the track leading toward the first safari camp, "Jackson is actually most valuable. Spots thing, you know. Why, only last safari she chattered at a bloody great leopard watching us from a euphorbia tree. Client missed him, of course, but one could hardly fault Jackson, what?"

Since the lady monkey was at that moment again delving into the Remington plastic shot shells, indulging her taste for green-dyed poly-ethylene, there remained some question as to the truth of Northcote's account, but we were willing to give Jackson the benefit of the doubt as long as her digestion held out.

The Mburo area does have a fair population of tsetse flies, and Jackson was working more effectively than any bug dope. She nabbed them before they could settle down for a solid cigarette-burn bite. The monkey was paying her way.

I secretly hoped that Northcote was right. Back in early 1962 I'd been in the Mburo area with another of UWD's hunters, Brian Herne. For nearly a week we'd played games with a very large gentleman lion, a cat obviously heavily maned from the gingery hairs he'd left high in the bark of our bait tree, on what was probably the last legal attempt to bait a lion in all of East Africa. If that lion was large, he was also smart, for he never gnawed on our zebra baits until hours after sunset, and he left them hours before the faint light of dawn. But perhaps that cat, or his elder son, still lived in the Mburo country, and perhaps, if Jackson was all Northcote claimed as a cat-spotter, we might see the whiskery simba.

"But the monkey certainly doesn't spot other game any faster than we do," commented Mike one evening as he daubed antiseptic on a nip where Jackson had mistaken friend for foe. "She doesn't give a tumble to ordinary game like waterbuck or topi or reedbuck or whatever."

"Strictly cats," confirmed Northcote from the other side of the camp-fire, where he'd been listening to the short-wave broadcast of a cricket match and idly scratching the sleepy Jackson's ears. "Strictly cats for her and it's time for dinner. *Chakula!*" he shouted at the mess boy, as if food settled the question of Jackson's merit.

But next day the monkey gave him the lie. We had driven high onto a burned-off hill and were glassing the opposite slopes while munching sandwiches out of the chop box. Jackson for once was quiet. She'd dis-covered a package of a headache remedy called Veganin that Northcote was taking for a jumpy tooth, and had eaten four or five of the codeine-based pills, enough to put a grown man to sleep. Suddenly she *"chir-r-r-r-r-d"* in alarm and rattled her chain in a leap to the Land Rover roof. While we had been sweeping the binoculars over slopes a mile distant the sharp-eyed monkey had picked up the slow movement of a black clot of buffalo only five hundred yards below us, where they dozed out the noonday heat in a clump of thorn trees.

"That one bull will make forty at least," judged Northcote quickly. "Good-o, Jackson! Shall we take him, Mike?"

"You two go ahead if Mike wants him," I said. "No shooting for me this trip save for lion and buff a lot better than forty. Furthermore, I'm feeding Jackson my share of the canned peaches for finding the buff that all of us missed!"

That the selected bull ran a mile after John and Mike had stalked to within seventy-five yards for a difficult shoulder shot through thick brush, that the bull had made it into wall-thick brush edging the lake, that two more .375 slugs were punched into its hide for finishers only after an hour of hands-and-knees crawling through the dark undergrowth, were hardly Jackson's fault. She, after all, had proved that buffalo were definitely in her repertoire.

In the Chembura country Jackson justified herself on elephant, sensing a pair of young bulls long before we did. We were not to discover her reaction to rhino until much later, but when we left the Chembura water-buck country with the yard-long horns of a record Defassa waterbuck added to my own trophy list, and when we stopped for a day of photog-raphy in Queen Elizabeth Park, Jackson established her abilities on an-other of the Big Five. As we drove through a patch of forest toward the Ivasha and its herds of topi a leopard stepped out of the brush. We all saw it, but Jackson saw *chui* first. It was certainly Jackson who reacted most violently and in all directions.

The leopard, amazed at the spectacle of a highly edible monkey riding in a safari car, merely sat and stared, but after chirping the alarm Jackson leaped to hide herself in Northcote's neck and beard. There she shivered in a fear that relaxed all sphincter muscles, so that the professional hunter drove on with his shirt soaked. Obviously Jackson could quickly spot all dangerous game. On some she reacted at both ends.

But even Jackson wasn't helping me much in the quest for a big and hairy lion. The two college-age boys had taken the prime leopard they sought, had shot their first elephants, and had racked up fine heads among the common game. We had crossed down into the Ibanda section of Tanganyika, where the flooding Kagera River divides it from Uganda on the north and Ruanda on the west. Mike had clobbered a wide-sweeping fifty-one-inch buffalo in that territory and had already run ample shooting tests on the new bullets Remington had sent on for that purpose. Yet the only lion I had seen, with or without the rich MGM style of mane I hoped for, had been a sprinter. He dived into cover at three hundred yards. I had taken respectable lion on earlier safaris into Kenya, Tanganyika, and Mozambique and had intended only to look for a cat with a better mane than this one. But no MGM type, it appeared, would materialize on this hunt.

It was the morning after my son, Kem, had taken a forty-two-inch buffalo after passing up half a dozen lesser heads that the lion business picked up. John and Mike and I left the Ibanda camp early, to reach the remains of the boy's buffalo by dawn's early light. Perhaps a pride of lions had struck it during the night. When we arrived, the *ndege* (vultures) had already spotted it and were rapidly reducing the ribs and spine to greasy bones. But on the burned ground edging the *karonga*, or brushy gully, in which the buffalo had died we hit clear tracks. A pride of lions, seven or eight from the pug marks, had apparently fed on the remains in darkness, then struck off across a freshly burned plain.

John and his gun bearer Celcio and I took up the track, leaving Mike, Jackson, and the bearer-skinner Marselino with the Land Rover. It seemed reasonable that the lions would stop and lie up in the next karonga, where there was both deep cover and water, but the tracks showed again on the far side, unblurred as yet by the rising breeze.

On fresh-burned grass, spooring up lion or any other game is a cinch and can be done at a fast walk; but once the marks lead onto an old burn where the soft ash has been blown away or head into heavy grass already mazed with the traces of wandering game, tracking is almost impossible. We hoped that the lions, one of which was leaving the broad forepaw marks of a heavy male, would stop at the next obvious point, a narrow valley choked with man-high grass and shaded by scattered thorn trees. One cat, the heavy-pawed male, had twice lain down as if to rest, the tracks showing that the others had stood waiting on his majesty. But they were not in the logical cover, and beyond it we could find no clear trace. Five miles of careful tracking had led us more than halfway round a circle.

When Celcio went back for Mike and the safari car, John and I circled out ahead to cut the track, but it remained a mystery. The pride of lions, once in an area of high grass and hard ground, had vanished in its own peculiar fashion. They had done so hours before, since the country was dotted with bands of impala, perhaps two hundred of them in sight at once, which fed as if no lion ever existed.

But Mike and Jackson had had high adventure during their wait. "First I knew of this rhino," Mike recounted, "was when Jackson chirped two or three times and then climbed up onto the roof. The *faro* was probably half a mile away. He wandered to within a hundred yards or so. At that point I had the long lens on my camera, got some good shots. Then the big lummox apparently saw the car, decided it was another rhino, I suppose, and charged straight at us. Came like a steam engine. I didn't know whether to grab a rifle or drive the Land Rover out of his way."

"We'd have been in a pretty pickle if you'd shot the beast," put in the professional hunter. "Totally protected here for several years."

"What I thought," Mike replied. "I stalled the Rover twice trying to barrel out of there but made it when the rhino was just passing the twenty-yard mark."

"So where was Jackson all this time?" I asked.

"She'd jumped over the back seat and was hiding under the spare tire —probably never thought she'd live to chew up another shot shell!"

We found two more rhino that day, on the way back to look over the mob of impala for an outsize head. We took pictures of topi and roan antelope. We watched from fifty yards a herd of buffalo, cows and young bulls, as they paraded down into heavy brush to lie up in the afternoon. It was an interesting day, with not a shot fired, yet all of us in Northcote's car as we turned back toward camp were depressed, convinced that we'd run out of both luck and time on the business of a proper lion. Even Jackson seemed subdued. Perhaps she'd been at the Veganin pills again.

When we were at least a thousand yards from where a few vultures still circled lazily over what little could possibly be left of the buffalo carcass, Jackson sounded off. Two squirrel-like *chir-r-r-r's* and she dropped off the roof to clutch Northcote around the neck. Automatically he stopped the Land Rover.

"False alarm," we all agreed.

We were in the middle of a wide-open plain, every inch of it burned clear, hardly bush enough to hide a mouse for half a mile. Inevitably our glasses swung to the point where grass and brush began again, to the *karonga* over which the vultures sailed.

"That a lioness on an anthill, or just an anthill that looks like a lioness on an anthill?" Mike asked calmly.

None of us could be sure. For my money the odd tan shape was just a freakish anthill. More optimistic, John took it for a lioness. The two Africans shrugged their shoulders and muttered something about *"Hapana jua*—I dunno." But Jackson was dead certain. She still clung to her master's beard. His shirt back was soaked by now, the final sign.

At six hundred yards there would be no doubt the monkey was right. Seven-power binoculars then brought up the unmistakable head shape, even the ears and eyes, of a lioness lounging across the top of the anthill. Jackson had disappeared behind the toolbox.

"There must be others with her," said Northcote quietly. "Probably the pride we tracked this morning, back again for a lick-up. If so, there's a good male."

"But she's staring straight at us," I pointed out, "and not a speck of cover in between for a closer sneak."

There was one possibility. Lions are often disdainful of moving vehicles, especially if they haven't been hunted hard. As far as we knew there'd been no safaris, nothing but poachers in the Ibanda area for months. Perhaps if we angled the Land Rover toward the *karonga* edge a half mile beyond that sleepy-looking lioness, we could leave it for her to look at, then slip off the other side and down into cover of the gully for a closer stalk.

It worked. At least it seemed to. When John and I dropped off the far side of the car with our rifles, Celcio, his head above the observation hole in its roof, could still see the lioness. She lay there undisturbed.

John and I knew that the stalk would be difficult. We had to stay out of sight, sound, and scent of not only the sentinel lioness but also others in the pride. They, for all we knew, could be lying or moving anywhere in the next half mile of gully. This would be a crawl job, with careful search in every direction before each slow move. The stunt would be to locate the male before the others located us.

We had crept only halfway when Northcote froze and beckoned me with palm-down hand. He'd spotted something. As I crawled alongside he put his mouth to my ear and whispered, "There's a fine lion lying a hundred and twenty-five yards ahead of us. You'll see just his head above the grass in a moment. But he's in the wrong place. Must be over three hundred yards short of the lioness. They seldom spread out so much—I think there are two prides."

At the moment it seemed unimportant. The family habits of lions or interpride hassles meant little to me when there was a hairy MGM type, or at least one with enough mane to be a passable imitation of that famous Hollywood trademark, within sure shooting distance.

I eased the .375 Weatherby, companion of twenty years of hunts in Africa and India, around our protecting grassy point and adjusted myself behind it. The 2½X scope hung steady on what had to be a bulge of mane on the resting lion. Now if he'd lift his head . . .

The lion did better than that. Perhaps suspicious sound had drifted to him; perhaps, and more likely, another in his pride had spotted us and moved in alarm. He stood up. For those long moments during trigger squeeze his forequarters were clear.

At the whomping shock of the three-hundred-grain bullet the lion dropped out of sight, but as we scrambled up over the gully lip the *karonga* fairly boiled with cats. Ahead of us, where the dead lion lay, we counted seven, six females and one young male, as they stood momentarily before drifting into deeper grass. Much farther on, up where the sentinel lioness had been, there were three shapes, or was it five, that oozed out of sight.

And as we walked cautiously in on the dead lion a vague memory nagged at my mind. Was I wrong in thinking that when he had stood up for the shot my scope showed a patch already blood-crimson behind the near shoulder?

The answer was clear as we stood over the lion and beckoned up the Land Rover. My bullet hole was there, centered in the shoulder but a mite high, so that at least fragments of the bullet had severed the spinal cord for instant death. But behind that shoulder, one high and one low on the ribs, were two great tears in the hide. They were well licked but still bloody evidence of a slash from the amazing widespread fangs of another cat.

John and I looked at each other in agreement. Now it all fell together: the tracks leading so steadily away from the carcass that morning; the evidence that one of the departing lions, the bigger-footed male, had lain down at least twice during that retreat; the afternoon appearance near the carcass residue of not one but two prides of lions. The male I'd shot had been the head of a family group driven off in the dawn by superior force. He'd returned later with his pride only to see the stronger pride, or the stronger male, still holding the ground. Indeed, they must have been in the area all day, even when we had sought for and found the original line of lion tracks.

"Wonder what the other chap looks like," said John. He had been inspecting my lion's fang wounds, and his eyes on mine were not twinkling but serious.

"We'll probably never know," I said sadly, "not unless we can find him —and he must be a real MGM type indeed—if I come back another year. And if I do, we'll have Jackson along and a special package of tasty Koda-chrome for her to chew on between cat spottings."

Northcote ruefully checked his still-damp shirt back. "Righto!" he finally agreed.

---

36 : De Mortuis Nihil Nisi Bonum

Jackson is dead. No longer will she catch tsetse flies and evacuate all over hunter Northcote's back. And no longer will she chatter in fear at the sight of the spotted cats who are archenemies of all the monkey tribe.

I'd like to be able to say that a hungry leopard crept into the sleeping safari camp one dawn and snatched Jackson from beneath Northcote's shotgun muzzle; or, to put it in the Disney fashion, that Jackson fell in love and wandered off into the sunset with a handsome Pallas male. Neither would be the truth. The far less romantic fact is that in full maturity Jackson became completely cantankerous. She snapped at every-thing and everyone in sight save Northcote, ultimately gnawed bloodily at the hand of a female child who merely wished to pat her monkey ears. She had to be, as the euphemism goes, put away. I like to think, however, that in some apish Valhalla Jackson is chewing up Remington shotshells, pain-killer tablets, and whatever passes for the celestial tsetse fly.

---

37 : What a Beautiful Morning

José Simoes stuck out his jaw and screwed up his face into a fair imitation of a Mozambique thundercloud. The situation looked dark. I tried to console him. "So there aren't any fresh lion tracks, and Jamuss did give us a bum steer," I argued. "Even so, we've had our share of fun already this morning."

With a first-rate trophy nyala, or *buindi*, as it is called by natives in Portuguese East Africa, on the truck and ready for the skinners, I wasn't disappointed that the waterhole mud showed no cat tracks. We'd even picked up a fat red river hog for a supper roast. As far as I was concerned it was a beautiful sunshiny day, and if the rumored pride of lions hadn't watered there last night, maybe they'd show up tomorrow night or the next. Then Simoes could get busy with his five-gallon can and the tin megaphone like a fireman's trumpet and roar up some whiskery old cat into spitting distance. That would be fun too, but right at the moment I was content with the nyala.

And a good nyala is a proper source of pleasure to any safarist. He's a handsome antelope. Not big—perhaps three hundred and fifty pounds in the biggest of bulls. Nothing like as graceful as the impala, for example; the bulls have something of the high withers and scraggy neck of the kudu. None of the compact power of sable or oryx. But handsome, his color ranging from gray-whites underneath through all stages of deepening blue-gray, so dark that the nyala looks almost dead black when you catch one at dawn gazing just outside a strip of jungle. An astonishingly long mane of stiff black hair springs from the bottom and the top of his neck, fading back along the spine. His sides are barred with pure white stripes, his face marked by the white lines and patches of the bushbuck tribe. A really handsome antelope, carrying his lyre-shaped horns proudly. And well this one might, since they were some thirty inches around the curve.

The nyala is rare, or certainly was a rare trophy until the great Klondike rush of safarists barged into Portuguese East Africa, because that's about the limit of nyala range. I'd taken most of the other members of his tribe, and had done a lot of wandering and hard work in the taking. The nyala has one close cousin farther north—the mountain nyala of Ethiopia, huntable only with the express permission of Emperor Haile Selassie. There's the bushbuck, of course, which is spread over most of English and French Africa and is almost as common in Mozambique as jackrabbits in Nebraska. There's the kudu, both greater and lesser, different in size but similar in stripes and body conformation. The horns of a youngish greater kudu bull look much like those of the nyala. The sitatunga also belongs on the nyala family tree; and certainly the bongo does, because the hard-to-get bongo bull I'd located in French Equatorial jungles some years earlier, though over one hundred pounds heavier and stockier than a nyala, and with dark mahogany hide, carried the characteristic striping and lyre-shaped horns.

Like most of their brethren, the nyala of Mozambique are furtive types. They hang out in the long panels of panga-thick jungle that stripe the Mozambique hunting country, and it's a task to delight the savviest and sneakiest whitetail hunter to pick a nyala bull out of dense cover. But at dawn and dusk they come out, each dark bull with his harem of two to four dainty red-brown females, to nip at fresh grass along the jungle edges. Then the gimmick is to find the nyala before he finds you, and to make the right guess on his horn length, the nyala being one of the very toughest on the African trophy list to estimate correctly. Plenty of them in Simoes's country to pick from, and this morning we'd picked a good one.

But Simoes was still very unhappy about the lack of lion tracks. The waterhole had attracted plenty of game, November being the end of the long dry in Mozambique. He pointed out their tracks to me. "There's *nzoo*, and *palla palla*, and *sfiri*. But no lion, no *kalamo*."

I could recognize the bucket-size round footprints made by drinking elephants, the round-ended buck tracks of the sable, or *palla palla*, and the neat hoofprints left by several families of warthogs that had come to slake their thirst and acquire a fresh coat of bug-resistant mud. The local brand of hammerheaded hartebeest—Lichtenstein's in this area—had been to water in numbers, and one whole end of the pool of thick green water had been tramped up by a mob of buffalo. Plenty of game watered here, but the lions hadn't hit this particular trough on their circuit.

Simoes gave up reading the waterhole sign. "Camp is about fifteen kilometers," he said. "You like codfish well enough to go back and eat *bacalhau* for lunch, then try the Magid waterhole this evening, or shall we stay here and open some canned sausages?"

"Let's take the backstraps out of this pig and toast 'em on sticks," I suggested, just to get a rise out of him.

But we weren't due for lunch just then. January, one of Simoes's ace trackers and a man who seemed to have wives in every village south of the Zambezi, had been off with two other blacks doing a little spoor reading of their own. He came trotting back, waving his hands for quiet and pointing toward the south. Obviously he'd seen something more solid than last night's tracks. Buffalo probably, since they're everywhere in Portuguese East Africa.

I couldn't catch the muttered conference between Simoes and January, but judging by the tracker's excitement, he'd seen something of greater interest than a few waterbuck or even buffalo. And since I'd already spent a couple of days alone with January, sneaking up on bushbuck and kudu until we could hit 'em with a tossed rock, I had respect for his hunting judgment.

Then Simoes turned and explained. "Eland. A herd of fifteen or twenty just over that little ridge a kilometer or so, and January says there is one tremendous bull in the bunch, a really old one. We go, no?"

What a beautiful morning! On earlier safaris I hadn't had much luck with eland. There'd been the massive old bull that Tony Dyer and I had happened on in the Northern Frontier District, but ponderous as he was— sixty-nine inches around the neck, as I recall—his twisted horns were no miracles of length. And everywhere else I'd run onto eland they'd been too small or too spooky to make the stalk worthwhile for an indifferent head.

The biologists may have other ideas, but it has always seemed to me that the eland is a second cousin in the bushbuck-kudu-nyala clan too. He has the same humpiness about the withers, the same vertical white striping, though his pinstripes fade as he ages. The same jumpy quality, too, with ability to use eyes as well as ears and nose in spotting danger. It always amazes me that a heavy eland—and a big bull is almost a ton of good beef—can leap like a one-hundred-pound impala. The cow that jumped over the moon must have made reentry over East Africa and met an eland bull.

Simoes was as excited as I was. He knew that if January said the eland was big, it was big. Moreover, this stalk was obviously going to be spiced with just enough difficulty to make it interesting to him as a professional.

The waterhole lay at the edge of a broken but open plain, with little or no cover. The parklike forest, here and there dotted with bush, which is typical of Mozambique terrain, spread to the south and west as the ground rose gently from water level to a ridge that was really just a roll in the ground. Having hunted the area before, we knew that just beyond this roll, about a half mile from the water, the cover ceased and there was another patch of open plain. If the eland had fed too far out onto it, we'd probably be out of luck. Normally he'd move slowly upwind, but the only good cover edging the plain was likewise on the upwind side, and a roundabout sneak from that direction would surely mean giving our scent to some wandering cow and so spooking the whole bunch. It seemed to me, as we made our plans to leave the truck and move out ahead—just Simoes and January, myself and my gun-bearer-tracker, Juan—that the direct approach was the best.

And Simoes, a straightforward type who believes that the best defense is a strong offense, felt the same way. We started for the plain.

We moved fast to the point from which January had seen the gray-brown shapes of moving eland, merely keeping a fringe of brush between us and the grass patch. The animals were no longer visible, perhaps just slightly over the hump, so the next two hundred yards were slow—dead-slow. Eland, like kudu, are not conspicuous animals. They blend well into gray-green-brown cover. But they see well, and it was a dead cinch that the herd we were stalking was protected by cows that acted as sentries even while feeding.

Humped over, heads and arms down to look like moving animals, we ambled slowly forward, only now and again risking a peek from under hat-brims to be sure no outrider cow was gawking at us. No concern about noise at that distance, and little about the breeze, which seemed to be a steady crosswind. But we were so much in the open it would be strike three if one of the eland saw us. Once Simoes froze as one of the cows lifted her head and essayed a small jump, but it was only skittish play. Finally we made the tree and could peer around the trunk.

"Where's the bull?" I whispered. The binoculars showed nothing but the brownish hides, the light-bodied shapes, and pindling horns of what were obviously cow eland.

Simoes couldn't see the bull either, not then. He muttered impatiently.

Then we saw *two* bulls at once. They'd stepped out on our side of the herd. No doubt about them—and no doubt about which was the big one. He was half again the weight of the younger bull. Even at this range, a full three hundred yards, the age-darkening and the scarring of his forequarters and deep-dewlapped neck were clear in the Bausch & Lomb glasses. His horns were heavier than those of any eland I'd ever looked at. Each was surely as long as a yardstick, and the straight conical points, beyond the twisted section, ran out over a foot. This was an old bull, no doubt about it, but he seemed to be shifting around nervously. Since he might move back into the herd any second, better try it from here.

But the shot didn't seem feasible. The grass made a sitting or even a kneeling shot impossible. Out of puff from our bent-over stalk, more stirred than I ever expected to be by a game animal that wasn't likely to bite back, I could not, when I stood to shoot offhand, seem to get the scope cross hairs squared exactly on the tender spot behind the foreleg. The shot had to be precise. This bull eland was big, beefy, and tough. If I merely stuck that one-hundred-and-seventy-five-grain Nosler slug into his lungs he'd die, all right, but in so doing he might travel miles, his tracks mixed into the herd spoor. Even Juan and January couldn't bloodhound him indefinitely on stone-hard ground. Better risk everything to make it sure.

To our right, no closer to the herd but perhaps a little higher, an acacia had fallen in some equatorial windstorm. If I could belly over into its tangle of upthrust roots and branches, I could probably see the herd better, and I'd surely find a rest to make the shot a dead cinch. *If* I wasn't spotted in the process.

There was no point in Simoes's coming. He couldn't help on this one, nor could Juan or January. I'd do it myself and cleanly, or it wouldn't get done.

And in just such a situation lies the real thrill of big-game hunting: once a mouth-watering, heart-thumping trophy has been sighted, to work out for yourself, and by yourself, the final stalk, the worming into position for the dead-certain shot. The fall of the trophy itself is anticlimax.

It was a long way over to that fallen tree on knees and elbows, the rifle cradled across my bent arms, binoculars forever flopping from under my shirt. A long and thorny way. It must have taken ten minutes. And when I wormed into the tree tangle and looked, the herd was still there, having fed only a few yards farther away, but the bull was invisible.

One gray-hided form showed, but it was only the younger bull, suffered to remain with the herd as long as he didn't challenge the old patriarch. Then another patch of dove-gray began to show, more and more, as two cows fed apart. *That* was the old one. The scope cross hairs crawled forward to the bulge of shoulder, then down to where the knuckle of elbow showed. Now squeeze easy. *Kurrang!*

At the shot the whole mass of eland moved crazily in a jumping swirl of dust. Even the old bull leaped once, twice—then he was down. Down for good.

I've said it is anticlimax after the trophy is down, even when the gun bearers and trackers and skinners and the truckdriver and the assistant truckdriver and various other assistants of undetermined duties all jump up and down and sing, and you and the professional hunter shake hands and agree sagely that this is a very large bull indeed, that his horns on the curve make thirty-six inches, and the tape makes neither of you a liar. Then you take the pictures. Sure, all this is anticlimax.

But not for the camp boys. After the picture taking was done and the mutual-admiration society had closed its session for that day at least, the natives were just starting. They had the job—and it's a stunt pretty much peculiar to Portuguese East Africa, where game is seldom skinned or even caped in the field—of tossing that bull eland, a ton of rich beefy meat, up onto the truck bed, alongside the fat red hog and the graceful nyala. And you know, with a little verbal assistance from Page and Simoes, they did just that. Did it in four or five heaves, too, so we all could get back to camp in time for lunch.

38 : Africa's Rarest Trophy

Sitting up in a tree most of the night ought to give a man time to think, and perhaps ponder his sins. But with a horde of jet-powered mosquitoes around my head, flying fighter cover for assorted bomber-weight bugs with junior H bombs in their stingers, it was hard to think very clearly. Why was I perched in this unlikely tree almost nine thousand miles from my home, peering gloomily at a fog-dank meadow in the middle of the Oubangui-Chari jungle? What was it that had brought me to this repellent-smeared but still bug-bitten, and thoroughly uncomfortable, pass?

If you're a trophy hunter, you'll guess the answer. There's a sort of madness that besets trophy hunters, a gnawing deeper than the bite of any jungle bug, and more insistent. If there's a sporting beast on earth that's hard to take, you want him. The harder he is to take, the fewer the sportsmen who've ever been before you, the more you want him. If he's a common beast, you want the biggest of head and horn. You can be satisfied with that. But the top sport of the game is to get the uncommon one, and the more uncommon the better.

Hunter Jean Gerin, sitting beside me stone-still in a cloud of mosquitoes, understood. So would another of our breed, Don Hopkins, who a few years ago had spent seven weeks in mud-smeared bamboo jungle trying for this same kind of beast. He'd got one at last—and, measuring its twenty-inch horns, decided it was too small to be a real trophy. Nearly fifty years ago Kermit Roosevelt got one. Aside from those two, though others may exist, we knew of no other Americans who had succeeded against this beast in fair combat. Two, in almost fifty years. The beast? The bongo.

The bongo comes as hard as that for good reason. First, there's the trip to his kind of country. The big jumps were easy enough even in the age of propellers—across the Atlantic, in my case, in a fast and comfortable DC-7 from Idlewild to Zurich, where I wanted to look up some Swiss hunter friends. After a short visit with them I went up to Paris, where I hopped across the Mediterranean Sea and the Sahara Desert to the cities of French Equatorial Africa. I got off at Bangui.

There luxury ended. In a freight plane loaded with groceries and jugged wine I had a roller-coaster flight over savannas and thickening jungle to Berbérati, then a day of pounding southward by safari car on a road that became a track and finally ended abruptly on the banks of the Sangha River. There Gerin had providentially stashed a German-made rubber boat rigged with a 35-horsepower Johnson outboard, incongruous among the log pirogues in which the Baya tribesmen waterbugged across the muddy stream to watch our loading. Next a blissfully fast trip down fifty miles of river to the ten-hut village of Bayanga, between lush jungle walls solid to the coffee-colored water, everywhere green save for splashes of white from a flowering tree like catalpa.

At Bayanga rugged adventure began. Into the jungle we plodded, heading a line of Pygmy porters, fifteen miles through a tropical rainstorm, hip-deep through mud-banked streams whose water felt oddly warm as compared to the soaking rain, along trails *panga*-slashed to Pygmy height where a tall man must travel bent double, with lianas cunningly snatching like snares whenever we hurried over hordes of fire ants that swarmed in the drier spots. No luxury in that, or in the tent and brush-shelter camp we finally reached in the jungle. Certainly none on the loose platform of poles where we perched in the tree.

Even so, this night we were doomed to failure. Jean could understand my mishmash of American and high-school French better than I followed his pure Parisian, but we had to agree that an evening ground mist, formed as the night air cooled over soaked jungle and marshy *sangha*, or meadow, had already blotted out half the grassy meadow we were watching. Even if the moon did show from behind scudding clouds, we would be blind listeners.

When Jean offered a wad of nylon netting and whispered "Voulez-vous dormir?" I gladly caught on to his idea of snoozing for a while and propped my rifle against the tree. Swathed in nets against the buzzers and biters, we settled down on the pole-floored perch to doze until morning. No bongo tonight.

Getting to this secret jungle spot was only half the problem anyway. Getting a bongo would be the tougher half. Hopkins had hunted forty days for one quick glimpse of bongo hide; one of Gerin's clients, before Jean had discovered a hot bongo area, had sweated and sworn for eight weeks without even that glimpse. The bongo may be a beast of size— a bull will heft upwards of four hundred and fifty pounds on the hoof— but this rare antelope is a tough one to beat in his home territory.

The bongo is a furtive type, living only in jungles so jammed with growth as to be almost impenetrable, green tangles where visibility is a matter not of yards but of feet. Even Tarzan would leave bongo country to the Pygmies and the gorillas. To make matters tougher, the bongo is a night feeder, with a quaint habit of gnawing the charred bark and pith of fired trees to season his usual leafy diet. He walks on tiptoe, so that his cloven tracks slant oddly deep into the forest mold, can slip through the tightest tangle of lianas by forcing his nose between so that the lyre-shape of his horns will wedge the growth back over his shoulders.

So agile that he can crawl under a dining-room table and then jump back across it without disturbing the diners, a bongo will stop to fight off dogs. This trait is taken advantage of by poaching Wanderobo in British East Africa, where the use of dogs is illegal, or in some sections of bongo range across the forested Central Africa, by light-skinned hunters who have used yapping shenzi dogs rather than make a true sporting try. Paul Du Chaillu first brought bongo hides from the West African forests a hundred years ago, though these mysterious antelope had been rumored for almost twenty decades earlier, but it was not until the twentieth century that the naturalists were sure how they should classify the bongo, or that whites of any nation hunted the rare antelope with success.

The physical facts are clear enough. A four-hundred- to five-hundred-pound bull bongo stands something over four feet at the shoulders, carries heavy white-tipped horns with a slow twist and a shape akin to the Grecian lyre—horns up to 39½ inches in the Aberdares of Kenya or to 37⅝ in the jungles of French and Belgian Africa, where bongo families most often appear. Big-eared like the kudu, the nyala and the sneaky little bushbuck, the bongo like them carries narrow white stripes on his body hide, from ten to thirteen on either side; but where the kudu is gray, the bongo's color can be deep mahogany or a bright chestnut red.

A handsome beast—and a pity he's such a tough one to hunt, I thought, pushing the netting farther from my face so as to foil any bugs with extralong stickers. But there would be other nights to lie quiet out there listening to the bird that filled the lush blackness with a call amazingly like the three notes of our American whippoorwill. Perhaps one night there'd be no mist and the moon would shine out full just as a bongo stepped out into our meadowlike sangha.

At 1:30 that morning it was no buzz-bombing beetle that roused me, nor the prod of the poles crooked under my hips. Something moved out in the middle of the two-hundred- by four-hundred-yard meadow, something that slurped and sloshed in its central marsh. Only one cloud layer masked the moon, and I could make out several shapes wavering in the mist.

Jean came alert at the first gentle shake. "Bongo?" he whispered.

I had been quick to wriggle out from under the netting and to line Bausch & Lomb 7 X 35 binoculars on those lumpy shapes. Disgusted with what they showed, I handed the glasses to Jean and muttered, "Nuts! They're elephants, four cows and two little calves."

Under any other circumstances, being able to watch a family group of elephants wallowing and squirting each other like kids in a swimming hole would be fun. Royalty was once treated to the same sight from a tree in Kenya, you recall, and now touring schoolteachers can goggle at the show, but here and to us the elephants were a blamed nuisance. Their rumpus would keep any bongo from the clearing; and even if we should there meet in daylight the biggest bull that ever wore ivory, he'd be safe from a bullet, because a dead elephant in the clearing meant a feast for every native and Pygmy village for miles around, no bongo for weeks. We blasphemed the elephants and rolled up again to wait for dawn.

By full sunrise it was clear that our second night of vigil had been no use. The lush-grassed *sangha* with its clear stream, quite likely the only sizable opening in the green jungle for a thousand square miles, lay empty and still, save for some odd brown ducks preening in its central pool. When Jean's gun bearer N'Gakoutou and a few boy-sized Pygmies came down from our camp to pick up the nets and water bottles and rifles, we checked the meadow edges and sandy streambanks for fresh tracks. Nothing save the elephants had visited us during the night, though we could still pick out the rain-blurred prints of bongo and one or two of those lesser marsh-loving antelope, *sitatunga*, that had fed into the clearing on the earlier evening, when a heavy shower had driven us from the *Hochsitz*, or tree perch.

"It takes patience," philosophized Tommy Aman over our camp breakfast, and Tommy should know.

A young Swiss friend who had already hunted most of Africa, much of it with my Zurich chum Jacky Maeder, Tommy could well know the answers on bongo. He had already taken a twenty-eight-inch bull only two nights before the day I had sloshed into camp after the first fifteen miles through—or rather under—Pygmy trails leading back from our river landing. He was staying on chiefly in anticipation of spending with me a few days trying to photograph the gorillas we knew were in the area, a risky job to which the French Equatorial authorities had gladly given us permission. Tommy, with his bull bongo's hide already salted, could be an authority.

The story of how he and Maeder and professional Jean Gerin had located our bongo territory was a saga in itself. Gerin had wandered miles in Oubangui-Chari territory trying to trace the source of the bongo hides that certain village chieftains had laced into their sunning chairs. But the payoff had come only after Maeder and Gerin had worked out with Mercedes-Benz mechanics the design of a Unimoc, the ultimate in safari vehicles, a six-cylinder, eight-speed, four-wheel-drive marvel that could carry hunters and boys and a load of four tons, and carry it up a 60 percent grade if need be. That got them part way into bongo country, to the river. Then from the Unimoc's top came down the inflatable rubber boat that

could carry men and a light outfit whizzing over the flooded Congo tribu-
taries under the thrust to its 35-horsepower Johnson.

The boat had made it possible to explore several hundred miles of
river, to quiz riverbank villagers and follow up a score of jungle leads.
Tommy and Jean had been two weeks on the job; I'd arrived only after
their explorations proved just what section of the rain-soaked jungle was
our best bet for bongo. This was the place. It would take only patience and
a hatful of luck.

"Plus one more practical item," I said to Tommy and Jean. "In the
States we have no use for those three-post German-scope reticles you use
on pigs and *hirsch* in Europe—not legal to hunt much after sundown
anywhere in our country. But the cross hairs in my four-power fizzled out
completely last night. Might be all right if the rain quits and we get a fat
full moon, but if it's all right with you that fat reticle—"

"Certainly you can borrow my .300 and the Zielsechs—just don't forget
the extra side safety." Tommy was gentleman enough not even to chide
the gun-borrowing gun writer. After all, I hadn't picked my arsenal for
this expedition with any knowledge I was doomed to be a night owl!

And a follower of Livingstone and Stanley, I reflected, gazing around
the encampment we had christened Bongoville. It had been chopped out
of a jungle underbrush by the *pangas* of Jean's own boys, the extra porters
and their Pygmy satellites we had recruited from the river village, a cut
area some fifty feet each way. Perpetual shade or a steady drip after each
rain came from the spreading tops of giant jungle hardwoods four feet
through at the butt and rising a hundred feet straight up without a branch.
A little green tent held netted cots for Tommy and me, with its outspread
fly for Jean and his gear. A whole housing development of huts thatched
with the broad *gungu* leaves had sprung up for the natives. Each lean-to
had its fire, and even now three of our Pygmies were smoking black their
share of Tommy's bongo and a tiny duiker antelope brought in for meat.
Their faces perpetually solemn, the little fellows also indiscriminately
smoked us and smudged off the daytime insects in the process.

Jean's No. 2 boy, Abba, was adding to the smudge as he poked up a
slow blaze under the drying poles draped with our spare pants and canvas
jungle boots, in a fruitless effort to warm away at least some of the mud
and water. A fruitless job, since we were soaked to the hips after each
trip of more than a kilometer or two outside the green wall.

Jean saw me looking over Bongoville and scratching at last night's bites.
"*Pas le Waldorf, eh?*" he smiled.

But he needed to offer no excuses. I knew that in Jean's own bush in
the semidesert of northern French Africa his safaris operated like the plush
hunts in Kenya, with refrigerators and thick mattresses for the general-bag

hunter, but here we were limited to what a few Pygmies could tote on their backs. Enough, anyway, it seemed as I dropped onto a cot to make up for sleep lost during the night watch. Tough trophies don't come with easy living.

By noon the onrushing express sound of an equatorial downpour confirmed what soggy clouds had earlier threatened. There'd be no tree-sitting that night, not unless we wore diving helmets. The intensity of a Congo-style rain, even after the wet season is presumably over, passes belief. Water falls in solid sheets. Even the G-string-clad Pygmies stayed under their *gungu*-leaf shelters, not once venturing out to snipe the cigarette butts I moodily flipped from our tent during a long afternoon of swapping hunting fables with Jean and Tommy.

By midnight the storm had poured itself out, and at 4 Jean and I were guzzling tea before sloshing down to the *sangha* and a dawn watch. No game showed before a watery sun lightened the clearing; but when we again checked the marshy edges for tracks, we found that a whole family of bongo had fed through during the night. They had trailed within thirty yards of our tree-perch while we were snoozing out the last of the rain. The rare antelope were using the *sangha* again. From here on it would be a matter of *"la bonne chance,"* as Jean phrased it, of having a wide-awake hunter and a full moon lighting clear skies if and when the bongo returned.

But not that night, nor the next, though the jungle at times seemed alive with furtive noises. We hunched on those poles for interminable hours, not daring to smoke because cigarette glow or hand movement, rather than the scent of tobacco, might betray us to a bongo standing back in the edge of green. Only the sound of Pygmy drums, a dim reverberation from some far village of forest nomads in the jungle depths, was sign of animal life. When the hands of my watch moved slowest, in the black hours after the moon had set, I began to wonder if this bongo try was worth the piper. Perhaps it would have been wiser to hunt with Jean out of Fort Archambault, where in the dry bush lion and kudu and sometimes oryx, elephant, and whole herds of buffalo were handy for the rifleman, or to have tried for the giant Derby eland in the middle country of brushy savannas.

Another facet of the trophy hunter's madness is that it is self-renewing. One good meal or one good sleep, or the sight of a fresh track—these are enough to keep the fever high.

When N'Gakoutou handed up our gear and the borrowed .300 magnum with its fat-lensed scope late that fifth afternoon, I had that certain premonition all hunters know. The day had been moderately clear, and although there would be a long dark spell between the sudden fade of the equatorial sunset and the coming of the moon, *la lune* would be roundly full. We were already sure that the bongo were far more wary of the *sangha* on bright nights, but at least I should have shooting light at times. The prospects were good. My trigger finger itched a little too.

The day birds quieted with the sun, and as the jungle walls of the little meadow blackened and its grassy center faded to a vague gray the night birds opened with their hooting and gobbling, as if to drown out the rising buzz of millions of insects. Once in the grayness a flight of loud-winged birds like curlews, big as our own water turkeys, zoomed by our tree on the way to roosting, but with their going the *sangha* settled into silence.

Twice during the early darkness Jean and I momentarily forgot stiffening muscles when the sucking sound of footsteps came, or seemed to come, from the far side of the meadow. Too far, and too dark, and perhaps only imagination anyway. Being a confirmed smoker, by 8:30 I was beginning to think that a few puffs might be worth the risk, but Jean was still sitting there quiet, only his jaws moving on what must by now have become a tasteless wad of French-made chewing gum, bought from the marketplace of Bangui. No smoking, we'd agreed, even if it did help ward off the mosquitoes.

Whorls of ground mist were forming along the little *sangha* stream as the moon wrestled up from the jungle trees and fought to penetrate scudding cloud layers with light. A stray beam slipped through our treetop and pearled a fluttering cluster of white-winged moths that for some strange reason wanted to light on the toe of my jungle boot. They jostled each other for position on the wet canvas.

But all philosophy as to the ways of moths and men suddenly fled. Those imaginary steps we'd heard earlier were real.

Even as I touched Jean and he nodded in silent agreement they came again, from over to the right, where we had twice seen fresh tracks after nights of evening rain. A stealthy *suck, suck* sound as hoofs were lifted from clinging mud. We strained forward in absolute attentiveness, eyes and ears forced beyond their normal sense. Something had materialized at the stream edge directly in front of our tree-perch. Materialized is the best word, because the ghostly wreaths of drifting mist were like ectoplasm, and the creature moving wetly before us appeared as a wraith. Its head was down, and it seemed only a ghost of a shadow. Then for precious moments the moon broke between clouds and the creature's dim body stripes were visible, white-tipped horns raking far back over the hazy outline of shoulders. A bull bongo had arrived.

Moving with infinite slowness so that no rustle of cloth or click of metal could betray our hiding place, I lifted the .300 magnum off my knees and tenderly eased down the safety. In absolute silence I slanted the muzzle against the sky so as to spot its reticle clearly and position my eye in the dead center of the scope. The three posts remained vague black lines as I swung the rifle down toward the animal, fuzzy indications against the light-hued stream edge that midway between them bulked bongo shoulder. Steady now. Right there!

Nothing was quite clear, and the light grew no stronger, even faded a shade as a cloud edge slid over the moon. Must shoot. With the last ounces of trigger pressure, blast and flash split the evening stillness.

Blinded by the muzzle flare, we could not see what had happened, nor could we at such short range hear the two-hundred-and-twenty-grain Silvertip hit home; but we could hear the bongo splashing in a desperate lunging run around close to the left of our *Hochsitz,* and as the crash of the shot died into echoes Jean and I heard him break heavily into the underbrush, fall, and bubble out dying breaths.

"Sure he's dead?" I queried of Jean in a voice that, now the shot had been fired, was as full of trembles as a quaking asp.

"*Oui.*" But even though the animal was down, Jean delayed congratulations. "*Attendez,*" he whispered, and we listened again for any slightest sound of life. None. The bongo was either dead there or had somehow slipped off into the jungle cover.

Within short minutes lantern light showed behind us in the trees. Abba and the Pygmies were making their way down from the camp, and Tommy and N'Gakoutou were cutting around the *sangha* edge from where they had been watching in hope of a *sitatunga.* Jean and I dropped down from our pole nest and joined them in a flashlighted search for the bongo. He must be close—but time dragged before one of the Pygmies spotted the carcass.

Bright chestnut-red he seemed under the lanterns, that hull, husky in the forequarters, with fine stripes vertical on his sides. A beautiful trophy— his horns long ivory on the tips, polished hard on the front of their twisting curve, more than three hand spans.

There was a tape in my pocket, and while the boys held their lights we spread it along the horns. Thirty-two inches either side. Now around the bases. Ten one side, nine and three-quarters the other. A beautiful trophy. What price a few soakings or a few bug bites? The trophy hunter's song rang in my ears. What price a hard hunt when a uniquely beautiful head was the prize?

After that all was anticlimax. The photographs next morning when the bull could be dragged out onto grass, the caping and salting and the lunch of sweet tenderloin, and the great smoking of precious meat by the Pygmies. The long slog back to real luxury at the riverside village of Bayanga, even two days of fruitless pursuit of the gorillas whose bellowing bawls we had heard across the river at night, the long haul back upriver, with the rubber boat and hard-taxed motor pushing a forty-foot pirogue cut from one great log. The trip in the Unimoc to elephant country, where the beasts that made the tracks never carried quite enough ivory to suit me; the short trip into Bangui and the fast flight to Paris and the pretty stewardess who plied me with chocolates as we dipped into New York—all these were anticlimax.

Riding on the empty seat beside me when we winged into Idlewild was a big rubber-lined bag, and in it were the partly cured cape and the cleaned skull and horns of a bongo, my hand baggage. And how else would you have carried, fellow trophy hunters, what so few have brought from the Oubangui jungle?

---

39 : And More Bongo

The success of my penetration into the jungles of lower Oubangui for a mahogany West African bongo set off a firecracker string of the jungle antelope hunts. Within a couple of seasons six more had been taken off the very *sangha* or meadow we had hunted. With their East African clients also demanding a try on the spooky striped bulls, the professional hunters of Kenya began planting salt blocks and building little tree houses at strategic spots in the Aberdares. The great bongo craze built up until a safarist's masculinity was slightly suspect if he had not at least made a serious try.

And it went beyond the men. A Texas couple flew me out to their jillion-acre *rancho* for a week of bongo preparation—we shot quail or geese in the morning, talked bongo all evening—because the lady of the house was bound and determined to be the first Texas-born female to have slain the rare beast. At that stage, having gone on safari was, even for Texans, becoming commonplace. She simply wished to top 'em all.

To ensure this triumph of gamesmanship, two hunts were laid on. The first was at my old stamping grounds, with professional Gerin. I shudder to think of the backbreaking struggles of the Pygmy porters who toted back into the boonies Jean's cases of wine and the lady hunter's cases of cosmetics. She had no less than five chances to shoot a big red bull, cashed in on none. Later, with a Nairobi-based hunter whose name I'll not mention because he's short-tempered, seven feet tall and four feet wide, she nailed one in the Aberdares. Or somebody did, anyway.

But for a time the rain forests were crowded with bongo hunters. Probably more of the science of stalking these bulls, certainly more knowledge of their habits and habitat, was then provided than had been discovered in the entire preceding fifty years. It was on the strength of such understandings, incidentally, that the present reserve areas in the Aberdares hills were established, so on occasion the side benefits of a hunting exploration are far-reaching indeed.

Bongo are also now known to inhabit certain sections of the Sudan, so the possible hunting belt extends virtually across Africa, but the big antelope with the lyre-shaped horns is still a rare and prized trophy, one of the really hard ones. Don't try for him if you're not willing to hike two dozen mountain miles a day, soaking wet, while feeding a bug and leech population like that on Guadalcanal.

40 : Why Hunt Elephants?

It happens every time. You're gabbing with solid American citizens, perhaps some not very savvy about hunting, talking about Africa. Somebody mentions elephants. Immediately pops up the double-barreled question: Why hunt elephants? Who could miss an elephant?

Who indeed? It has been done, I am told. But the safarist seized by a buck ague so colossal as to ensure missing a hulk too big for a two-car garage is a rare bird. Such a total miss has naught to do with our case, anyway. The fact is that successful elephant hunting demands that from moderate to ultrashort range you be able to hit a five-gallon can—the elephant's heart—nestling in an odd position behind the shoulder; or perhaps a loaf of rye bread—the brain—which is tucked into the stern end of a lumpy, bone-armored head somewhat bulkier than a fifty-gallon drum. So the question deals not with missing five to seven tons of elephant entirely, but with knowing the pachyderm's anatomy well enough to punch a bullet precisely into vitals hidden by his very bulk. The penalty for even slight misplacement is quite possibly your own demise. You just don't "miss" elephants, friend, not more than once or twice a lifetime anyway.

Far more interesting, of course, is the question of why anybody should want to hunt elephant. To the average "civilized" mind, conditioned by all the Disney, Daktari, and Tarzan nonsense, and chiefly experienced with those docile, small-eared Indian elephants common to circuses and zoos, the great gray creatures of Africa must likewise be slow-moving hulks, utterly noncombative. Presumably they too divide their time between toting around Hollywood musclemen dressed in loin cloths, and gamboling in the waterhole. This is a false portrait, as are so many on the TV tube. The elephant is gray, and normally moves slowly, to be sure. Yet in his shambling run he can get up to almost 25 mph, like when he's chasing you. Olympic sprinters do little better. Anger one elephant or a herd and you have turned loose a hurricane. And as for toting Tarzan around, well, the grown African elephant has not been successfully domesticated, to any degree, since the days of Hannibal. There is in the nature of the great beast a very sound reason why every African professional hunter off for a busman's holiday tackles either buffalo or elephant, likely the latter.

That reason is not simple. Nor is it easy to convey in words. When of thirteen safaris I made my first, years back, I felt no urge to hunt elephant, but took out a ticket chiefly because the arms writer of another magazine had made his first safari, the year before, without hunting elephant. A mighty poor reason, perhaps. But after that first hunt, up in the sandy *luggas* (washes or dried riverbeds) of the Northern Frontier District, I was converted. Now, for my money, the bull elephant of trophy proportions is the number-one hunting challenge in Africa. Not necessarily the nastiest tempered or the most dangerous—those crowns go either to the buffalo or the leopard—but the greatest hunting challenge. I say this after nine elephants taken, and a thousand encountered, in nearly all the safari areas of the Dark Continent.

That first bull wasn't such a muchness. I had set as acceptable ivory weight for the trophy the modest minimum of sixty-five pounds per side. Most people agree that eighty is very good; one hundred or over—and I've been lucky enough to beat that only once, with one hundred and twenty-three—rates as most excellent. There are today perhaps only two sections of Africa where you face reasonable odds in trying for a one-hundred-pounder. But sixty-five will do to start with, I had told Tony Dyer back in 1956 on the Merille *lugga*. Even that came hard. We scoured around for days tracking elephants, glassing elephants, following up misinformation from the nomadic Sanburu tribesmen who watered their goat herds at shallow wells scraped in the *lugga*. The elephants we found one day were forty miles away the next, that being their idea of a casual overnight jaunt in times of scarce water. Every respectable bull seemed to sport a broken tusk or, as is not usually the case, was unapproachable within a mixed herd.

But finally long search paid off. We located the right bull in a bunch of five, and from fifty yards I made an acceptable heart shot. Nothing to it, so far.

But Tony hadn't told me about what would happen next. The remaining four bulls—shaken for a moment by the rifle blast—as if by a quarterback's signal wheeled and headed for us. We scrambled up onto a rocky knoll. The elephants charged, screamed, finally stopped and backed off. This was just a demonstration. But I had learned what it could be like to be caught in either a stampede or a deliberate charge. What do you do when seven tons, or seventy, come down on you? Good question.

That first safari was easy to remember when I hunted the Belgian Congo a few seasons later. We were operating on the Rutshuru Plain north of Goma, a panhandle between Albert Park on the Congo side and Queen Elizabeth Park in Uganda. This brushy flat then had, I suspect, the heaviest elephant population in all of Africa. What it is like today, after the bloody revolutions and upheavals that began in the Congo within two months of our hunt, is hard to say. One windless day we found, my Swiss friend Tommy Aman and I, a group of thirty or forty elephants feeding in dense twelve-foot bush, by spotting their backs from afar. With no professional hunter along to question our bad judgment, we pussyfooted in to look for possible trophy ivory. Sneaking around on hands and knees and looking *up* at bull elephant is an excellent stimulus for the adrenal glands. When a bull elephant starts tearing up the very brush you are hiding behind, to stuff it into his face, it becomes even better.

When another bunch moved in behind us it was time to go. High time. There were almost entirely cows and calves and the female of the species is vastly more troublesome than the male. Even in open country it is wise to give a bunch of cows a two-hundred- to three-hundred-yard berth. No telling what idiocy of maternal fierceness may possess them.

This trait was behind a charge we faced in the Congo. In a forty-acre patch of jungle around a waterhole, Aman and I were spooring up big footprints that might well mean a big bull, were close enough to hear the purring rumbles that are the sign of full-bellied elephantine contentment. When the rumbles quit we knew the beasts were alerted. Two crashed down past us, small and probably cows. Then a huge-bodied elephant, the tallest I've ever seen but with absolutely no ivory showing, moved out, stopped fifteen yards away, unreeled a firehose length of trunk to sniff in our direction. Our bearers tried to disappear down a wormhole; Aman and I stood with rifles ready. The critter made up its mind, rolled back its trunk and hiked its ears in the signs preparatory to a real charge, grunted into gear. Two hard-jacketed slugs in its brain halted the elephant seven paces from us. It was a cow, a pregnant cow, in whom we had not the slightest interest, save that she go peaceably away. But who can account for the vagaries of a pregnant lady?

The Congo authorities called it *defense legitime*, no count on our licenses. Defense, no doubt about it, and, if not legitimate, then desperate.

The point I'm making here is that not only can a wounded elephant jam a tusk through your gizzard, or squash you into peopleburger, but an unwounded one, especially a female, may come up with the same idea. Its reasons will appear valid only to the pachydermatous mind. Crocodiles kill the greatest number of native blacks, I am told, the buffalo is the runner-up, the lion and rhino probably fight for the show spot. Elephants do not rate high in that sweepstakes because they're big enough to be avoided and are generally smart enough to avoid man—but they can indeed put the careless hunter into the obituary column. And isn't the element of personal danger one of the three factors that distinguish those animals that really challenge the hunter?

The two others are difficulty of terrain and the cunning or sensibility of the game. Elephant country holds none of the gut-busting physical difficulty of sheep and goat mountains, of course, though bulls are common in the giant heather regions of Mount Kenya above eleven thousand feet. Most of the stories told by safarists who claim to have tracked elephants for endless sole-burning miles are highly exaggerated. But where the elephant of Karamoja Bell's day roamed fearlessly in the open, today's pachyderm hangs more in dense bush, where he's hard to locate. And remember that any elephant, casually wandering from one patch of feed to another, ambles at five to six miles an hour. That will force a mere human into a puffing trot. There is certainly a degree of physical difficulty.

Far more interesting are the elephants' reactions to being hunted, their intelligence, and their abilities to sense the hunter. On the first two scores the animal with the tail on both ends is hard to beat. Tsayo Park got into serious trouble from overgrazing by elephant herds because the pachyderms knew as precisely where the park lines lay, where elephants were and were not protected, as if there had been actual fences. In Zambia this past fall, one open-country section of the Luangwa Valley, up near the boundary escarpments, was filthy with elephant when Phil Harkin and I first poked into it. There were a few around the second day. But after the third the word had somehow been passed. The elephant had bugged out for farther and thicker places. With a very high IQ, they know, and I think they can communicate.

Game animals come equipped with various levels of sensor, just as do humans. Our powers of scent are downright lousy, our hearing is only fair, but our eyesight is excellent, for example. The moose smells and hears well but has poor eyesight for distance. The sheep has absolutely superb eyes, a good nose, doesn't much give a damn what rock noises he hears. The Cape buffalo is a toughie because all three of his senses work efficiently. And so on.

The elephant—well, those huge flapping ears, effective as hide-cooling fans, will also funnel abnormal noises into remarkably acute ears. His trunk is as sensitive to threatening smell as is radar to an incoming plane—and it can be raised to sniff the upper air currents or swept down along the ground like a vacuum cleaner to snuffle out a footprint. We were, on one occasion, investigating a small waterhole in Kenya, when we were driven back from it by the arrival of a dozen elephants. One might turn out to be a good bull, so we stayed close to watch. The leader stepped cautiously into the clearing, paused. Surely he would come to the water. Then that trunk tip swept across where I had stood five minutes before. Silently the leader wheeled and the group oozed off through the bush. Not crashing away in heedless flight; no. Silently. These six-inch pads of gristle that elephants use for foot soles squdged down so gently that no twig broke, and no branch cracked as tons of weight swept by it.

The elephant's weakest sense is his eyesight. Stand still and he has a tough time making you out. Move and he can spot you from across a football field. By astute use of the elephant's visual defect and by moving only against a good breeze, a careful man can work up into touching distance, if he has the nerve. The Pygmies of the Ituri have done this for centuries. Smeared in elephant dung to kill their human pungency, they sneak in under a bull's belly, stab him in the bladder, and wait for him to die—a method I offer free for those who would prove their courage by killing an elephant with bow and arrow or other inadequate weapon. None of these stunts would be possible if elephantine eyes were bird-sharp, and few men would be able to stalk into dead-certain range for even a rifle.

For the targets are not large on an elephant. Remember the five-gallon can and the loaf of bread mentioned early in this piece. The problem is to calculate instantly the angles that will get a bullet surely into an execution area through any intervening flesh or bone. This is a neat trial of judgment.

When we were flying home from Zambia this past fall, the stewardess, a snappy brunette from Rome, asked the inevitable why-do-you-hunt-elephant question. I answered it as best I might. She had somewhere come to know the truth—that among Africa's mammals the elephant is doing remarkably well, with the only real threat to it being not hunting but the human population explosion, since, after all, a herd of elephants and a native farmer's banana patch can come together with only one flattened result. Control for reasons of expanding humanity kills vastly more elephants each year than trophy hunters ever could. I recall watching John Blower, then the Chief Game Warden of Uganda and essentially a man of protectionist views, nonchalantly signing an order for the indiscriminate slaughter of fifteen hundred elephants in one reserve. Such control killings are still common. And finally, in these days of low ivory prices and high taxes, the professional ivory killer is long since kaput. All this the Roman girl understood. What I found hard to explain to her was the emotional element in the hunt of my Zambian bull.

We had looked at two hundred or more, over three weeks and at from fifteen to two hundred yards, searching for trophy ivory. Hunter Rolf Rohwer reported a bunch of good tuskers, from which his clients had already taken two, watering at a hidden pond two hours' hike back into the *mopane*, but they had gone, driven off by the earlier shooting. Nothing we located seemed good enough. As we stood examining the total wreckage of a *baobab*, a tree eight to ten feet through the trunk, which had been felled and ripped apart by bulls hungry for the damp pulp that passes for *baobab* wood, we heard a lesser tree crash down in the forest. Only elephants could do that.

It was long minutes before we found the bunch, mostly young bulls, noisily feeding by walking down *mopane* trees and then eating the leafy green topping. Nine, but no big ones. To the right we heard other munching sounds. Three bulls. The two finest stood on a small island created by a loop in a deeply eroded creek bed. One carried ivory of a weight excellent for the region, curved and bulky tusks so long we could see them either side of a heavy-trunked hardwood. Would go seventy-five pounds each tusk.

The stalk would not have been hard save for the steep-walled creek, its bottom choked with dry leaves. The only quiet way to cross it would be to fly. As we crept over the edge nearest the big bull, he was standing broadside at fifteen yards. A heart shot. Just below the top of the crease made by the foreleg would do it. But my foot dislodged a chunk of clay that rattled down into the leaves. The bull whirled to face us.

There wasn't any place to go. The creek gully was too deep to jump back into. Surprised and perhaps even frightened by our sudden arrival, the bull was going to charge. Either my shot would be right or the Zambia newspapers would have front-page news. His brain should lie dead behind the center of the trunk base on a line between the two eyes, said my racing mind. The rifle lined up there without further thought. But as he rolled into motion the bull lifted his head. That changed the angle. I must shoot lower by anyway six inches. Right there.

At that moment, to my heightened consciousness, the wrinkles crossing the elephant's trunk seemed as coarsely visible as masonry on a wall. The rifle sight lined automatically and my trigger finger tightened automatically. As the rifle belted me in recoil, the elephant dropped out of sight, instantly dead from only three hundred grains of lead and steel that had bitten into a hidden brain located as precisely as if I had used a T-square. For a moment I had lived quite outside myself, had compressed days into seconds.

That was part of what I couldn't explain to the stewardess, plus the supreme satisfaction at having faced the bull in fight as fair as ever conflict between man and beast can be, to slay him with a little projectile thrown as accurately as David slung stone at Goliath. Come to think of it, it is difficult to make things clear, isn't it, save to another hunter?

---

41 : Supermarket Leopard

"Phooey and double phooey!" was Bob Johnson's comment as we waited by the safari car, and he pinched his nose to shut out the smell of death and corruption. "That warthog—what's left of him—is stronger than the whale that washed up near Atlantic City last summer!"

"He's mighty powerful downwind," I agreed. "But that should do the business on the leopard."

This bait had done no business, however. That was evidenced by the discouraged way in which professional hunter Tony Dyer and his trackers checked the ground for pug marks and looked for claw scratches on the trunk of the acacia from which hung the warthog's remains. All it had drawn was flies—millions of them. In a day or two it would be so far gone that even a spotted cat wouldn't relish it. Too bad. Should have been a good set, with the headless boar slung under a tree branch on a likely game trail between the escarpment and the Mara River, which marks a Kenya game-reserve boundary. But probably no cat had followed the game trail; certainly none had smelled the bait.

"Strikes me he could hardly miss that, though," said Bob. "Almost knocks a man out of the safari car fifty yards away."

"Needs to be a bit strong for a leopard," said Tony, who had given up the search for cat sign and was swinging himself behind the wheel. "Nothing delicate about *chui's* sense of smell. Likes his meat well aged, our spotted chum."

Roy Newing and I followed them on this midday bait inspection, trailing along in our DKW jeep, a 3-cylinder creation that could cross swamps like a railbird and scuttle up slopes like a rock rabbit as long as you kept the pint-size engine screaming in low-low gear. Back along the Mara and up onto the plateau toward camp we jogged along smoothly, with plenty of chance to talk leopard.

"You know, Roy," I suggested, "a first-rate leopard is number one on Bob's trophy list. On the way down from Copenhagen he was buzzing the stewardess about it and he's been harping on spotted cats ever since we left Nairobi."

"We should've had action by now, with all those baits out," answered Roy. "Pity we can't hunt them as we did in Nigeria—used to shine their eyes at night with a bloody big flashlight around the villages, and blast Spots with buckshot."

"No wonder you had so many people chewed up," I responded. "But I've got a bright idea as to how we can improve our baits, even if leopard do have a lousy sense of smell."

There wasn't time to expound on this bright idea right then. Tony had pulled his car to a halt and was out flagging us down, beckoning quiet and caution. As Roy cut the motor of our little vehicle, the Kenya-born professional hunter stepped over to my side. "Sizable bunch of eland just ahead," he whispered urgently. "They've probably spotted us, but perhaps you and I can cut around between them and the escarpment and get into range for that 7 mm. magnum of yours."

I was already out of the car with the Mashburn rifle ready, and off we started. "Quick like a long dog now," spoke Tony.

When my good friend of the East African Professional Hunters Association speaks of a long dog he means a greyhound. At least that was my conclusion when we finally pulled ourselves up out of a gully and stood at the escarpment base to check on the eland. We had traveled half a mile at a trot. Even so, the eland herd had moved faster.

They were making off along the cliffs at their traveling trot—steady, tails swinging, no stops to look back. There was a good bull with the bunch—an old one, judging from his color and the weight of horn that showed in my binoculars—but they weren't going to stop this side of the Uganda border. Bob Johnson, the New Jersey friend whom Tony was guiding most of the time, had already taken his eland trophy over near the Kuku Plains. I had an eland head that was too big for any wall in the house pranged up in the NFD thornbush on an earlier safari; so missing out on this herd was no great cause for sorrow. It was just as well that the eland had won this round.

On the way back to the cars there was time to talk over the leopard scheme. It sounded good to Dyer—messy, perhaps, but effective. He recalled working a similar stunt on a perversely smart old dog leopard, one that fed on ordinary baits only under cover of darkness, never showing for the men who watched for him until greed overcame his feline caution. "Let's try it," he agreed. "There was leopard sign around the water hole beyond a bait Bob and I put up a mile or two west of camp, and perhaps the Page-Newing method will work. You and Roy set it up tomorrow."

Roy and I knew where that bait had hung, and by noon we had Operation Supermarket well under way. He had driven over to the escarpment edge, where, a full week before, we strung up a fat stud zebra along lion tracks. The zebra had drawn nothing but flies and the attentions of some long-legged hyenas, but under the ministrations of the equatorial sun and a million blowflies it had become a pungent and puddinglike horror. The boys, Guyo and Kalofia, didn't much like the job, but eventually got it cut down and lashed in towing position behind the DKW. We thereupon ran away from it, on a wandering course of three or four miles, to Bob's bait tree. That smeared trail *had* to be easy to follow, even for a leopard suffering from a bad head cold.

The stage around the leopard tree was then set with fresh topi meat on the ground and tied to low branches. One hindquarter was lashed in the tree up where the leopard would prefer to feed. A veritable butcher shop, all in all.

And it worked. In the faint light of the following dawn Bob and Tony, in their blind fifty yards or so from the bait area, finally made out a moving lump on the tree limb. This resolved itself into a spotted lump, and then, as the minutes stretched and the light grew, into a fine hulking leopard. Bob's shot galvanized the cat into an arching leap that dropped it—stone-dead—into the thick grass.

Tony was beeping his horn as they approached camp to join Roy and me for breakfast; so I had the steel tape all ready. Seven feet six inches. A very fine male leopard had visited our supermarket.

I still had a leopard to get, and for two or three days Roy and I watched our more conventional baits. But they were doing no good, just ripening further every twenty-four hours. So, one morning we made a new move. In a matter of hours we cut down and dragged the grisly remains of two sets to make an even grislier supermarket in a valley below camp.

On this route from the escarpment down to lower country we decorated the bait tree and the surrounding brush with enough fresh meat to hold the vultures in daylight and to keep the hyenas snapping and growling all night. We made scent drags to that bait tree from every direction, advertising our supermarket for leopards. Then we built a brush blind.

When, in the mine-shaft blackness that comes just before African dawn, we trundled the DKW slowly down the grade, figuring to stop half a mile short of the bait and pussyfoot to the blind, the car lights picked up eyes ahead. One pair, two pairs, half a dozen pairs—a whole mob of hyenas, all moving away from the bait. *Away* from it. Either they'd finished the whole business—which would be quite possible for two or three hyenas, let alone this mob—or something had driven them off it. That something had to be either a leopard or a lion.

Either one would do, I thought, as we felt our way in the velvety dark toward the blind, but a spotted cat would be preferable as vindication of the butcher-shop technique. In the blind, Roy and I squatted, stiffening with dawn cold for what seemed hours before the east reddened enough to make it worthwhile to peer at the bait area. The supermarket was set well down into a hollow about a hundred yards away. Nothing but darkness down there.

Ten minutes later one of my legs went numb, and as I shifted to relieve it my own cautious rustle was broken by a sharper noise from the hollow, a scratch. Claws on a tree? We heard it again. Then a chopping, ripping sound made faint by distance but unmistakable. There was a cat feeding down there.

But even when the light had warmed almost to picture-taking strength the brute wouldn't show. Whatever it was, lion or leopard, it was feeding on one of the chunks of bait that had been left on the grass. We'd been fooled by our own scheme. As the day brightened the cat might well leave without showing itself.

The hyenas had done their work, however, leaving little on the ground but scraps. After a few hors d'oeuvres the cat moved to the steak counter. Even as I watched through the shooting hole in our blind a lithe and spotted form reared up out of the grass and fastened its claws into the dangling hindquarter of zebra that the bone-cracking hyenas hadn't been able to reach. Its near shoulder was completely exposed.

The whang of the 7 mm. magnum was echoed by an "E-e-e-e—yow!" from Roy. There wasn't any doubt about that hit; the leopard collapsed like a rain-wet paper sack.

The cat wasn't as big as Bob's. The tape read only seven feet and an extra inch. But that didn't matter much. We had vindicated the Page-Newing method of leopard baiting, and this time it was our horn that was beeping when we rattled into camp for breakfast. I was so elated I immediately bet Bob that I could go out and do the same thing with a lion. The wager? One dollar, American.

One nice point about supermarket baiting is that all the slightly used baits that have attracted no attention are put to use. To make our lion set we cleaned up the country, dragging in mortal remains from several points of the compass. For fresh bait I shot a stud zebra. He provided enough meat to stock the supermarket counter in a mighty attractive display, one calculated to arouse the most sluggish lion appetite.

We built our blind in the big economy size, with chopped grass to sit on and a heavy branch at the bottom of the peekhole—or firing port. If the lion the local Masai insisted was ranging in the area came into our store, he was going to run into a one-hundred-and-seventy-five-grain Nosler slug for sure.

We didn't win the dollar. Lost on a technicality, because we didn't catch us a lion. For a while we thought we had one. Long after we'd tiptoed into the blind, after the scarlet flush of an equatorial dawn had widened beyond the Mara, my first peek through the hole showed a lioness —at least what seemed to be a lioness—working on a suspended hind-quarter of zebra.

I waited ten minutes, then peeked again, this time with binoculars, searching in the grass patches edging the bait area for the ponderous maned head of her boyfriend. But he wasn't there. And what had seemed, in the half-dark, to have the dimensions of a lioness had suddenly grown spots. What I was looking at was the leopard of all leopards!

Roy elbowed me aside to look for himself. "Gor!" he whispered. "And neither of us with a license."

That was the brutal truth. No ticket. That leopard was safe as a babe in arms. We watched it sitting on its haunches and feeding steadily, hoping that the light would warm enough for photography, but the huge tom leopard, with one final growl and a twitch of its tail, went away before full daylight.

When we walked to the bait area I took out my steel tape. From the toothmarks in the zebra to the ground was 68½ inches. "And that cat, Roy, wasn't standing up. It was sitting on its haunches!"

"With some three feet of tail he was over eight feet long, perhaps eight and a half!" Roy shook his head regretfully. "Who'd believe it?"

I did, and I still do, because it was my tape. Tony did, and I guess he still does, because he took a client back there a few weeks later and tried for that leopard. They didn't get it; never even saw it. But then they didn't use good old American merchandising, the supermarket method.

42 : Home Is the Hunter

As a personal friend of twenty years' standing, it has been interesting to watch the growth of Tony Dyer, the professional hunter mentioned in the earlier pages. Born of Kenya colonial stock—his father had been part of the British raj in India—Tony got his lore on animals and hunting, a degree of understanding of animal habits and skills as tracker and sure nemesis unrivaled by any professional today, on his family's farm. He was less than ten when he took his first eland as a practical matter of providing eating meat in large chunks, and his youth afield was enriched by associations with Onyango, the wily gun bearer, and various Wanderobo who for a time sponged on the Dyers, did a bit of vermin trapping, and, more importantly, taught the young scion the ways of the wild. Tony had only completed his apprenticeship by a year or two— his mentors were men like Sir Philip Percival—when the Mau Mau problem reached its peak in the early 1950s, so that for a time his quarry was man, high in the freezing-cold bamboo jungles of Mount Kenya.

As a professional hunter, few if any rate higher. A good many African hunters, it must be noted, are excellent camp administrators, chauffeurs, and mechanics, but frankly rely on gun bearers and trackers for the details of where an animal went and why. But, with Tony, it was he who did the tracking, who was the final arbiter as to hunting procedures, Tony, who, without thinking, enriched his campfire conversation with vast quantities of naturalist's lore.

Save for trips with close friends, however, Tony left the "white hunter" game in the middle 1960s to develop ranching interests on lands of his wife Rose's family, and is now a prosperous sheep and cattle breeder who cops a tray full of blue ribbons at every Nairobi Fair.

He has, however, maintained close connection with the world of safari by becoming a kind of perpetual president of the East African Professional Hunters Association. That, to a degree unmatched by any other group of outfitters, affects the course of conservation and of hunter licensing in the Kenya-Tanzania-Uganda area. And more recently, largely single-handed he has fostered the development of an International Professional Hunters Association. This could conceivably regulate the major outfitters of the world as effectively as the East African Association. And somewhere along the line there has been time to father almost a basketball team of curly headed boys—though I doubt anybody plays basketball much above Nanyuki.

On one of my hunts, Tony was fresh from the hospital after a battle with a buffalo which had started when a client shot badly. Tony had ended up with a ripped thigh, among other things. That thigh was still so tender that bouncing in a safari car was exquisite pain, yet for one reason or another—I have always thought it was a deliberate move to get back onto the bronc that threw him, so to speak—Tony and I spent much of the safari sneaking around in brush full of buffalo, daring them to start a scrap. We got it finally, the Cape buffalo not being minded to let any-one knock chips off *his* shoulder. Having stood together through it, we are therefore the closer friends.

43 : Safari Rifles

One of the stock articles written at least once by every firearms writer, whether or not he has spent much time on the Dark Continent, goes under the heading: The African Battery. It's a never-miss subject, like a piece on why the .30-30 is really a lousy deer cartridge.

But I for one have come to think there is no such animal as an African Battery, no ultimately balanced set of rifles and calibers so near perfection that any safarist must either carry the combination or feel handicapped, doomed to an unsuccessful hunt. It is possible that in the early days of African hunting, when safaris went on for two or three months and the shooting involved many dozen head of game, beasts dropped every day to feed the camp, furnish baits and so on, that a three-rifle battery was highly desirable. But it does seem an absurdity in the present age of fifteen-, twenty-one-, and thirty-day safaris and total kills per hunter nearer fifteen to twenty-five head than the awesome bags of yesteryear. After all, in this day and age you do not traipse casually about slaying anything within range. Each and every animal bagged—or for that matter hit and lost—counts on a license list that is becoming shorter and more costly every year. Furthermore, the modern hunter has a very different idea of what constitutes sport.

It is quite reasonably possible today—in fact it's done all the time—to make a one-rifle safari, use one caliber for everything from Thomson's gazelle to Tembo the elephant. Common sense indicates that in any attempt to save air baggage weight you should avoid a bean-blower caliber, since it is obvious that it is better to be overgunned on the smaller stuff in order to avoid being undergunned on the big tough brutes like buffalo, elephant, and such. The usual caliber choices are the .338 Winchester magnum and .375 Holland & Holland magnum, though one-gun safaris have been made with the .300 and .378 Weatherby magnums, the .404, the .416 Rigby, the .358 Norma magnum and no doubt others.

The British have long held the quaint idea that the diameter of a bullet is the sole index of its power, so in certain formerly British areas, notably Kenya, you run into a legal demand for rifles over .40 in caliber for the hardskins. This would suggest that you might approach a buffalo with a .45-70 but would be a criminal to do so with a .378 Weatherby, a paradox which verges on the silly. It has been my private experience that such laws are, like the speed regulations on our highways, largely ignored when conditions seem to warrant. Most professional hunters, once they have come to realize that a client can really shoot, does not get the wind up, and knows animal anatomy reasonably well, are not inclined to waste time peering into said client's rifle muzzle to see how big the hole is; and in Zambia, Mozambique, Angola, and Botswana, for example, the game people show very little curiosity about caliber.

One problem with these middle calibers for the one-gun enthusiast is that of getting proper solids, bullets so strongly jacketed that they will positively not break up or upset or mushroom or be bent into banana forms by harsh contact with the noggin of an elephant or the shoulder bones of a buffalo. Bullets jacketed in copper, or in gilding metal—and the flat-pointed bullets Winchester uses in .375 loads are gilding metal—will not penetrate reliably. To make an effective frontal brain shot on an angry elephant, after all, requires that the slug punch through over two feet of bone honeycomb, springy and energy-absorbent, before it even reaches the inner nerve center. Bullets done in honest steel (which will react to a magnet, naturally) or for U.S. reloaders, the heavily nickeled bullets now being made by Hornady in .338, .375, and .458 diameters, will work properly. I have dozens of recovered solids which prove the point. If you can get and load correct hard-nosed bullets to complement the expanding bullets you'll need for the lighter species, there's no reason why a safari cannot be made on a one-gun basis.

The classic African combination, of course, was always three rifles. The first was a "heavy," which in British terms meant a shotgun action taking two rifled barrels for such finger-sized cartridges as the .470, .475 #2,

.465, or one of the earlier rounds of the same sort. All of these toss from four hundred and eighty to five hundred grains of slug at somewhere between two thousand and twenty-two hundred feet per second and approaching two and a half tons of striking energy. Items like the .577, the .600 and so on are strictly for those with no feeling and little sense, however effective such *ballista* may once have been on pachyderms, for example. All this type of equipment had evolved from guns such as that god-awful cannon toted by early explorer Sir Samuel Baker, which was essentially a 4-gauge shotgun lobbing a quarter-pound lead ball.

There is much mystique about the British double and its Central European imitation, much rationalization about the speed of the second shot, the relative reliability of having two firing mechanisms, the "automatic" pointing of a side-by-side gun. The double rifle is certainly a beautiful object, a delight to fondle, but the mystique is largely bunk. They are little if any faster for a second *aimed* shot, and they are a damned sight slower for the third and fourth, should they be needed, unless you've spent a lifetime practicing stuffing in cartridges from between your fingers. Two locks isn't all that much more reliable than today's bolt actions. The instinctive pointing bit comes into play only when the shooter is in dire trouble, about to be overrun by some large and angry critter, and the vast bulk of today's safari shooting on large or dangerous game is done from a moderate distance, under the careful supervision of a professional who abhors the thought of involving either client or self in a battle. There, for Joseph American, a scoped bolt action is likely to be far more useful than an iron-sighted two-barrel. Few doubles will shoot particularly well; all of them have persnickety digestions, were originally sighted and the barrels regulated for only one batch of ammunition. When you come right down to it, the reason for the double rifle was that when the Britishers probed into tropical areas and met oversized beasts they needed oversized cartridges, and the basic shotgun action was the only one then available that could handle such lusty rounds.

So for my money, if you want a "heavy," make it a .458 Winchester, which does all the .470 ever did and with better ammunition, comes relatively cheap from numerous makers. For real muscle, go to the .460 Weatherby, which develops the awesome paper energy of some 8000 foot-pounds. Don't monkey with calibers for which ammo is hard to get anywhere and unknown in the boondocks. The African countries have plenty of .458 fodder—the average American brings over a hundred rounds, fires two into a tree, six to ten at game, gives the rest to his professional hunter! As an aside, let me remark that the major difference in the effect these two cartridges have on elephant—and I have used both on several bulls—is that the .460 into his bean will stun an elephant for ten to fifteen seconds even if you don't line your shot right to penetrate the brain, but the .458 won't. There is, it must also be admitted, a difference of the same order at the butt end, though neither can be considered comfortable to shoot.

The rifle called "medium" has classically been Holland & Holland's trusty .375, one of the most versatile cartridges we have ever had, accurate, potent at the receiving end but not murderous to the giver. Its brother cartridge, the .300 H&H, is rapidly passing away because of more modern items like the .300 Winchester, .308 Norma, .300 Weatherby, but the balanced and effective .375 hangs on, and properly so. Its record on the cats, the large antelope like eland, on buffalo and even on elephant—the meat hunters of Mozambique shot up .375 ammo like Chinese firecrackers when they were operating—is irreproachable. There are cartridges like the .358 Norma magnum and the .338 which offer similar ballistics but neither seriously threatens to displace it.

The large-sized .30-calibers are often shot as mediums; that is, they are used on game of "middle rifle" weight with fair effectiveness. The chap I took to Zambia a few years back had a .300 Weatherby which he shot well, and so used it on all manner of game, all save elephant. Lacking solids in .30 caliber, Tembo he did not try. And it worked OK. It is not, however, my feeling that anything smaller than .33 caliber or with bullets lighter than two hundred and fifty grains can reasonably be called medium.

The "light" rifle may seem heavy by our standards in that a .243 Winchester or 6 mm. Remington deer rifle, for example, should be used in Africa only by people both highly sensitive to recoil and not insensitive to the appeal of common sense. These real lightweights belong on the seventy-five to two-hundred-pound animals like puku, impala, Tommies, Grants, and such and only on them. I say this in spite of the fact that I am responsible for the commercial appearance of these two cartridges and because of the fact that I've already tried them on African critters. Zebra they have on occasion killed, for example, and they do well on light-framed antelope where nervous systems can be shocked all apart by velocity—but I also know of a professional hunter whose license was lifted because he endangered both his client and himself by plinking a lion with a .243. What we properly mean by "light rifle" here is the .264-.270-.30-06-.280-7 mm. magnum breed.

Among those make your own pick, if possible taking on your hunt a musket equipped with a 4X scope with which you are familiar and in which you have real confidence.

Roughly ten years ago, when entering the exhibit hall at an NRA Convention, I ran into a gun-scribbling colleague who burst out with the exciting news that he was Africa-bound, on what would be his first safari. He rattled on about how thoroughly he'd checked out his battery, prepared his .470 and his .465 and his .475 and his .505, even I supposed, his four dollars and ninety-eight cents. Halfway through his account of the loads for these I stopped him with the question: "Fine, now what are you taking over to do your shooting with?"

The answer to that is the so-called light rifle. Through it you'll burn five or six times the ammo you'll shoot through the "medium" and ten times the amount you'll bump out through the "heavy." It's the so-called light rifle that'll do the heavy work, numerically accounting for at least 80 percent of the trophies you take. I suspect this is why, though in Africa I've used items like the .280, and the .270, and the .30-06, and even the .300 Weatherby, I lean toward the 7 mm. magnum clan, either Mashburn or Remington chamberings, because—and especially with Nosler bullets—the percentage of problems, when I did my share even reasonably well, was down at the vanishing point. The reliability or surety seemed higher. I felt in far better shape when with the big seven- and one-hundred-and-seventy-five-grain Noslers I was forced to take control of a large antelope like the one-ton eland, or a tough guy like the lion. But if you prefer one of the other calibers, I'm not going to sulk in a corner —just plan to use the bullets which are in that caliber rather toward the heavier than the lighter side, preferably Remington PSP Core-Lokt or Nosler, and things will work out OK. Zero such rifles, incidentally, so the group centers three inches above point of aim at a hundred yards. That will put you back on at from two hundred and fifteen to three hundred yards, depending on whether your musket is a .30-06 with one-hundred-and-eighty-grain bullets, a .270 loaded hot, or a 7 mm. magnum with Spitzer 175's.

When there has been no commercial reason, which is to say when I have been Africa-bound on most of my thirteen safaris to date without having to worry about what is, in the trade, referred to as field-testing a new model or caliber, the two basic rifles in my kit have been a .375 Weatherby and a 7 mm. magnum, the latter usually of the original or Mashburn persuasion. These have been so much used in Africa, India, and other parts of the globe where gun bearers are common that they no longer have much bluing on the barrels, that having been polished off by dark and grimy hands. These calibers have served me well.

Unless my memory is slipping, the .375 Weatherby—which is merely an improved form of the Holland, about two hundred foot-seconds faster, not the hard-kicking .378—has so far accounted for five elephants, some three dozen buffalo, many of them on what amounted to control work for Mount Kenya ranchers, two rhino, three or four lion, five leopard if we include a pair from India, two tiger, gaur, wild water buffalo, and so on. A good many of these creatures are in the dangerous category, but I have not yet been eaten or stamped flat, despite charges from several of them, while toting the souped-up .375. As a matter of fact, it is my observation that its paper figure of five thousand foot-pounds of energy with a three-hundred-grain bullet at under three thousand yards is just as deadly as the five thousand foot-pounds of paper energy deriving from the fatter five-hundred-grain bullet of the .458 at some two thousand one hundred and thirty feet per second. It fixes elephant as well or better, assuming equivalent solids.

Zurich friend Tommy Aman and I were working on elephant in 1958, in the Belgian Congo just before the upheavals there. One day we spotted on the Rutshuru Plain two bulls very different in tusk form but both in the seventy-five-pound class, as good as we'd seen. By discreetly waiting until they fed closer, we were able to take both at once. That is, I whanged mine with the old Weatherby and a three-hundred-grain Hornady slug, and he dropped in his tracks. But Tommy apparently didn't nail his just right with his .458, because it started off at a shambling run, with Tommy still blasting away. When his rifle was empty I took a try at the spine and dumped the elephant right there. Lucky? Mebbe, but another exemplification of the old saw that it ain't what you hit 'em with but where you hit 'em. The man who gets into a fight with a dangerous animal does so, ninety-nine times out of one hundred, because of some mistake of his own; but if I must get into a scrap with a buffalo or a big cat or an elephant, I'd rather have that warmed-over .375 in my hands than anything else I own or ever expect to own.

The 7 mm. magnum, I feel, is close to perfect as the caliber for all the lesser African game, including, I might say, the leopard and possibly the lion, for all our North American species that live in mountains, and for all the Asiatic types of both high and low terrain that weigh under a ton or generally don't eat people. Respected colleagues have advanced the notion that the 7 mm. magnum isn't a damned bit more effective than other calibers in what we agree is the light-rifle category where African game is concerned, but I suspect they advance such theories as an exercise in academics rather than out of conviction supported by experience. The idea certainly doesn't jibe with published ballistic data. Big 7's of one brand or another have been in my hands on every continent of this world, have accounted for so many hundreds of head of game that I won't mention figures here for fear of being called a liar by some or a murderer by the sneaker-clad old ladies, and the sum total of that experience is to lead me into the statement that for game from seventy-five to a thousand pounds, especially at ranges beyond rock-throwing yardage, this category of cartridge is the most useful we have. It hurts you little, hurts the game a great deal.

Whatever your African battery, take it with you on the plane, in the necessary number of hard-shelled cases with polyethylene liners. Bolts out of actions. Locked cases. If the guns are fancy, slip into your gear one or two cloth cases to use to protect them against dust and scratches in safari car travel. Shipping guns ahead usually means only trouble. On any stopovers en route, put the guns into bond at the airport, for the legalities of bringing a firearm into Italy, for example, are almost as bad as getting a pistol permit in New York City. If you're a decent shot, ammunition allotments for a thirty-day safari need be only something like forty to sixty rounds for your "heavy" and "medium" combined, a third to a half of these solids, and sixty rounds of "light" with no solids. Most calibers can be picked up overseas if requested beforehand but remember that rifles shoot differently with different lots, brands, and bullet weights.

A multipiece cleaning rod with solvent, patches, screwdriver, and such goes into my kit because I don't frankly want old Mgugu the gun bearer slipping gooey British oil into the bore to make my rifle shoot off, nor do I want to face the dire possibilities should he manage to switch bolts. A surgeon friend of mine had that happen and he's lucky to have a face left. Tend your own rifles. The bores don't need cleaning during the hunt anyway, not with modern ammunition.

Shotgun? Well, the sandgrouse shooting, or driven francolin, and at times waterfowling in the African way are about as fancy scatter-gunnery as you can get anywhere, sandgrouse being faster than whitewings in a Mexican field. For these, it is, of course, desirable to have your own gun, plugged off to two shots if it's a pump, left home if it's an autoloader, the British idea of gentility still being the two-barrel. But busting guinea fowl, a very desirable and rewarding activity because it produces table fare unrivaled anywhere, is more practical meat getting than sport. You spot a bunch of guineas trotting along, descend from the car with your trusty scatter-gun, walk in their direction with disarming nonchalance, or perhaps unobtrusively, like a stalking leopard. This is to give them time to get you thoroughly spotted as a menace. Next, give that up for a faster walk, followed by a trot. Break into a dead run, and finally, as the birds are about to fly, screech to a stop and blare away at them. My observation is that a ground-sluiced guinea tastes just as good as one picked off in full flight, perhaps better. So if your safari area doesn't have sandgrouse and no driven shoots are planned, figure to rent a shotgun over there. It won't fit, and it'll kick your eyeteeth loose with dynamite-loaded German shells, but it'll stop guineas. The few you can get close to, that is.

44 : The Marsh Walker

The termites that built the anthill on which I sprawled in the African twilight had expected me. Every knob of that cement-hard dirt pile poked into a tender spot. And as the fiery ball of the sun disappeared beyond the papyrus swamp, evening chill came fast and misty. The air was suddenly filled with darting batlike shapes, some form of nighthawk chasing insects, not ordinary whippoorwills but a type of nightjar I'd never seen before. Their flickering wings carried large white dots, and long slim pennant feathers projected eight or ten inches back from the tips. Oddballs, even for Africa. But darting bullbats weren't *sitatunga*. There weren't going to be any of the long-hoofed lyre-horned antelope feeding out of the swamp tonight, that was for sure, and it was too cold just to look at birds with fancy feathers.

"Screwy deal," I said to professional hunter Dave Williams as we jounced back toward camp. "There I was with Brian Hearne sailing around in the Sese Islands. They, so the story goes, are so filthy with *sitatunga* that the boss here, Ernest, got Prince Bernhard his trophy in less than a day and picked up one for himself in an hour. But we couldn't do a bit of good because Victoria Nyanza was four feet above normal water level and the swamps were small oceans. So now we come chasing three hundred miles up here to Katanga where nobody but you *ever* saw a *sitatunga*."

"Service is the motto of Uganda Wildlife Development, Ltd.," broke in Ernest Juer from the rear of the Land Rover. "Speed and service. When Dave radioed in to our Kampala office that he'd seen *sitatunga* here regularly, night and morning, we simply passed the word to you and Brian when you called in to fuel the launch at Bukakata. Here you are, what?"

"Speed, all right—eight hours in the launch with the diesel threatening to throw a con rod—and then six hours in a Land Rover with your Monte Carlo Rally technique. Plenty of speed. With two-way radio sizzling through the air, plenty of change in modern Africa, too. But I wonder what happened to Dave's *sitatunga* herd."

The *sitatunga* didn't move out into the swamp edge next morning either, though we were watching before daylight. Odd, because the animal is essentially a creature of habit. He dwells in swamps so thick a man can scarcely force his way through the seven-foot papyrus. The hairy antelope—in reality a bushbuck type that is related to the bongo, the two types of nyala, and the kudu family—grows seven-inch hoofs to support his weight in the marsh. The *sitatunga* can swim as well as he can run, and hides by sinking into a pool until only his nostrils show. But once happy in an area and in a routine, he's usually likely to stay in that spot and repeat that routine.

When the dawn watch drew a blank, we were not too down in the mouth. I had another day or two. We ground off into the rolling grassy hills to prospect for buffalo and to spot campsites for future safarists with Uganda Wildlife Development, Ltd. With one boss of UWD in camp with us, and with my friend and former Chief Game Warden John Blower back in Kampala making serious *sitatunga* medicine, we'd keep trying for a good one. "For the honor of the company," muttered Ernest, who quite obviously knew what I was thinking.

UWD does have other unique approaches to safari matters, ideas that will, I suspect, be widely imitated in the hunting areas of Africa as time goes on, that are already being imitated in Tanganyika, for example. The company is government-backed, and Uganda became independent in October of 1962, a few months after I hunted with UWD as its first client. Hence UWD can guide matters of game control and hunting to bring maximum long-term benefit to the country.

The UWD philosophy, as Juer and Blower express it, is conservation with the rifle. Game is not to be clobbered, but cropped, as a given species and area can stand harvesting. All fees for trophies taken go direct, as cash, into the coffers of the local governments—Uganda is lucky in that the tribal kingdoms visited by early Nile explorers still exist as state-like regions—so that the locals know exactly what a game animal is worth in hard coin. Any ultimate profits of UWD are likewise funneled back into the central government, earmarked solely for conservation use. Excess meat and the edible end-products of controlling the herds of buffalo and hippo that have threatened to eat themselves into starvation under the obsolete total-protection methods of Queen Elizabeth Park are sold to create further income from game. Our own states, Wyoming for example, know precisely what maintaining healthy herds of pronghorn or deer or elk means in tourist dollars. Uganda, through UWD, is applying the same principles, that's all.

"We'll be able to run twenty-one-day safaris," Juer had explained, "for roughly twenty-six hundred of your dollars, including the air fare on

Alitalia jets, to give a man eight or ten trophies and at least fourteen hunting days, plus two park visits for camera work and a couple of days of Nile perch fishing."

"You must be talking about Coolidge-type dollars," I scoffed, "the old kind that bought six or seven gallons of gas. Today's inflated bucks will get you only three."

"No, we can operate in the black," Ernest continued. "Special hunts for Karamoja kudu or hundred-pound elephant will, of course, run closer to standard Nairobi prices. Wish me luck, anyway, since this operation means a great deal to Uganda game management." *

"We could stand a dollop of luck ourselves, Page and I," ventured hunter Dave Williams as we turned back toward the swamp edge in late afternoon. This day we'd looked over a few beetling old buffalo bulls, but none were quite as heavy or wide across the mustache-shaped horns as the freakish piebald bull, almost albino white, that I had passed up a week earlier in the Lake Mboru country. There'd been fine bushbuck but we didn't need a bushbuck and some later safarist probably would.

"Those *sitatunga* must barge out sometime," Dave reassured himself. "They were regular as clockwork before you chaps came—always showed back in that sort of bay in the papyrus, where the surface is all green and looks like a lawn but is really muck up to your hips. Fed into easy range of the anthills on two evenings, too."

As he, Ernest, and I left the Land Rover to the gun bearers and hiked the last half mile toward the swamp edge a traitorous thought came into mind. *Sitatunga* are furtive, nervous. Why else would they spend their lives in impenetrable hippo swamps, in muck too thick to swim in and too thin to stand on? Perhaps Dave had watched too often, had spooked the mud-walking antelope.

But I had already come to realize from earlier days spent with Dave in the game-crammed Semliki Valley before he moved to Katanga and before Brian and I had tried the Sese Islands, that Williams was too much the professional for any such carelessness. Our doings with a certain fine buck Uganda kob, chosen from the ten thousand head that throng the four hundred square miles of the Semliki, and a certain near-hassle with a buffalo had proved that. It would be the *sitatunga's* own immediate whim, not any earlier freak of man-betraying wind, that would determine whether or not we saw them this evening.

---

* The good wishes were hardly needed. Since my experimental hunt with UWD, although techniques and prices have changed, the firm has been almost solidly booked by safari visitors, many thousands of East African pounds in trophy fees turned in, the size of controlled game areas doubled. Tanganyika developed a closely parallel system.

The anthill hadn't softened a bit since I last sprawled behind its crest. The same hard knobs rammed into the same tender spots. While I dulled my knife carving out reasonable elbow holes and digging knee rests in the sunbaked clay, getting ready just in case, the sun dropped again below the papyrus, the air cooled quickly, and those strangely feathered bullbats began their bug-catching dance.

In the short African twilight hippo bulls grunted irascible love calls from the depths of the papyrus reeds, multiple piggish grunts with appeal only to fat lady hippos. Dave and Ernest had crouched behind anthills a hundred yards or so back, well beyond the wings of a stage all set but darkly empty. Without even breeze-ripples of the papyrus tufts, the only ground movement was the slight form of a jackal, skittering nervously along the swamp edge.

A hundred hippo love grunts later I checked the scope cross hairs against the wall of reeds. Fifteen or twenty minutes more, then quick darkness would blank us out for another day. Too bad. I could exist without a trophy *sitatunga*, but it would be nice to pair the lyre-shaped horns of a swamp-walker with the heavier twists of his jungle cousin, the bongo. Ten minutes more.

Then there was a faint stir of movement far up in the head of the green-surfaced bay. The papyrus had parted, and two, three, then four brown-shadowed forms were moving into the clear. The last was the best, clearly a bull but smaller in the body than I had imagined, perhaps two hundred and fifty pounds. In the glasses it seemed I could make out faint ivory tipping on the horns. Him or nothing. But they'd have to work closer.

It was a turtle-slow race against time. The *sitatunga* must feed much closer—to the two-hundred-yard mark anyway—before I could be sure of dropping him in this light. And every dawdling minute meant that much less ability to see.

The prodding knobs of the anthill were forgotten when I edged the 7 mm. magnum up and over into position. The cross hairs were on the biggest antelope, wavering until he turned almost broadside, then steadying as I held breath and squeezed.

Recoil slid me down below the anthill lip, so I did not see him fall, nor was I able to watch the others run across the soft mud and into cover, their oversized hoofs making them light as water-striders. But the whoops from Ernest and Dave in their box seat gave me the word. The bull *sitatunga* was down and dead.

By the time Dave's skinners had wallowed out to the animal, then wallowed their way back again, dragging him across the slime, it was black dark. With the flashgun forgotten in camp, there could be no pictures, but when the Land Rover rattled up to the swamp edge we could at least measure.

"I read 27½ inches on the right side and 27¼ on the left," called out Dave. "No new record, but a very nice swamp-walker indeed."

"And you'll note," put in Ernest, "that you didn't even get your feet wet. That's UWD service, what?"

And it was. The combination of two portable radio transmitters and smart thinking on Dave's part, with only a very small chunk of patience on mine had done the business, brought into range one of the toughest to bag of the twist-horned antelope. This was a sort of team trophy. Where the *sitatunga* now hangs in my dining room there isn't any little brass plaque. If there were, it wouldn't have my name on it, but rather a line like: Through the cooperation of Dave Williams—and Guglielmo Marconi. Wasn't it Marconi who invented the radio?

45 : The Cautious Crocodile

Our stewardess shuddered in exquisite horror. She had been assigned to the Rome-Lusaka flights long enough for African tales of gore to become commonplace, but the account of crocodile activity I had just given her was too gruesome for any young lady. It had involved the messy fate of a thousand Japanese soldiers who in the mid-1940s were trapped in a Burmese mangrove swamp. They were chopped up less by the British bombardment than they were by an invasion of blood-hungry crocodiles. Only twenty survived. By this tale our pocket version of Sophia Loren was shaken from her uniform cap right down to her "alligator" pumps.

"And therein lies the paradox of the crocodile," I said to Art McGreevy in the next seat, my companion for the safari in Zambia. "He's uglier than sin and associated only with death in its more vile forms, yet is the source of footgear and handbags for the most beautiful people."

The croc certainly qualifies on the first score. Beauty the saurian cannot boast, not unless you find attractive a length of armor-plated hide— *Crocodilus nyloticus* of the African rivers can make close to twenty feet, they say, and his sea-going cousin from the Australian coast has measured closer to twenty-five—which has a yard of peg-toothed mouth gaping at one end and carries at the other a slab-sided tail muscular enough to whip the feet from under a stud zebra. The croc appears to have a specific gravity of just about 1, so he barely floats in water, or can walk around on the bottom. Hence his leg muscles aren't much for support, and he collapses into a loglike slug when sunning himself on a mudbank, but his frame packs surprising power and speed. I saw twenty-footers imitating driftwood trunks on the shores of Kenya's Lake Rudolf, each weighing close to a ton, totally sun-sluggish since they are fully protected in that area. But turn a boat as if to land and these monsters would whip into the water with ponderous agility, almost as fast as a gecko.

The croc is a well-organized animal for his job, which is to seize and haul back into deep water about anything he can clamp his beartrap jaws onto. He can stay underwater for endless minutes, or ooze along with only his nostrils and eyes showing. His eyes and his ears are rigged for submarine operation, the ears having sliding covers that keep out the water but seem to reduce not at all his ability to hear either an antelope drinking upstream or a man with a rifle walking along the shore edge. His eyes have extra see-through lids that work precisely like a skindiver's mask in sharpening underwater vision. I thought about those eyes every time we waded Zambia's slightly muddy Munyamadsi River.

The area of our safari in Zambia, the valley of the Luangwa River, a chunk of acreage roughly three hundred miles north and south and perhaps fifty the other way between two escarpments, is among other things first-rate crocodile territory. It should be, with the Luangwa flowing all year round and a whole series of feeder rivers which are either bank-full floods or strings of drying pools that hold crocs even in the dry months.

"But they're game animals here," explained Peter Hankin, chief professional of the Luangwa Safaris operational group. His son Philip was due to squire me about in our hunting block. "Your license is good for only one crocodile. Otherwise hide hunters would be in here and would exterminate the breed."

I can see reason for some degree of protection even on a predator with as few friends as the crocodile. And he has almost none. Most students of dangerous beasts feel that the crocodile accounts for the bloody deaths of more African natives than do the buffalo or the elephant or the lion taken separately or together.

But even that bloody history has to be balanced off against possible species extermination. And the hide hunters, shooting at night with lights, and preferably picking off the smaller, younger crocs for their more workable hides, could in providing shoes and handbags for the fair ladies of this world clean up the crocodiles as effectively as they ever threatened the egret or the Somali leopard. One croc on the license would be plenty for me, however, if he was a big one.

"And I can't see how busting one will be much sport anyway," I confided to Philip later on.

"You may regret that remark," he replied cryptically.

I certainly did. From here on out please understand that while shooting just any old croc may not constitute the highest form of hunting sport, I seriously consider that shooting a specific crocodile, one selected for trophy size, for example, offers as great a stalking and shooting challenge as does picking off an antelope as big-eared and spooky as, say, the kudu.

The crocodile is ugly as vice and twice as hateful. Nobody in his right mind would eat one. In desperation I once ate roast alligator tail in Bolivia, found it like chicken that had been fed a steady diet of codfish, and the Bolivian alligators are I suspect less likely to chomp on carrion than are their African relatives. But they are not stupid and most definitely not insensitive. And you do not, regardless of what the hide hunters do at night, shoot them casually in daytime hunting. The bullet must be spotted precisely right. If you do not slip the bullet in just fractionally behind the nearly invisible earhole (to blow his doorknob brain into smithereens) or hit a mite farther back to break his neck vertebrae, it's impossible to kill a crocodile quickly enough to keep him out of the river. Once in, he sinks, and that's that.

The first time we waded the Munyamadsi to hunt a prime patch of buffalo and elephant country beyond it, we met the granddaddy of all local crocodiles—ngwena in the Chuyanja tongue spoken in much of Zambia. We had eyed the river pretty carefully before slipping off our shoes and sliding into the cool water. The four natives with us made a particularly careful inspection. No doubt some of their ancestors had been taken by crocs. No eye knobs showed, no swirls broke the surface for at least fifty yards either way, and we had selected the shallowest fording place in a mile. Halfway across, we paused, partly in bravado, partly because the cold mud slishing between our toes felt so good. An upstream mudbank that had been hidden by a bend was in full view. A saurian as long as a Cadillac limousine nonchalantly slipped off the bank into deep water, the boil showing he had turned downstream in our direction.

"Wow! See that character?" I exclaimed to Philip when we, after a dozen quick strides, stood on dry land. "I'll nail his hide to the barn!"

When we returned from trying to locate a head of forty-six inches or better from three different bunches of buffalo that morning, the supercroc was back on his mudbank. With glasses, and concealed at three hundred yards, we studied him carefully. An ordinary crocodile, like an eight-footer, occupying the far end of the bar, gave us a comparison. Grandpappy was distinctly more than twice as long.

"He'll make seventeen feet anyway." Philip's guess coincided with mine.

I picked the 7 mm. magnum from the hands of Jemusi, who had the job of toting my camera bag and whatever rifle was not slung on my own shoulder, checked the chamber, and with Philip made a long sneak that ended at the undercut riverbank perhaps fifty yards from the mudbar. Cautiously we peeked over. The big croc was gone. Had he seen us from three hundred yards? Had he somehow smelled us upwind? Or had he, as the natives insisted, felt the vibrations of our footsteps? Or had he just decided to swim off on his own?

Two days later it happened again. We sighted the big croc from several hundred yards downstream, sneaked into possible shooting position, found him long gone. Uncanny. We built a blind and waited two hours. He never returned. He *knew*.

The lesser crocs weren't quite that jumpy, but even they, after their sandy siestas had been interrupted by humans a few times, began to slide off into the water and knobs-only watchfulness at the slightest suspicion of an approach.

"Crocs may be reptiles, and their brains may be the size of a small orange, but they certainly get smart fast," I said to Philip. "Let's leave this section of the river alone for a few days, let 'em cool off."

Philip agreed. He even refrained from pointing out that he'd said it would be tough to take a specific trophy croc in fair daytime fight.

But the idea of resting the area didn't work out so well. A hippo, it seemed, ended his days in the Munyamadsi, not far from the steep-banked section with its beaches and bars that we had named, for obvious reasons, Crocodile Alley. Every saurian in the river, and a hundred or two from the Luangwa itself, came to dine on the defunct hippo. And a dead hippo is a lot of dinner, a couple of tons of edibles, and while crocodiles can go a long time between feedings, they are pretty casual about what is considered edible. The more rotten a carcass, the better they like it, very possibly because while their jaws have great closing force, they are not designed to bite off chunks as a shark does but rather to tear by grabbing and twisting or shaking violently. The deader that hippo got the better the crocs liked it. Yet they fed not constantly, but in waves, and no matter how sneakily we approached we never could catch out on the bank, sleeping off a surfeit of hippo, a really big crocodile. Certainly we never fooled the Big Daddy of the river. Ordinary crocs sunned by dozens, but never a really huge one.

"Not much left of that water-horse but skin and a bad smell, either," mused Philip. "A day or so more and these crocs will spread out again up and down the river."

"Lion we bagged pretty handily," I said. "And a kudu was no great problem, nor respectable buff, and we've even fooled a leopard—but these crocs, or that croc, has had us whipped for nearly a week."

I had come to the realization that a beast I'd always regarded as vermin, hardly fit prey for a trophy hunter, could be, if you become selective, as tough hunting as any of the fancier critters that hang on den walls. So far, the denizens of the Munyamadsi had had no reason to rely on their green-mottled armor. They'd beaten us on three scores—sight, scent, and sound.

On our last two-way crossing of the river we weren't even thinking of crocodiles. A runner had come over from one of the far villages with a tale of elephants. There were many huge *njovu* with great white teeth, as he recounted the story. We splashed across, this time with great disdain for any lurking reptiles, to track down the hulking gray sources of his report. The elephants weren't there. They seldom are. Tracks, but small tracks and traveling fast to extend a lead already too great for sensible pursuit. It was noon before we returned to the river edge, striking it a half mile below the Crocodile Alley section.

"The rest of the hippo must've broken loose and floated downstream," I commented to Philip as we started over the bank. "Look at those crocs on the sand!"

We hastily pulled back out of sight. Perhaps four hundred yards above, a bar projected from the far shore. There were a dozen reptiles sunning on it. A very large one, precisely how large it was hard to tell from two furlongs, occupied the place of honor. Utterly relaxed, he was several feet longer than the others.

No conversation was needed. With a quick wave to the bearers to stay well behind us, back from the river's edge, Philip and I swung off in an upstream circle. We could approach the undercut bank from behind a clump of thornbush that grew at just the right point.

I kept thinking about the croc's ability to sense vibrations. Was it really a myth? If they couldn't hear my feet, they might at least pick up my heartbeat. This stalk held more excitement than sneaking up on a record-sized impala, or getting up close enough to a bull elephant to gauge his ivory!

As we slipped out toward the bush, I glanced automatically upstream. Were we hidden from any crocs up that way? Too late. A huge saurian, pausing not to consider anything more than the flicker of movement he had spotted from over two hundred yards, slid into the stream. He looked very large—could've been Grandpappy, the Monster of the Munyamadsi. But the one we'd seen first, if he still snoozed under the opposite bank, would be big enough.

At a quick glance he had looked like a fifteen-footer, with a full yard of peg-toothed mouth open to let some type of tick bird clean his gums of bits of hippo. Now if his belly was full enough to keep him snoozing I might well have it made.

Leaving Philip at the bush, I dropped to the sand and with loaded rifle began to crawl, first on elbows and knees, then belly-flat to the sun-hot clay, toward the edge of the river. Within two feet of it I stopped, pushed the rifle barrel forward and over the edge, strained to lift my eyes just enough to see the bar forty or fifty yards away.

Two of the crocs were already awake and moving toward the water, but the big one was still fast asleep, almost straight broadside to me. Now, just barely behind the ear.

The slight click of the safety brought open one slitted eye. I saw it move in the riflescope. But I also saw the cross hairs rest with deadly steadiness on the leathery plate hiding the crocodile's brain pan. Too late for that reptile. The rifle bucked and the top of his skull lifted off. The croc shuddered once.

Abelo the skinner and Gosamu who carried the water and Jemusi who toted the camera and Amoni who smoked too many cigarettes and carried as little as possible ran a dead heat to the riverbank. They were more pleased than Philip and I. Why not? The toothy horror that lay dead on the bar across from us might well have eaten one of their grandmothers.

A trickle of blood ran from the defunct croc into the stream. It could bring back the reptiles that had oozed off downstream at the shot. I fired again into the water, and Philip blasted another waterspout. Then we waded across, running the shallow places. I wanted the boys to repeat the wading process so I could photograph them from beyond the limp carcass of the crocodile, but they'd have none of it.

Fifteen feet of croc isn't as much as seventeen, but it's as much as two and a half tall men lengthwise in the mud. That size of croc isn't pretty, either, because it's a sharp reminder of what the world must've been like a few million years ago when teeth, claws, and armor ruled the earth. But that much croc can be satisfying, and now I'm completely over any crocodile fever. Just one problem. What to do with all that belly skin? How many suitcases will it make?

46 : Death in the Morning

The man was dead. He had been gored, trampled into the red sand, tossed like a bundle of rags, ripped again and again by black horns. He was bloodily, messily dead—destroyed by a bull buffalo in an utterly senseless attack.

Now, it isn't often that an African buffalo charges a man for no reason at all. Yet one had murdered this native without provocation. The evidence was still clear in the sand. During the night the buffalo herd had moved up from the river, through the crop fringe of the native shambas, and on into the hills. But one bull had dropped out of the herd and stood for hours in a patch of bush not far from a footpath that meandered among the huts. In the freshening dawn the native and his brother had come along that path. And then—for no reason at all and from at least sixty yards—the Cape buffalo had rushed him, smashed him.

The tracks were clear—deep-cut marks of spread hoofs. Here the bull had angled out of his hideaway and rushed down on the hapless native with the power of a locomotive. Then the prints blurred into the smears of brutal murder, finally showing clear again where the buffalo had slowly returned to his hideout, leaving behind the bloodied bundle that had, only moments before, been a living man.

As I've said, this kind of blind, insensate attack doesn't happen often, even among game animals as massively dangerous as the Cape buffalo. When one does charge, it is usually because it has been wounded—has good reason for attacking man. José Simoes, the professional hunter who was studying the scene with me, agreed with me on that. Only once or twice in his years of hunting Mozambique, first for meat and later with clients, had he run into a situation like this.

José had been one of the professionals back when meat hunting was big business. In those days there were between forty and fifty working hunters, each with a trained squad of some thirty natives, who hacked away at the vast herds roaming the Marromeu and Cheringoma plains below the Zambezi. José had had his close calls in the course of shooting hundreds of buffalo, many of them with an ordinary .270 and soft-points, in order to provide sugar-plantation workers with meat. It had been dangerous work.

"It was not the danger that stopped me, though," he said. "The buffalo is not usually like this, a murderer of unarmed men, but honest and brave like a Miura fighting bull in facing his equals. I have dared buffalo to come and fight me because I knew we could do fair battle together, but this was pure murder."

As a guide, José displayed that combination of guts and stubborn—even foolhardy—courage that the Scandinavians call *siseu*. This I knew, for he'd been alongside me in one scrap with a pair of black Mozambique bulls, and there was no questioning his bravery—or that of Juan Cazadore, the long-limbed black gun bearer he had assigned to me. Juan and I, looking for a fifty-incher to outdo the pair of forty-six-inch trophies I'd taken in Kenya, had also met the bulls of Portuguese East Africa. We'd run into no crisis—merely a stroke of bad luck. The trio of oldsters we'd found had run behind a big clump of bush, and when they reappeared I broke the neck of the wrong bull—not the fifty-plus giant I had marked earlier. The kill had one broken horn, more than a foot of it having been smashed off in some herd fracas, yet the horns were still almost four feet in spread.

It was the government, José told me, that had put a stop to the practice of running the black Marromeu herds with trucks, as our Sioux once ran the bison of North America on horseback. It was government action, inspired by José's conservation-minded friends, Dr. Palhinha and Señor Tavares, that had reduced the number of meat hunters from forty to twenty, then to eight, and eventually eliminated the practice. Economics had helped. Stiff restrictions put on in 1954 limited the buffalo and elephant kill to thirty tons of meat, and required a tag of one hundred escudos, or three dollars and thirty cents, for each animal. The tariff was four times as much for an elephant worth less than one hundred dollars at railhead. These restrictions, plus the rising prices of trucks and supplies, had soon put the casual meat hunters, and finally many professionals, out of business. It was, I knew, a source of great relief to José, both as a person and as a safari outfitter, that the buffalo herds were scattering and growing ever thicker over the rich graze and parklike forest that covers much of Mozambique. He respected buffalo. But from the evidence before us, this was murder, an unprovoked charge on a defenseless black.

"Hard to understand," I offered. "Sometimes they won't charge even with reason!"

"That is so," agreed José as he studied the clues in the sand.

There had been several buff dropped by my rifle up on Mount Kenya, I recalled. None of them had charged, nor had the second bull of the pair that Bob Kuhn and I took on the Rift Valley escarpment. Maybe I'd also been lucky with the brave bulls in Tanganyika, and certainly we'd been fortunate with two in the impenetrable thickets beyond the Mara. My

friend Bob Johnson had faced a charge on our 1958 hunt and lived to tell
of it. Somehow or other, in my hunts in British Africa, and in French- and
Belgian-controlled areas as well, the buffalo I'd met and shot at close
quarters in densest cover, though dying bravely enough, had never seen fit
to charge. Which was all right too.

But common sense indicated that my string of good fortune must have
an end. There had been times enough when buffalo, unwounded and unseen until the last moment, could have committed murder with me or anybody else as the victim. They didn't—so why had this bull rushed down on
a native who bore neither weapon nor malice? That was a puzzler for both
José and me.

The night before, on the way back to Simoes's North Camp, we had
come back empty-handed from hunting a kudu area. The camp needed
meat, and just at dusk José had taken a chancy shot at a reedbuck. Perhaps
it had been hit, perhaps not, but the little buck couldn't be trailed in the
darkness, which drops over equatorial Africa like a curtain when the sun
goes. So at first morning light José sent Juan Cazadore, a superb tracker
usually assigned as gun bearer during my safari, to investigate while we
organized for the new day's hunt.

It is to Juan—afraid of no animal, few men, and, judging by the number
of his wives, no woman—that the rest of this story belongs. Carrying into
the dawn light the five-shot Cogswell & Harrison .375 that had been on
his shoulder during the days when he and José had hunted buffalo and
meat elephant together, Juan had hiked the straight half mile or so to the
last trace of the reedbuck.

As he sought its blood spoor he heard the dead man's last scream, the
affrighted howls of his brother, and the bellowing of the blood-mad buffalo.
Quickly he ran the five or six hundred yards to the scene. There the
murder evidence became as clear to him then as it was to us now, an hour
later. And then Juan had taken onto himself, alone, that part of the white
man's burden that involves the execution of animals dangerous to the unarmed blacks.

Juan told his story simply. He was sure from the tracks, he said, that
the bull had gone back into the very clump of brush from which it had
made the fatal rush. But no blotch of black hide was visible, no stir of
movement. José circled at fifty yards, deliberately gave the hidden bull his
scent, but the buffalo refused to stir from cover. José knew what he had to
do. With no one to back him—just his rifle and its full magazine—he
worked into the tangle of a fresh-felled tree that had been burned off its
stump by the natives in clearing the area, and stood by its trunk.

Then he shouted at the buffalo, taunted it as a matador in a bull ring of Spain cries *"Toro!"* until finally the brush parted and a ton of black fury, its horns already blood-tipped, launched itself at him.

It took every shot from Juan's .375 to stop that charge, and he hit the bull hard every time—in the head, in the shoulders, and finally in the spine. It lay before us now, a black hulk only five steps from where Juan had stood, perhaps fifty from the huddled body of the black it had earlier smashed into death.

There was little more we could do. "I must send the truck to notify the D.C. of all the details," said José, "and we will take this man to the village of his father for burial. That is all."

But it wasn't really all. There remained points on which I for one will forever wonder. Why should a buffalo in the prime of life, accustomed to the villagers' activities, unwounded, bearing no evidence of illness, charge down on that defenseless African to gore and stamp him like that? What murderous instinct had prompted the bull hiding in the bush by the path that morning? I doubt we'll ever know the answers. The ways of Africa, its animals, and its people are often strange indeed.

---

47 : This Trophy Business

Longhairs and intellectuals tend to decry trophy hunting as an exercise of competing egos. As is so often true of aphoristic cracks by people who are themselves strangers to the subject they're commenting on, there is part truth, but only part truth, in the accusation.

Humans are naturally competitive. Ardrey, in fact, would have us as very highly competitive and aggressive animals, the descendants of a hunting ape who fed himself and his family by slaying game with a club made from an antelope thigh bone. Were we not naturally competitive, life would be minus not only football games and track meets, but also bereft of most technological development either good or bad and, it seems to me, much of our real sense of unity with family, tribe, or nation. There is grave question, however, as to how far the competitive urge should properly be carried into hunting—or fishing—activities. Fishing derbies usually degenerate into a sadly low level of sporting ethics.

Hunting is a basic competition to start with, anyway. It always involves some conflict of man against nature, whether you consider nature the steepness of the sheep mountain, the bitterness of a subfreezing duck blind, or the highly developed cunning of an old buck deer. I know from long personal experience the agonizing lung-bursting competition of one runner against another; but I honestly doubt that there is great difference between that, in severity of strain, and the effort of a determined hunter, perhaps a mite soft from the exigencies of modern life, to make that last ridge beyond which, he hopes, his ram may be in range. The athlete recovers sooner, that's for sure. But so long as the competition is between man and the animal or natural forces, it is a healthy one. It brings out the best, really, in both man and game.

It is only when this competition involves man, while still applied to hunting, that the egghead criticism becomes justified. Compete seriously with your hunting partner for the bigger bull, and a friendship may be destroyed. At least one divorce among my acquaintances started when man and wife got into a dog-eat-dog competition on their second safari. I once told a long-time friend that I doubted I'd ever take him on another big-game hunt because he was just too disgustingly lucky, as indeed he was. The words were halfway out before I had enough wit or sense of proportion to turn them into comedy. The wrong sort of competition can be destructive.

Probably more important is the effect of overdeveloped man-to-man competition on hunting ethics, especially among those individuals, often successful, who feed on the urge to win. Listening to a gathering of such people, each outbragging the other on some recent accomplishment, may essentially be high comedy, but when you know that one notable in the trophy race has bought prize heads, or shot them under jacklight, or paid off a Yukon Indian to keep a Dall ram in view all summer until the season opened, or shucked out major money to bribe officials into granting permission on a protected species, or suborned a guide to sneak into a park area, or used a helicopter or light plane when such is clearly taboo, or any of the dozen or so dubious practices that have been resorted to by men determined to win at any cost, such becomes direst tragedy. It can only destroy the moral tone, the ethical level of the whole sport.

Nor are the ladies entirely immune to such human failing. I distinctly recall one of the fair sex who was firm in her wish to be the first Texas lady ever to slay a bongo. She got the bongo, too, after spending thirty or forty thousand bucks and failing on several chances, but I'm not at all sure that the victory was worth the cost. Even so, her attack was far more ethical than that of the horn buyer or the murderer who bribes his guide to let him shoot game beyond his license.

The effect on guides or professional hunters of such competitions among men, rather than between men and nature, is profound. The Nairobi professional who fattens his client's pride with the information that his latest Thompson gazelle, or kudu, or whatever, has just made the Rowland Ward record list, and backs that statement with a phony measurement and citation of an edition of Ward that was printed two decades back, has not enlarged his profession, only his customer's hat size. Many years ago, I caught my head shikari feeding up his sleeve the tape with which we were measuring a tiger. He was just a bit more obvious about it. Surely any man should be able to do his own fibbing.

Competition against an absolute, or a set of norms, as in the Boone and Crockett Club record lists for North American game, or even the Rowland Ward lists when they are properly handled with up-to-date books and measurement methods, is of a very different color. Here the search for a top-quality specimen is not so much against other men as against luck or the forces of nature. You want a record-level mountain caribou? You go to the likeliest area for such, as I did in British Columbia in 1970; you look over as many stag caribou as time and strength permit; and if one seems probable to score over 390—which means a supercaribou indeed, the hatrack to end all hatracks, you bend every effort to kill it cleanly. And *maybe* you succeed.

In the whole program this is called selective shooting. It is the highest form of hunting activity, since the stag or bull of this level is, most of the time, well beyond his breeding prime, is no longer transferring his physical attributes to future animals. Verging on the period of age and senescence, he uses up feed but makes no contribution to his kind's welfare; trimming him from the herd is of actual benefit to it.

This style of competition, against the norms of the species, has to be grossly overdone to become sinful. Quite evidently, of course, guides and outfitters cannot be expected to produce "record-level" trophies for all their customers; and equally evident the man who hunts with no other end in mind, purely the acquisition of a set of horns Boone and Crockett wide, with no feeling for the auxiliary pleasures of hunting, the comradeship of the campfire, the spiritual uplift of mountain fastnesses, the simple challenge of outwitting an animal on its own terrain, has cheated himself.

Essentially, competition, as the TV-watcher conceives that term, has no place on the hunting scene. We hunt perhaps to beat ourselves, or to triumph over nature, perhaps to beat on their own ground animals of greater strength or sharper senses, but not, if we are ethical beings, just to beat other men.

48 : The Monarch of Kudu Valley

"You've tagged this place with the wrong name, Mac," I said as we creaked wearily back into camp. "Shouldn't be Kudu, but Hoodoo Valley."

"Righto," our professional hunter agreed in pure Kenya jargon. "The way these blahrsted blighters have been giving us the twist, there's a hoodoo in it somewhere. Bloody awful, that's what."

"You can say that again," Bob chimed in with straight Connecticut Yankee. "These kudu make whitetail look stupid."

My own ideas as to the comparative cunning of deer and the shamba-raiding kudu behind our Kandoa camp in Tanganyika had come to tally with those of my artist colleague Bob Kuhn. The big twist-horned antelope of East Africa could not only see farther and smell farther and hear better than any whitetail that ever jumped a windfall, but they could drift off into tall grass and *myambo* bush like striped gray ghosts, then ooze into sight again five hundred yards away where least expected. Never did they make the false move a deer so often will. One herd, living in a valley no more than three miles by two, had kept us bamboozled and bewildered for four straight days.

Not that we hadn't expected trouble with kudu. On our fast flight across to Europe and on to Kenya, Bob Kuhn and I had talked little but African game. During the southbound leg toward Nairobi, by the time our aircraft was skimming past Mount Kenya we had about agreed that buffalo might be tough to kill, but kudu would be hard to hunt, especially in cover thickened by the rains.

On safari with Tony Dyer a few days later up in Kenya, where kudu are rarer than hamburger in a ball-park sandwich, I'd fallen onto both greater and lesser kudu trophies, but they had been unadulterated luck. To get a fifty-inch whopper down in Tanganyika, where we'd come now with Owen McCallum, the hunting maestro Hunters Ltd. had lent us for the second stage of Operation Africa, was going to be rugged. Mac had already made that clear.

"You'll paint no pictures of kudu while they stand around, Bob," he had explained as we rattled south on the Cape to Cairo Road. "And you, gun writer, will get no setup shots like that last impala," he had said to me. "Without time to get into the Ugalla country, we're going to have to hunt kudu in Kandoa, where they've been chased before. Right back of where we'll camp there's a little valley, like a crater, with an old boss kudu we hunted for a week last year and never got a shot at. He spots his blasted cows around like a lot of ruddy guards. With their big ears flapping, there's just no way of getting at the old man. This bull runs over fifty inches, too; might be sixty on the twist."

"Could we push the bunch into rifleshot?" I asked.

"We tried that, too." Mac paused to concentrate on wheeling the safari car through a swatch of frightened *gombies* that a cattle herder was trying to whistle off the road. "We used all the boys in camp and a couple of locals, even tried driving the car into the valley, since the grass was all burned off then. Got closest that way—four hundred yards, and they took out like bloody rockets. These kudu know all the answers, and if you get even a bash at the old man you'll be lucky."

We made the one hundred and seventy miles down from Mto-Wa-Mbu, where we had stopped to make photographic acquaintance with a couple of buffalo, in very good time. By 4 o'clock our camp was a going concern, and a two-hundred-shilling kudu ticket was burning a big hole in my pocket. So we tried the valley herd the first time. We were *not* lucky.

Even so, Asmani, an ivory-toothed fount of local hunting information, hadn't given us any bum steers. He had said there were *tendalla mkubwa* everywhere behind the hills. The knotted handkerchief perched on his woolly head Topsy-style may have earned him the nickname Rabbit-Ears, but he knew a carrot from a kudu. They were 'most everywhere—everywhere we weren't.

With Asmani picking the path, the 7 mm. Mashburn magnum on my shoulder, and Methui, Mac's gun bearer, swinging along behind with the .375 Weatherby in case we bumped into something tougher than a kudu, we made a silent procession around the western edge of the craterlike valley. Some of the grass was burned, and the bush had dried down enough so that in spots we could see as much as a hundred yards. But only from the point we finally climbed, cleared by fire and running out into the bowl several furlongs, could we see the whole valley. There were a few acres burned clear, even one or two smoking logs where woodcutters or casually passing Warangi had performed their usual July function of firing the shoulder-high grass. Everywhere else baobab trees and more baobab trees reared above brush, and brush burst up through walled grass. Tough country to hunt. So we sat and looked.

Mac saw kudu first. A cow, mooching along on the edge below us at five or six hundred yards. Then with the glasses we could pick up more

until the count was ten. A pair of very young bulls (spikes in U.S. par-
lance) moved out from the euphorbias to the east and joined the herd. No
master kudu? No real *ndume?* Had he died or been picked off by some
luckier gent? Then a fair bull trotted out from the eastern side of our
point, momentarily showing clear as he crossed a burnt brush patch to
catch up with the cows. One—two—two and a half twists, enough for a
trophy. But he was already at four hundred yards and going, too much of
a shot so early in the game. We watched him sidle in with the cows,
shouldering them around as if he bossed the whole shebang. But he was
only the second-ranker. When another bull loped out of hiding and put an
end to such presumption, even without binoculars we could spot him as
the master bull. White tips on his full-twist horns caught the sun even at
that yardage, and if he wouldn't go well over fifty inches a steel tape must
be rubber. But he stayed smack in the middle of the herd of constantly
shifting cows.

"Want to try a stalk?" asked Mac. "I doubt we can get into range even
if we find him in that grass, but we won't spook 'em out of the valley by
trying."

For the first hundred yards off the ridge we had good cover, but then a
stretch of burn left us naked as goldfish. That may have done it. Even before we were submerged in the sea of shoulder-tall grass, so Methui said
afterward, the kudu began to ghost off. Mac and I caught one glimpse of
white-striped flanks, and when we fingernailed up the slick sides of a
baobab to get above the ten-foot *myambo* brush two cows and a small bull
focused eyes and ears on us from a furlong out. But we never saw the big
bull again that first evening.

Kuhn had it right the next night when we sneaked up to a glassing
point on another hill. From there we'd seen the group of hump-shouldered
antelope, and lost them in the brush on another stalk. He announced a
proper method of plugging the master bull kudu. "Bring up a couple of
four-inch mortars," was Bob's idea, "plant 'em on the hills back of camp
and lay down a barrage. I'll spot for you from that chewed-up baobab over
there." Unsporting, maybe, but apparently some such desperation was the
only practical scheme for beating the combination of dense cover, keen
senses and savvy of the valley terrain that kept these kudu completely safe.
Frustration was too weak a word as we slogged back to camp and called for
"*Magi moto!*" to wash the thorns and ash smears from our feet and legs.

A bull kudu, close to five feet at the shoulders and over five hundred
pounds, pushing six hundred on occasion, with a rack fifty inches or so on
the beam though with spirals instead of sprockets, is like a smart bull elk.
He's a browsing animal rather than a grazer, true, nipping off leaves of the
myambo by preference, and he's not shaded in brown or tan but is smooth-

haired gray with multiple light stripes down his flanks. He carries a whitish line of crest and throat hairs rather than the dark and full neck covering of our bull wapiti. But in acquiring unto himself a harem of slick cows, and in using them as protection for his regal self, he's a dead ringer for the wisest elk that ever whistled in the Bighorns.

Occasionally a kudu is spotted from a car and knocked over by some lucky lad suited in khaki fresh from the needles of Kharmali in Nairobi. This nicely laundered safarist thereafter figures his spiral trophy was a soft touch. In the same way, the dude who rolls off a saddle horse and pots an elk, any elk, may decide elk hunting is merely a horse ride. But working kudu that have been hard hunted, bulls that never grew those long horns by being dumb, is a tale with another theme.

Bull kudu run with their cows all year round, rut or no, and they never take a midday snooze without picketing the bed with bright-eyed and funnel-eared ladies of the harem. When trouble crackles in the thicket, it's the cows who take the rap by moving first. If they don't get shot at (which is not only illegal and unethical but unwise because cows are hornless), the master bull delays not in moving up to protection in the middle of the bunch. Only seldom—as we once saw the old boss kudu of Kandoa do— will a kudu pull the mule-deer stunt of standing on an open ridge to look back. Thick stuff, even dense hawk's-bill thorn and *myambo*, is pie for a kudu. He lays those heavy spirals back along his withers and greases away like a sneaking whitetail in a cedar swamp. In the short grass of October it's possible that a Tanganyika kudu may be as easy to approach as a Wyoming elk is in bugling time, but in June and early July below the equator, when the grass is up over your ears and the bush is still green from the rains, the advantage is all with the kudu.

Mac had never hunted North American game, of course, but after we'd swapped stories a few tired evenings over the spuds and roast impala he agreed with me in grading the kudu's vision as sharper than that of either deer or elk. Not only do they spot movement, but they seem also able to identify stationary humans, which our deer critters don't do well. Their sense of smell we ranked as good as any in the antelope family, and kudu cows certainly work their noses overtime.

The ears—or rather the kudu's reaction to sound—I'd personally rate away ahead of any of our North American critters carrying hatracks. Kudu near the native castor-bean farms or shambas pay no mind to sounds of chopping or pan-beating any more than do whitetails outside a Maine logging camp; but give them a twig snap in the brush, and they take out, right now. They don't follow the example of our deer in wasting fatal seconds trying to spot the source of a noise. Nor do kudu bolt, to run blindly into trouble or a waiting rifle. They move at a trot, rarely a run, and sneak through cover. Still-hunting kudu in heavy grass makes trailing Michigan swamp whitetails a game of mumblety-peg, and British Columbia elk a test only of leg muscles.

On the morning of the fourth day, we figured we had the master bull in a box. With the sun so high that it had long since burned away the dawn chill, we were peeled down for fast action when we spotted his white-tipped horns above the green brush. He was moving in behind a particularly fat baobab, fully fifty feet around the trunk.

"If he doesn't come out of there, it's five bob to one he's lain down. It's long past feeding time now," was Mac's verdict.

Two pairs of binoculars, Mac's and mine, stayed on that green patch for twenty minutes. Thirty. No movement. Must be settled down in the shade for the midday hours.

"Let's take Idi," I said to Mac, "and leave Bob and Methui up here with one set of glasses to spot for us. If the old man is asleep, alone, the three of us might just get in on him."

"Righto," Mac agreed, and picked out a series of baobabs and cindery patches to give him a line on the fateful green clump.

We sneaked in there on little cat feet, easing rubber down onto crispy crunchy burnt grass, tenderly sliding our worn khakis past scratching thorns. We were twice as quiet as man is meant to move. But past the edge of the green growth, to within fifty yards of the baobab—and there, staring straight at us, was a cow kudu! Beyond her another winnowed the air with ears and nose. Where they'd come from is still a mystery, since in the morning of glassing the area only the big bull had shown.

"That tears it," Mac sucked through his teeth. "Let's back out of here now before they're sure of us."

With snail movements we oozed out of sight, but that one unfortunate glimpse by the sentinel cows had done the business. When Idi and Mac tried a flanking movement calculated to drive the whole herd past where I might get a shot, the "whole bunch of bloody blinking expletives and cuss-words broke out over the profanely named ridge," as Mac put it. Flim-flammed again.

"When these characters scram, they don't even do you the courtesy of waving a white rear end at you the way our Connecticut deer do. They're downright unmannerly," was Bob's supper comment after we had gone scoreless that fourth day. "And they certainly gave you and Mac the business this afternoon when you waited for the bunch to move into that euphorbia patch. What spooked the cows, anyway?"

Mac and I hadn't been sure. Maybe one of us had twitched his nose to shake off a tsetse fly. We'd been standing in deep shadow on the down-wind side, and had kept a curtain of brush between us and the advance guard of a herd that was feeding toward the forest to lie up for the day. Our hideaway was so dense that we could barely spot the kudu, but they'd somehow sensed us and ghosted off so suddenly that we never did know for sure whether there'd been a bull along or not.

Four days of it—no runs, no hits, all errors. The next morning was the last dawn chance we'd have if we were to get through Arusha into Nairobi and catch the plane for Ethiopia.

Overcast, it was a good morning to hunt. The kudu would probably feed later in the day, and there'd be less revealing glint from binoculars or gun metal. "Furthermore," said Mac, "it's Sunday, and that's my lucky day. Remember the buffalo?"

"Could be," I agreed, gulping another cup of *chai* against the pre-dawn shivers. "But also remember that the hyena we saw yesterday evening wasn't one of those lucky striped ones."

We had no plan of campaign for the last go. Already we'd tried everything the Kandoa general staff had to offer. Maybe some senile or idiotic kudu would pose for us. We'd look and hope.

Past the big baobab with the scarred trunk, where the Warangi had slabbed off bark from which to twist ropes, we sneaked up onto the lookout point. Another fire had burned the day and night before on the south slope, but even so one small bunch of kudu moved across the fresh burn. They were a mile away and no big bull. A pair of warthogs snouted around in the brush a furlong below us, and in the dawn quiet we could hear them grunt over a choice root. There was less animal movement down in the valley than we'd seen on any previous morning.

Then off to the east, working downslope, my 7 X 35's picked up a gray movement, a bull kudu, still too far off to assay his horns.

"Mac, if that one moves anywhere in range, or even out of range, I'm going to take a crack at him," I whispered. "Let's sneak down to that point by the stump, where we can cover this side of the burn."

The bull fed along quietly as we worked down into position. His line should carry him past the point at close to six hundred yards, we agreed. That's much too far for a sane sporting shot, but between a rock and the stump I was braced for a solid sitting hold, and I'd shot the 7 mm. Mashburn magnum enough at all ranges, with hundreds of head of big game to the rifle's credit, to make an educated guess as to the curve the fast-moving one-hundred-and-seventy-five-grain Nosler slug would follow. Once I was set and solid—nothing to do but wait until the bull kudu moved into a clear spot, if he would.

"That's the old one, all right," Mac muttered quietly from under his steady binoculars. "He'll tape better than fifty, and the horns go into their third twist."

That remark didn't ease the tension, nor did my heartbeat slacken when the kudu stopped and seemed to look straight at us from behind a tangle of green acacia. The 4X scope cross hairs bulked fat, and his gray body, although I knew it would weigh a quarter ton, seemed too small for a fair target. About six hundred yards. A kudu's body should span between twenty-four and thirty inches at the withers. Between one and a half and two body depths of holdover should do it if he'd step clear of that brush. Now!

The *whomp* of the rifle was still jarring my ears when Mac shouted. "You hit the bugger! I could see no bullet splash and he stumbled a bit. He isn't even running!"

By that time I had recovered from recoil and had picked up the bull kudu in the rifle scope. He wasn't sprinting as a scared and unwounded animal would. He was at a walk, slow and sick-moving. I fired again, but this shot was too low and flared dust under his belly. Even that did not speed the bull beyond the painful walk that carried him into thick brush. He'd been hit hard by that first lucky one.

In seconds we had lined his point of last showing with a fat-trunked baobab, and assigned Bob and Methui the lonely job of waving us to the right spot from their vantage point on the ridge. Mac, Rabbit-Ears and the sharp-eyed Idi fanned alongside me down into the brush, beelined for where we'd last seen the kudu. Ash from the seared grass blacked our shins and stuck to sweaty faces. Without blood sign it would be a tough job to find that wounded bull.

And there wasn't blood sign. Perhaps there was hair back where he'd been hit, but no red spots showed in the dragging prints that lay clear wherever the grass had burned to ground level. Only if he stayed on the burn could we follow the track fast and easily.

But his prints, surprisingly neat and small for an animal of the bull kudu's size, moved into shoulder-high grass, grass mazed with meandering trails. Which way?

A hand motion sent Asmani squirming up the nearest baobab, his callused toes digging into the slick bark until he reached branches fifteen feet above ground. Now which way? Idi was convinced the proper trail lay south, toward the opening of the valley and the water any wounded animal craves, but Asmani, eyes popping, pointed towards the easterly ridge, perhaps a hundred yards up. Even my ignorance of Swahili let me understand that he was telling us the bull was close, very close, moving slow, very slow.

Off we ran, Mac and I, stumbling through the grass and tearing brashly through thorn clumps. Lyred horns wavered over the brush a hundred yards ahead, but the striped body of the bull was not visible, no shot possible, until he began to stumble across a burnt patch.

Winded, I brought the rifle up for a try at the shoulder. Dust puffed off hide, the bull staggered, then rolled for the count. The master kudu of the valley was ours after five days of struggle, and Mac was beating me over the shoulders with most un-English lack of reserve. I was too happy to speak.

When we taped the horns—fifty-five long inches around the curve, a superb trophy in any man's language, worth five or even fifteen days of struggle—when we'd admired the massive dove-gray body with its white markings and mane, and when we'd taken a bookful of pictures, Mac and Bob and I sat under a baobab as the skinner went to work. We sat quietly, thoughtfully.

Finally I spoke what was probably in the minds of all three of us. "You know," I said, "this kudu is one of the two or three best trophies I'll take home from Africa, but I'll never look at him on the wall without realizing one thing. We didn't beat the old bull quite fairly. We didn't outwit him or outstalk him. He wasn't defeated by man—he was beaten only by one of man's newfangled gadgets, a hotshot modern rifle."

"Plus a pocketful of luck and a baobab tree," reminded Mac gently. "It took all three." And so it did, to bring down the master bull of Kudu Valley.

---

49 : Look Out for Mama!

The small, dark but important-looking gent was throwing a real tizzy, African-style. No sooner had our safari car rumbled into the clearing around his Kukangu shamba than he buttonholed white hunter Tony Dyer. With hardly a pause for the *"Jambo, bwana"* of greeting he launched into a flood of Swahili, both hands violently accenting his excited harangue.

On the middle seat of our hunting buggy, gun bearer Onyango and the two skinners—the Pygmy Shabani and his helper Kibuphi—were flashing acres of white teeth at the small man's tale of woe. But artist Bob Kuhn and I, not savvying much more Swahili than the word *k'faru* that emerged from the sputter, were totally stumped. For minutes there was no damming the flood of deep and fierce indignation.

"What's wrong? Don't tell me somebody stole his chickens and he wants to blame it on the Mau Mau?"

Tony waved the excited Meru to silence and explained. "No, this is most important to him, and it may be a good break for us. This chap is the headman here—his family and one or two others live inside that *boma*. He's popping his cork because a rhino has been raising bloody hades here for three days, won't let them work their fields. It seems *faro* knocked down the sides of their irrigation ditch and won't let them clear it, and this morning the rhino chased his third wife—the young-looking one over there holding the *m'toto* in her arms—up a thorn tree."

"Big deal," I said. "No wonder he's some scared and a lot mad—especially that business about putting his new wife up an acacia."

"Who wouldn't be?" offered Bob. "He probably figures that job is reserved to him. But what's with the rhino now?"

"These people are really terrified," replied Tony, "and they don't dare to look for him, but we certainly will. Which *bunduki*, friend Page, the .458 or the .375?"

As I climbed out of the car I was already pulling the big .458 Winchester bold-action out of its saddle scabbard—which is a far better way, incidentally, to tote carefully sighted rifles over roughest Africa than the usual clamp racks—and was fumbling five-hundred-grain solids into its magazine. Bob collected his cameras and we were off up the narrow water ditch to rid the world of the rhino.

"The animal must be sick, the way it's been acting," Tony said as we cut into the brush. "If we locate it, the kill should be an act of game control, won't count on your license."

That was fine enough, but I was ripe for a rhino anyway. We'd earlier prospected for *faro*, Tony and I, up in the giant heather that grows above the ten-thousand-foot level of Mount Kenya, above the forest belt where Tony had played deadly cops-and-robbers with Mau Mau terrorists during the emergency of the early 1950s. We'd already hunted miles of the high-grassed Kinna country near the Tana, misled here and there by ambitious but misinformed local trackers. A pigheaded steam engine of a rhino was one beast I'd dreamed of meeting, but we'd been out of luck to date.

The irrigation ditch was bone-dry as we hurried along its edge, with the glint of small fish, *barbe*, lying dead in its bed. The rhino had really crippled this little village. Small wonder the headman had been so excited. No *faro* tracks in the mud, though. Perhaps the beast had lummoxed out of the country.

A quarter of a mile from the shamba all three of us were halted simultaneously by a chorus of shrieks and angry masculine howls from behind.

"Now what?" wondered Bob. "That third wife up a tree again?"

"Maybe she fell out of it this time," I figured. But then we heard the unmistakable bass shouting of our skinners and gun bearer. Must be real trouble.

Back we went on the double, Tony's long legs scissoring from one edge of the ditch to the other while Bob and I sprinted to keep up. Around the last bend the *shamba* clearing opened. Two of our boys were standing on the safari car top, and a cluster of natives perched in the forks of a tall tree, a sort of watch tower, that grew inside their thorn fence. Every hand pointed in the same direction.

There was the rhino, in the jungle edge only a hundred yards from the huts. We slipped as quietly as possible across the opening. I remember wondering why there were no tickbirds with this rhino, and what sort of horned deviltry its fist-sized brain could be cooking up.

"There's your shot!" whispered Tony. The beast had turned enough to show a forequarter clear. There was no question of assaying the horns as trophies; so up came the .458, back went my shoulder and down went the rhino. "Give him another," suggested Tony, but I had already shucked the bolt and whomped another solid into the mud-gray beast. That concluded the entertainment.

Actually the show had just started. When they realized that their four-legged enemy was vulture feed, a small army of Meru poured from the shamba. Kids, young men and girls, the old headman and his three spouses came dancing and shrieking around us and the dead rhino. The bwana's slugs had done a job for them and, as Bob suggested slyly, "Now mama number three can keep out of trees."

There was a great celebration, with the headman, a Mohammedan, ticking off his prayer beads in loud-voiced thanksgiving. But the rhino's horns weren't so much, just over twenty inches on the front. The beast had been made violently cantankerous by some sort of ulcerous skin disease, and clearly was sickened by some internal illness that manifested itself in great sores, so it had given me no more battle than a tired steer. I didn't hop with any excitement, and even felt relieved when George Adamson, head game ranger for the Isiolo country, later confirmed the "act of game control" status for the kill, took over the horns, and okayed my trying for another rhino on the Northern Frontier. It was something of a letdown, even if the hog-headed and armored beast had been dispatched with cavalier neatness.

"Never thought you'd be playing Sir Galahad over here, did you, Page?" joshed Tony a few days afterward as we jogged northbound, with lion, eland and plains-game trophies bouncing in the Austin five-tonner behind us. "Saving damsels in distress and all that."

But the best his ribbing could get out of me was a grunt. My thoughts were on the real buster of a rhino that might be waiting for me somewhere in the thorn bush. There'd better be one. So eventually there was, but not until we had made our elephant hunt in the far north, had scouted our Grevy zebra and strange gerenuk, had run into buffalo where no buff should be, and had finally turned back to the range of hills called the Shaaba, which lie northeast of Isiolo. Nary sign of good rhino anywhere. For three days the few local sheepherders prophesied rhino over every rise of lava rock. We looked at zebras by the hundred, a herd of elephant using our waterhole, the odd Grant's gazelle mincing across the grass flats, but nowhere could we find the round-toed print of *faro*.

One of the odd parts of an African safari, whether you're blundering through the country in a borrowed jeep or hunting with all the skilled help offered by an expert from Nairobi's Hunters, Ltd., is that the unexpected can be expected to happen. You hunt elephant, but shoot buffalo; hunt lion and end up with a ton of eland; look for a nice eating-sized gerenuk and come back to camp with a trophy Grant's. We should have known, therefore, what to expect when, one fine morning, we left the Shaaba camp to prospect the flats north of the range, our object two or three unmarked zebra hides.

Tony stayed in camp that day. Accounts to tot up, a job to be done on the fuel-injectors of the diesel-powered Austin. Andy, a developing young hunter (termed a "stooge" in the rugged East African slang), could four-wheel the safari car through the thorn for us. Onyango, veteran of hundreds of engagements with various brands of African fauna, including two hundred and fifty rhino kills in earlier times as a game scout, to permit native resettlement, would go along in case of emergency, though our greatest emergency to date had been no more serious than a rock-cut tire.

"No trouble on your zebras," counseled Tony as we loaded up the car, "and you might well run onto a good oryx back there. Your judgment is as good as anybody's on them after glassing a couple of hundred, Warren; so if you see a good bull, take him."

The zebras came as expected. A nice young unscarred stud first, whacked in the shoulder from a hundred yards with the .375 Weatherby magnum. Then a careful skinning job and pictures as the vultures, Africa's disposal squad, dropped out of the sky for their horrid jostling devouring. But now the temper of the day—a day planned as a picnic with rifles more than as a serious hunt—began to change. We spotted a herd of dagger-horned Beisa oryx, and a lead pill from my 7 mm. dropped a dark-hided bull with trophy stickers spanning over thirty-three inches. We picked up the stud zebra Bob wanted and, as an unexpected stroke of fortune, found a fine bull oryx that stood long enough to be dropped by Bob's .30-06. A big day!

Then we ran out of luck, almost. The track we'd been following over the sweeping grasslands petered out in a maze of lava boulders that slashed at tires and racked the car even at a low-low crawl. No dice to go farther. Every alley came to a dead end.

"Might as well return to camp the way we came," said Andy in his quiet, clipped tones. He added in word-sparing fashion, "Difficult for the car." Since that was the understatement of the year, there was no disagreement from either Bob or me and we swung around on the return track. A fine day anyway.

But you can always expect the unexpected in Africa. Perhaps I'd had some sort of premonition when I put aside the 7 mm. used on plains game and propped the .375 Weatherby slugger between my knees. Just seemed sensible in case we might see the one buff I still had open on my Kenya ticket. But it was no buffalo that, without warning, wandered out of the thornbush several hundred yards ahead.

One rhino. Two rhino. Three rhino. From the slim horn and lesser bulk, the first was a cow, a *mamanuki*. Then came the family pride and joy, *m'toto*, stumping to keep up on ridiculously short legs. And finally the old man strolled onto the scene, a real old left tackle of a bull, with a length and heft of horn that set Andy's feet to stabbing at the brake and my hands scrabbling for a fresh load of solids.

The car was still swinging behind a screen of thorn when I dropped off, stood for a second to be sure that the magnum was filled with four cartridges, each carrying two and one-half tons of punch—slick-nosed Kynoch bullets over eighty-two grains of DuPont IMR 4064 powder—then headed for the rhino. I could hear Bob cussing about an entangled strap on his telephoto, and the skinners were still muttering *"Faro"* as they clambered up through the car's camera hatch to watch proceedings from the roof. Andy and Onyango could come along or not, as they wished, but I proposed to salivate this rhino properly, without tracking him halfway across Africa.

The Dark Continent has more varieties of sticker-bush than a monkey has fleas, each with sharper and more tenacious thorns than the last, but for once I could find no fault with the dwarf acacia and the wait-a-bit there on the Shaaba plain. They made a fine cover for me as I scooted from one clump to the next toward the family of rhino. The wheels between my ears were whirring with the thoughts that rhino can hear a watch tick (but there was enough grass to muffle any stones my hurrying might roll); rhino can smell as well as deer (but the wind was crosswise of the line of stalk so that offered little concern); rhino can't see a barn beyond thirty yards or so unless it's moving (but there were plenty of clumps for me to sneak behind). This was going to be a sure thing. I was resolved to stick the rifle muzzle smack into Mr. Rhinoceros's leathery, flickery ear and scrag him but suddenly.

At the next-to-last thornbush I stopped to look matters over. The bull was standing still fifty yards ahead, apparently ruminating on the days when, as a young bachelor, he didn't have family responsibilities. His solid-bodied front horn reared up well over two feet, I estimated, perhaps thirty inches. And the second horn was well developed. His tickbird escorts may have spotted me, but they showed none of the chirping and swooping excitement that would tip him off to danger. The *mamanuki* and her *m'toto* were busy off to the left a few yards closer, nipping on the tasty-tender tips of thorn scrub. At the next bush I'd be where I could see every crease in his muddy hide and drive a steel-jacket in with all the precision of a stiletto. Then I looked back over my shoulder.

Andy and Onyango were a clump or two behind, each holding a rifle in one hand and waving wildly with the other, excitement in every line. Something haywire? Must be important. I'd never seen rock-nerved Onyango stirred before, not even when we were playing hide-and-seek with buffalo. So I bellied back the few yards to them. "What's up?" I asked.

The gun bearer was too wound up to turn his Swahili into English, but Andy explained with customary quiet brevity. "Concerned lest you get too close. What of the cow if she charges?"

He had a good point. Eagerness had made me forget that the *mama-nuki* would, if her consort fell to a rifle bullet, probably go berserk. She'd charge everything in sight, sound or scent. Making like a rock behind a thorn clump wouldn't help matters because she would tear up the clump just because it was there, in her way. We could get ourselves into a real pickle if we had to shoot the cow or the calf in self-defense. One professional hunter, I remembered hearing, had done just that, and had lost his license for creating such a situation. Even worse, he'd lost face in the New Stanley bar, where more beasts are slain nightly than have roamed the veldt for the past thousand years. I had to look out for Mama.

"Why not shoot from here?" suggested Andy cautiously. That wasn't quite the way to carry out my original ear-poking intention, but it would keep us well clear of the cow should she rampage, and from a sitting position I could slug the bull right through the shoulder crease. The grass was high, but from one angle the rhino showed clear. Cross hairs steadied on the mud-smeared hide, my forefinger tightened, the Weatherby set back in recoil.

Even as I jacked the bolt, *mamanuki* stormed over toward her collapsed mate, her stumpy legs pounding up a great wash of dust. She whirled before him, rushed in and horned the bull in a frenzy, like a housewife screaming, "George, you lazy lummox! Get up, the house is on fire!"

But George was deathly ill, hardly up to squelching even a small blaze. Then she whirled again with that peculiar rhino deftness, like a fat girl doing a square dance, and began a constantly pivoting circle, snout high to locate the source of danger. It wasn't really funny, not with all that furious power behind a two-foot horn.

Onyango jabbed me and said, *"Mamanuki!"* adding something that meant scram in any language. He and Andy turned to hightail it for the car, out of the maddened female's way. Discretion here was the better part of valor, said their departing backs. But I had to stay a few seconds more, to watch the bull in case there was need for another three-hundred-grain solid. Before backing out of the danger zone, rifle ready, I slid in a replacement round and watched Mama every second until it was clear that her frantic charges were carrying her off the wind, clear of us.

With the bull gone the way of all good trophy rhino, we waited until our car-top watchers could see the cow and the calf well off in the bush, no longer a potential problem. Then we turned the safari car in for the fun of measuring—27½-inch horn and very heavy, supergrade for a Northern Frontier District rhino—the pleasure of hand-shaking and the big job of caping off the ponderous head and slabbing off inch-thick back hide as material for whips and shields. We didn't get into camp until black dark, didn't finish the telling of the tales to Tony until supper was cold and the lemon squash bottle empty. Time was of no concern after such a day.

Tony sat quietly toasting his shins at the campfire until the last bullet was shot and the last dust had settled. The fire glint showed quiet laughter in his eyes as he called for chow. "As for you, brother Page," he said by way of finale, "it strikes me that as a happily married man you're always tangling with females when there's a rhino around. Seems to be a case of watching out for one lady or another, what?"

As the man did when St. Peter said, "Let's look at the record," I had to agree.

---

50 : The Hunting Trail Ahead

Often men secretly wish they'd been born in another and remote age, probably because the immediate present, any present, can seem mighty dull. Bill Ruger, maestro of the Sturm Ruger Company and so perhaps the greatest success story of the modern sporting firearms business, has several times privately assured me that he wished he had been born a feudal baron, or failing that an early Victorian gentleman of means and adventurous spirit, on the order of Sir Samuel Baker. The yen to have participated in the great Dark Continent explorations of the nineteenth century is understandable enough, gun-maker Ruger being an Africa buff of the first rank; but he has never specified, in the matter of the barony, whether it was such features of feudal times as *le droit du seigneur*, or the generally bad plumbing and heating systems in the castles, that so intrigue him. But any man's birthwish of this sort is essentially romantic, that's sure.

On the other hand, very much more seriously and for two quite different reasons, I consider myself lucky to have been born and to have lived in these first two-thirds of the twentieth century. Our generation has been privileged to know or partake in, after all, the most incredible advances in human technology: the airplane and finally the supersonic jet; communication from crystal set radio to intercontinental color television. Now men are voyaging into outer space, with the moon only a sort of waystop. The Industrial Revolution of the last century was picayune by comparison. But, as one with an inclination toward hunting and a very real veneration, some might say worship, of the world's wild places, I more importantly consider myself lucky to have lived during what will probably be the last days in which wild game and wild places will flourish in such quality and vast quantity that they can be enjoyed by *all* men of the hunter's turn of mind. It seems doubtful that the generations beyond our sons will be granted any such privilege.

That gloomy statement is not made lightly, with an eye to creating a cheap sensation. But unless revolutionary steps are taken the odds are clearly against the wilds you and I have known.

In the first place, while pills are obtainable almost anywhere and a few states have passed easy abortion laws, the population explosion really is not being taken seriously. Politicians talk volumes but enact nothing in the way of positive controls even in those countries where the intellectual and social levels make the problem clearest and simplest of solution. The Vatican continues to preach anachronism. Zero Population Growth is a movement confined to university campuses. The incredible increase in the number of people continues. More and more they spread into those areas which are least developed, where wild space is still left.

It is a horrid but imaginable prospect that the mass of people in these United States, now some two hundred million, will hit three hundred million, half again as many, by the year 2000. Can you imagine half again as many cars on the highway, half again as many people trying to jam into Yellowstone Park? Can you picture again as many vacationers trying to force their campers into a lakeside parking area even today packed tighter than a slum? Some among us can envision with remarkable clarity the further effects of such maggotlike multiplication on every wild area, from the back woodlot which becomes a subdivision to the chunk of national forest which becomes a supersized picnic place. But who among us has the vision to imagine a whole world of 2000 A.D. in which 7.5 billion humans, over twice the present 3.6 billion, wriggle in a struggle for food and *lebensraum?* What price hunting or the penetration of remote earth places then?

Our present splurge of interest in environment and in ecological restoration has brought attempts to undo or at least to delay the ruinous effects of pollution by man's waste, noise, chemicals, and the poisonous end results of power production and auto exhaust. The idea, it seems, is to retain enough timber or pure air or pure water for man to continue to exist in his environment. Of course, each and every one of these activities has already been the subject of warning after warning by hunting-minded men and organizations. Yet the new environmental interest may itself boomerang to the disadvantage of the hunting fraternity. Not that the problems aren't real and the solutions urgently needed. They have long been. But paradoxically the very excitement generated by these belated discoveries, the hullabaloo stirred up by the sensation-seeking press, politicians, and TV, has been such as to exclude from the problem-solving those very individuals and organizations who have always led the way.

The environmentalists, remember, have little or no time for the sportsman-hunter. The recreationist segment, for example, views all uninhabited areas, all green space, as part of a playground for the masses which they will chop up with roads and parking lots and picnic tables, at whatever detriment to the area's animals or natural beauty, so that these masses can without effort enjoy what is left. The average recreationist has absolutely no concern for the hunter—or for the game which might with the help of the hunting fraternity have continued to thrive in the area. And most other environment-minded groups, whether their intentions be noble or ignoble, omit hunting as a possible proper use of the land.

Perhaps worse, major governmental agencies, presumably charged with the care of our resources, show little concern with the wild places, hunting areas. The number of game migration routes and wintering areas destroyed by dams created to justify the Army's Corps of Engineers is horrifying. The Forest Service started years ago to peddle off the whole North Tongass National Forest of lower Alaska, ostensibly for the economic development of our forty-ninth state, reportedly to Japanese-financed companies and certainly chiefly for the use of Japan's millions. Meanwhile they stoutly assert in white papers the fiction that the ruination of the salmon streams and the slashing down of ages-old rain forests will not also destroy the best population of brown bears we have left. Both the Forest Service and the

Bureau of Land Management abet programs of highway building, either for the fullest "commercial" development of wild regions or to ease entry into them by thousands upon thousands of campers and weekenders, the very messiness of whose presence quickly ruins whatever wild qualities such lands may once have had. Yosemite has riots and a smog problem. Much of what Roosevelt saw in the Yellowstone area is buried under parking lots and campsites.

Outdoor magazines financed by hunter subscription have printed a thousand warnings of these and like dangers. Often they win a victory. But theirs is a tough battle, waged as it is against governmental bureaus whose major purpose, as in any bureaucracy, must be to expand and to create further projects to justify their existence. Particularly is the battle rough when each of those bureaus carries on whitewashing public-relations campaigns that involve expenditures of taxpayer funds far beyond the reach of a private budget.

Not that our publications themselves are as pure as Snow White. However militantly they inveigh against DDT types of insecticides, or the shenanigans of Washington bureaus, or the cupidity of the cattleman, none has really gone to work on one major menace confronting our remaining wild and near-wild domain and its inhabitants, the gasoline-powered vehicle. The phrase as used here refers to all those devices meant to extend man's ability to reach remote areas: the airplane, the four-wheel-drive car, and all that growing family of little buggies tracked or wheeled like the ATV and the snowmobile that on gasoline carry man over snow or up mountains or across waters where for centuries he could move only on his own two legs or at best on the back of a horse. Three and a half *million* of these screaming menaces, chiefly trail bikes and snow buggies, had been sold by 1970s end.

Two decades ago the effect of the float-equipped airplane on backwoods trout ponds was fully known. Surely by 1965 the effects of four-wheeler penetration into Rocky Mountain areas extending even up into Alberta and British Columbia, a penetration vastly accelerated by the bulldozer tracks cut for uranium or oil explorations, was also becoming pretty clear, even if not as sadly obvious as it is today.

So there was, years ago, ample opportunity for forward-looking editorial minds to question very sharply the ultimate results of such of the newer man-extenders as the trail bike, the ATV, the snowmobile; and perhaps even to formulate early in their development programs of use-direction that would avoid the really serious damages that now cause outcry. For the magazines, opportunity to control our future was there. But so, alas, was the possibility of lessening juicy advertising revenue.

Even the politically effective and in some ways responsibly oriented groups like the Sierra Club and the Wilderness Society and the Audubon Society, to mention only three of many, have forgotten that their founders, the figures revered in their pantheon of saints, were usually hunters. Teddy Roosevelt most certainly was. So were people like Seymour, Dan Beard, Gifford Pinchot, and more of like importance in early conservation. Audubon was a hunter, by his friends considered a superb shot. The famous naturalist Hornady was even considered by some of his contemporaries, I am told, to be a bit of a butcher. It was the hunter who around the turn of the century came to realize that all was not well, that a bit of primary preservation was then indicated and must be followed by a long run of *conservation*, of scientific or biological resource management.

And it was the hunter who for the past seven decades got up the hard cash needed to accomplish this, to bring back the whitetail to the point at which their numbers are vaster than they were when the Pilgrims landed, with deer in virtually every state and hunting seasons necessary for management controls in most; to bring back the commercially slaughtered buffalo to the full extent concomitant with our modern West of fenced-off ranches and merchanized farming; to maintain duck and goose populations in a high degree of health despite the attempts of agriculturists and industry to drain or fill in every bit of marsh; to supply us with new game birds, the pheasant and chukar, and to maintain others like the quail and the dove at acceptable levels. Never forget that while the hand-wringers wring their hands the hunters cart corn to wintering birds or airlift hay to starving elk; that the hunting fraternity thirty-five years ago taxed itself with an 11 percent levy on firearms and ammunition that now produces over thirty-two million dollars a year, some four hundred and forty-five million so far, entirely earmarked for matching with state funds to purchase wild lands or to carry out research needed to restore faltering species; that the hunting fraternity antes up over a hundred million dollars annually for the licenses which support all state conservation efforts, those for bluebirds or juncoes as well as for pheasants and deer. A conservative total to date for the hunter's contribution is two *billion* dollars.

Nor has the ability to start effective conservation agencies completely died out among modern hunters. The National Wildlife Federation, however protectionist its magazine may presently seem to some, began life as a hunter-fisherman group. As very few know, the effective Wildlife Management Institute is actually supported exclusively by the sporting-arms manufacturers, hence by their hunter customers. And to prove once again that the concern of the hunter knows no national or even continental bounds, organizations like the African Wildlife Leadership Foundation, today probably the most vital educational influence for conservation among Africans, and the Texas-born group which as Game Coin is building a world reputation, both spring from luncheon-table meetings of confirmed trophy hunters. The safari clubs of San Francisco, Los Angeles, and New York are similarly active. The idea that a bunch of men who like to brag a bit on the kudu or the Cape buffalo they've bagged can also cook up an effective program of wildlife management training for native blacks, and can maintain that process until the whole course of African conservation is affected by their graduates, must really shock some of the longhairs. Yet it is basic to the sportsman hunter's ethic.

You as a hunter must never let anybody forget such facts. Without the urge to hunt we would have had no significant conservation effort in this country prior to our present burst of emotional realization. It is pure tragedy that the environmentalists and the protectionists and the recreationists are happily trying to gloss over the importance of twenty million or more hunters. Never has there been so cavalierly dismissed a minority so large or so gifted with so much potential.

A further force militating against the future of the hunting fraternity is not as new as the environmentalist cry nor as inevitable as the spread of population. This is the hate-firearms, hate-hunting group. Originally, most supporters of firearms *control* meant just that. They sought a system under which firearms could somehow be regulated, so that individuals were not stripped of their rights as citizens to hunt and to shoot in a civilized fashion, yet crime involving firearms could be reduced and the likelihood of assassinations of the Kennedy type could be rendered minimal. These men were perhaps going at the problem entirely from the wrong end, but their aspirations were in the beginning limited.

Few leaders in such areas today are, however, concerned with mere control. They are confessedly and admittedly striving for the abolishment of firearms, for the disarmament of every American who does not wear a uniform of military or police sort. John Glenn's Committee flatly said as much, for example. So has the *New York Times,* which has become so nearly paranoid on the subject it distorts the facts of ordinary news. Personnel of the Johnson-appointed Violence Commission have vaunted that their proposed proscription of the hand-sized firearm is only a first step, to be extended to the long shoulder-fired arm which is the sportsman's mainstay. Rep. Mikva of Illinois, in offering his handgun-seizure bills, brags on that same intention. More ranters and ravers have crawled out of the woodwork, and quite unsurprisingly, all those steak-eaters who inveigh against hurting animals and that financially powerful group some mistakenly denigrate as "little old ladies in sneakers," have joined their parade.

This slant on firearms and the sporting usage of them has been loudly echoed by the big-city press, albeit less so by the smaller and more independent papers of the country. It has been preached repeatedly by the major television networks with the notable exception of one, although again the small-town or small-city TV station usually has local programs offering a different, even healthier, point of view. One of the major networks, ironically enough the one television colossus which had easiest access to basic expertise on the relationships of arms and men, for a time made a career of antigun editorializing.

More subtle, but probably more influential in the long run, has been the erosion of understanding of wild things and their ways as a result of the Disney nature-fakery approach, the "Bambi" idealization of animals as anthropomorphic, possessed of human capacities and attitudes. Quite possibly one of the greatest sins ever committed upon young minds, in terms of their understanding of life, these films and their TV counterparts, the "Daktari" sort of thing in which tigers are said to live in Africa and all hunters are portrayed as black-hatted dastards, will have a very profound and very bad effect on the directions of conservation in today's generation and the next.

The true relationship, or lack of it, between normal firearms usage and crime, between the hunter's gun and conservation, indeed most questions of constitutional justice or even the simple facts of wildlife management—all these attract far less attention in today's media, especially in television, than do emotional outcries damning the hunter and his tools. It may well be wishful thinking to say that the basic antigun climate is likely to improve during the next generation, short of a miracle.

For the very long term I do therefore envision a slow change in our American hunting system. It is now essentially democratic in that under our law the game belongs not to the owner or the lessor of land but rather to the state, the people. This concept will slowly, between now and 2000 A.D., swing toward approximations of the European scheme. Under that, the game belongs to the land, to its owner or to those who may lease the land, perhaps for the production of game and for use by hunters. In the old countries the state exerts only a degree of control in that it prescribes broadly applicable seasons, which are as much matters of custom as of management. It is true that in some areas, as for example on the moose hunting in Norway, the government actually indicates through its game wardens what the crop of animals should be for a given season even on private property. But truly private management of game animals and birds is far more general in Europe than here.

In the one of our fifty states still possessing large quantities of open space of which none is public land, all privately owned, the trend toward Europeanism is already marked. In Texas, ranch lands are leased by individuals or syndicates solely for the purposes of hunting, lease payments now passing seventeen million dollars a year. The owners are expected chiefly to cooperate by keeping off nonleaseholders and by arranging crop or cattle production so as to be helpful to the indigenous game. Hundreds of Lone Star ranchers have already found their deer hunting to be worth considerably more than their beef herds, and good turkey and quail areas command very fancy hunting-lease rates.

Scattered over other states both eastern and western are two other manifestations of a similar trend; the licensed commercial shooting preserve, where pen-reared birds are released to the fields in such numbers as to comply with the law's needs and the demands of pay-as-you-shoot gunners; and the syndicate-leasing of one or several farms for the private usage of duck clubs, gun clubs, and the like, with the landowner well enough paid to cooperate in respect to crops and general game management. Game-reserve areas, both fenced and unfenced, where deer and a wide variety of both domestic and exotic species can be sought for a head fee, are also spreading in Pennsylvania, Michigan, Florida, Texas, Tennessee, and New Jersey, plus a dozen other states. At the same time, state game or conservation commissions are everywhere buying up wild land, whenever financially possible, for the usage of their licensed hunters although that splendid public effort, alas, probably produces game less efficiently than do some private methods. The state of Pennsylvania now owns over 1.3 million acres of game land. Essentially, then, the swing is toward an era of hunting and land usage of which the hunter must directly pay, either by per diem fees or heavier licensing, much as he does overseas.

This is hardly democratic, since it pegs the privilege of hunting to the ability to write a check. Yet do not for a moment believe that John Citizen in Europe, whether in Sweden or France, Italy or Denmark, cannot hunt. The common sight of a Frenchman lustily pedaling a bicycle with a shotgun slung over his shoulder belies that. Scandinavians can acquire hunting opportunities with only a small effort. Italians fire more shot shells per capita than we do. Each Italian village has an area posted as its *Riserva di Caccia*, a sizable chunk of land perhaps grazed by village cattle and certainly used by the charcoal makers, but essentially the hunting area of the local club, a happy group who may not shoot many pheasants but in the local tavern can tell splendid lies about the ones they missed.

But John Citizen's hunting in Europe isn't really much good unless he is well enough heeled to pay the price for it. The six-hundred-acre hunting grounds once owned by riflemaker Larsen of Denmark, complete with its keeper and all the attentions needed by an amazingly rich population of pheasants, roe deer, ducks in season, had cost him annually, even after realizing income from the sale of birds and the subleasing of farm ground, about as much as it costs an American golfer to belong to his local country club. Mass bird shooting, where driven game can really be piled up for sale (as a marketable crop off the land) at five to eight hundred birds a day, or those uppercrust reviers where a whole staff of jaegers is needed to supervise the welfare of *hirsch* and chamois on a mountain acreage, will understandably come much higher. But such hunting can be both sporting and superb when correctly handled, and under such intensive management the quality of the game is unquestionable. And when you come right down to it, many Americans even today will find at year's end that they are laying out money in even bigger chunks in order to pursue deer and elk and birds and such on publicly owned land.

Assuming that the forces of population and land use, and the limitations placed upon firearms by either the well-meaning or the ignorant, do accelerate any Europeanizing of American hunting, hopefully we will also have sense enough to adopt much of the *waidgericht* or hunting code. Average hunters over here must somehow develop the deep respect for game animals that leads the European to offer his fresh-killed trophy a last supper, a final bit of greenery. They must somehow achieve that complete understanding of the primitive sources of man's hunting instinct that calls for the jaeger to smear his hunter's brow with fresh blood. We may perhaps develop other rituals, but certainly as sportsmen we must somehow advance from the casual, "gut it out and go get the truck" attitude of the meat hunter which so typifies many Americans afield. The European approach, I say from some experience, is more fun, if "fun" be the right word. Rewarding would be better. By it the hunter is somehow far more tightly related to his game and to the terrain in which it moves.

To say that we are trending and will continue to trend closer to the European systems of licensing hunters, even with our hunter safety programs as simple and childish as they presently are, is restating the evident. It may be something of a millenium, but perhaps one day each embryonic U.S. hunter will have to go through the complete course of sprouts, show detailed knowledge of natural history, demonstrate real skill at cleanly shooting the game, pass all the really tough series of tests that have, among other benefits, almost entirely eliminated accidents from the European hunting scene.

Of course, there can be no such thing as Europeanizing the African continent. I think that hunting there will hang on rather longer than some expect, because I think that the emergent governments are perhaps more keenly conscious of the tourist dollar than many give them credit for being. But eventually, and probably sooner than eventually, the octopus of population spread will strangle the Dark Continent's great game herds. It is not reasonable to expect that a man, his wife, and a passel of kids can share a patch of pea vines and banana trees with an elephant or a lion, and as things now stand the man can easily outbreed either.

Don Hopkins, who spent more of his early and middle years on safari than anyone I know unless it be his spouse Marge, in about 1950 said to me that the hunting in Africa had gone to the dogs as compared to ten years before. I felt the same way almost annually until my thirteenth—hope not last—African hunt in 1968. Quite obviously hunting in 1975 will not be like what it was in 1950, nor like it was in 1925. Nothing is.

But where Kenya has been thoroughly picked over, more of its choice sections turned into parks, even more land made the sites of native settlement programs, and much the same has happened in Tanzania and Uganda though perhaps not to such degree, the southern areas seem to be holding up. The Luangwa Valley in eastern Zambia, as one prime example, is so carefully manipulated by opening and closing its blocks that it offers superb hunting for a fairly restricted number of safaris annually. Unless the Zambian government embarks on some cockeyed expansion of game-cropping schemes to satisfy native protein demands, the quality of the hunting can be preserved almost indefinitely. Almost, that is. Ultimately that fertile land along the river will be taken over by unchecked population growth, and the roar of the lion or the grunt of the hippo will no longer supply the bass for nightly symphonies.

I have often wryly felt that hunters would be happier if they deserved the opprobrium heaped on them by the ignorant and the emotional, if they really had shot off all the game. The fact is, of course, that the man who hunts for sport has never brought any species to the brink of extinction. Quite the contrary, it is the hunter who has brought so many threatened species back from the abyss. But the hunter-haters don't know that, wouldn't admit it if they did. And after all, one might well be hanged for a sheep as a goat. Yet we can be thankful that hunters have never actually thought that way. Theirs has always been the primary impetus behind true conservation. I regret only that these noble impulses do not guarantee them a better future.